The Cambridge Introduction to
Literature and the Environment

The degrading environment of the planet is something that touches everyone. This book offers an introductory overview of literary and cultural criticism that concerns environmental crisis in some form. Both as a way of reading texts and as a theoretical approach to culture more generally, 'ecocriticism' is a varied and fast-changing set of practices which challenges inherited thinking and practice in the reading of literature and culture. This introduction defines what ecocriticism is, its methods, arguments and concepts, and will enable students to look at texts in a wholly new way. Boxed sections explain key critical terms and contemporary debates in the field with 'hands-on' examples and comparisons. Timothy Clark's thoughtful approach makes this an ideal first encounter with environmental readings of literature.

Timothy Clark is a specialist in Romantic, Heideggerian and post-Heideggerian poetics and in environmental criticism. He has held appointments in Finland, Australia and now works in the English Department of the University of Durham. His books include *Derrida, Heidegger, Blanchot: Sources of Derrida's Notion and Practice of Literature* (Cambridge 1992, paperback edition 2008), *The Theory of Inspiration: Composition as a Crisis of Subjectivity in Romantic and Post-Romantic Writing* (1997, 2000), *Charles Tomlinson* (1999), *Martin Heidegger* (2001) and *The Poetics of Singularity: The Counter-Culturalist Turn in Heidegger, Derrida, Blanchot and the Later Gadamer* (2005).

The Cambridge Introduction to
Literature and the Environment

TIMOTHY CLARK

CAMBRIDGE
UNIVERSITY PRESS

CAMBRIDGE UNIVERSITY PRESS
Cambridge, New York, Melbourne, Madrid, Cape Town, Singapore,
São Paulo, Delhi, Mexico City

Cambridge University Press
The Edinburgh Building, Cambridge CB2 8RU, UK

Published in the United States of America by Cambridge University Press, New York

www.cambridge.org
Information on this title: www.cambridge.org/9780521720908

First published 2011
Reprinted 2012

Printed in the United Kingdom at the University Press, Cambridge

A catalogue record for this publication is available from the British Library

Library of Congress Cataloguing in Publication data
Clark, Timothy (Timothy John Andrew), 1958–
The Cambridge Introduction to Literature and the Environment / Timothy Clark.
    p.   cm. – (Cambridge Introductions to Literature)
Includes bibliographical references and index.
ISBN 978-0-521-89635-1 (hardback) – ISBN 978-0-521-72090-8 (paperback)
1. Ecocriticism.   2. Nature in literature.   I. Title.
PN98.E36C53   2010
809'.933553 – dc22   2010042725

ISBN 978-0-521-89635-1 Hardback
ISBN 978-0-521-72090-8 Paperback

Annelle
(For Anne)

Contents

Science and the struggle for intellectual authority

The animal mirror

Illustrations

Preface

This book offers an introductory overview of the arguments, methods and concepts of literary and cultural criticism that concern environmental crisis in some form; a body of thought and work that is both varied and changing fast. A working definition of the subject, sometimes also called 'ecocriticism', would be: *a study of the relationship between literature and the physical environment, usually considered from out of the current global environmental crisis and its revisionist challenge to given modes of thought and practice.*

Introductions to environmental criticism have usually taken the form of critical anthologies in which the diversity of the issues is represented by a loose plurality of essays by different people. This study aims, ambitiously, for a tighter synthesis. The model is the kind of lucid conceptual introduction more familiar to other schools of literary or cultural theory, a systematic overview of the critical methods and arguments engaged with the intellectual and ethical challenges of environmental issues. The sequence of twenty short chapters includes readings of specific texts, inset box sections outlining some important concept or debate, a list of further reading and some inset sections called 'quandaries', open invitations to further thought.

Environmental issues pose new questions to inherited modes of thought and argument. To try to conceptualise and engage the multiple factors behind the accelerating degradation of the planet is to reach for tools that must be remade even in the process of use. Ecocriticism is one site of this crucial intellectual transformation.

Acknowledgements

Thanks to David Carstairs for permission to use 'Roadside reserve'. Thanks are also due to Richard Kerridge for a generous and helpful report on an earlier draft of this text; to Hilltop Publishing for permission to use the cover illustration by Judy Hammond for *The Wind in the Pylons* Volume I, written by Gareth Lovett Jones; and to Oxford University Press for permission to reuse Charles Schwartz's drawing of geese from Leopold's *A Sand County Almanac* (1949). Warm thanks are due to Ray Ryan and Maartje Scheltens of Cambridge University Press for their help and expertise.

Introduction

The challenge

We live in the age of unintended consequences.[1]

Ulrich Beck's phrase captures the peculiarity of a world in which day-to-day trivia seem weirdly politicised, often in disconcerting ways. What are the unintended consequences of being a motorist, taking a flight, eating meat or of simply flicking a light switch? Beyond this, the growing environmental crisis imposes kinds of retrospective irony: 'It is as if Western society has deliberately set out to destroy the integrity of the ecosystem.'[2] Is the Bible in part at fault for granting to humanity 'dominion . . . over the whole earth'? Lynn White Jr's controversial question from 1967[3] fed into a growing realisation that one of the distinctive features of western thought has been the depth and destructiveness of its assumptions about the human relationship to the natural world. At issue may also be conceptions about personhood, property and ethics:

> Questions about preservation of the natural environment are not just technical questions; they are also about what defines the good and moral life, and about the essence and the meaning of our existence. Hence, these are not just academic or technical matters, to be settled in elite dialogues between experts. These are fundamental questions of defining what our human community is and how it should exist.
>
> Robert J. Brulle[4]

This crucial, exciting but sometimes bewildering intersection of issues is the space of ecocriticism, or the study of literature and the environment.

Some deep schisms divide and energise modern environmental politics. So-called *reform environmentalism* remains the most familiar and dominant

1

variety. It holds to the mainstream assumption that the natural world be seen primarily as a resource for human beings, whether economically or culturally, but it strives to defend and conserve it against over-exploitation. For the most part reform environmentalists advocate measures within the given terms of capitalist industrial society ('sustainable development', carbon offset schemes, conservation charities with glossy magazines, etc.). Environmental politics becomes essentially a matter of long-term prudence for human interests and quality of life, the protection of aesthetically attractive landscapes and their associated leisure pursuits. Reform environmentalism also informs a new kind of consumer piety, with its sometimes extraordinary language – such that buying a slightly less destructive make of car becomes 'saving the planet'.

In contrast, more radical stances see environmental problems as far too serious to be addressed by the fine-tuning of inherited political and economic institutions. They demand a rethink of the material and cultural bases of modern society. For one radical grouping especially, the 'deep ecologists', the essential problem is *anthropocentrism*, the almost all-pervading assumption that it is only in relation to human beings that anything else has value. Deep ecologists urge a drastic change in human self-understanding: one should see oneself not as an atomistic individual engaged in the world as a resource for consumption and self-assertion, but as a part of greater living identity. All human actions should be guided by a sense of what is good for the biosphere as a whole. Such a *biocentrism* would affirm the intrinsic value of all natural life and displace the current preference of even the most trivial human demands over the needs of other species or integrity of place.

Others, specifically ecofeminists and thinkers in so-called 'social ecology', offer varieties of the position summed up by Murray Bookchin, that 'the very idea of dominating . . . nature has its origins in the domination of human by human'.[5] Ecological problems are seen to result from structures of hierarchy and élitism in human society, geared to exploit both other people and the natural world as a source of profit. Critics advocate fundamental political reform, moving towards kinds of small-scale, often anarchistic societies without inbuilt institutions of injustice.

For these and other radical environmentalists, things such as carbon-offset schemes, or other measures imagined to be able to engage environmental degradation through a few adjustments to the market-led economy, seem inadequate and irresponsible. The current state of the world erodes the very legitimacy of given institutions and laws, often instilling the grimmer conviction that the industrial market economy and the modern state are essentially and structurally committed to the process of an endless capital accumulation

Figure 1 Flooded road (Stuart Key)

and that this will end only with their own demise – either in the form of their political overthrow or, more likely, through environmental catastrophe.

Anthropocentrism

Anthropocentrism names any stance, perception or conception that takes the human as centre or norm. An 'anthropocentric' view of the natural world thus sees it entirely in relation to the human, for instance as a resource for economic use, or as the expression of certain social or cultural values – so even an aesthetics of landscape appreciation can be anthropocentric. Anthropocentrism is often contrasted with a possible *biocentric* stance, one attempting to identify with all life or a whole ecosystem, without giving such privilege to just one species.

The term *anthropocentrism* may perhaps seem too sweeping. After all, even 'biocentrism' is a stance taken by human beings and is hence 'anthropocentric' in a weak sense. Normally, however, 'anthropocentrism' in environmental discourse names the view that human beings and their interests are solely of value and always take priority over those of the non-human.

The literary and cultural criticism

Ecocriticism is necessarily a provocative misfit in literary and cultural debate. It is also a newcomer, having been around as a definable movement for less than two decades, though forms of recognisably ecocritical practice may be rather older (Raymond Williams's *The Country and the City*, for instance, is from 1973).[6] As a defined intellectual movement it is largely datable to the founding of the Association for the Study of Literature and the Environment in 1992, originally in the United States and then with branches in Europe, India, the Far East and the Antipodes.[7]

No distinctive method defines environmental criticism. Its force is best characterised in terms of its various challenges. Many ecocritical studies may be much like other research in cultural history, excellent as such but differing only in taking the environment in some sense as topic. A broad archive is now building up, tracing different conceptions of nature and their effects throughout the history and cultures of the world. For instance, one critic will consider the contributions of English women to emerging 'ecological' issues in the early modern period; another traces notions of nature made possible in Germany by the romantic period science of Alexander von Humboldt's *Kosmos* (1848–58); a third studies how writing haiku helped Japanese internees in the US get through their time in detention during World War Two.[8] Other environmental critics, however, move beyond the stance of being cultural historians and allow the distinctiveness of the subject matter to open up a sharper questioning of inherited conceptions in critical argument, for example, of the nature of linguistic representation and evaluation, canon formation, the aesthetic, of conceptions of personal identity and so on.

This book highlights what seems most distinctive about environmental criticism, where it most challenges inherited modes of thought and analysis. One challenge can be expressed in the following terms. Most criticism today is *contextual*, aiming to situate a text in a cultural or cultural-historical context. Thus a reading of *David Copperfield* (1850) will place the novel within the cultural politics of the early Victorian period, its determinations of class and gender, the history of publishing and the changing make-up of readerships. Yet culture itself has a context – the biosphere, air, water, plant and animal life – and more radical ecocritical work tends to be, so to speak, *meta-contextual*, opening on issues that may involve perspectives or questions for which given cultural conceptions seem limited. To use a term first coined by Henry D. Thoreau, environmental criticism may be *extra-vagant* – from the Latin for wandering beyond the boundaries.[9] A peculiar feature of environmental questions is how very soon they reach the limits of the competence of any one intellectual discipline. The issues often require an environmental and scientific literacy as well as a critical and historical one.

Environmental issues can pose new questions to given frameworks of critical thought, artistic practice and criteria of judgement. Is the classic realist novel, for instance, inherently anthropocentric in its customary focus on personal development, family, the social and political, with the environment featuring usually, if at all, in the guise of 'setting'? The basic conception of most novels may at first seem ill-suited to concerns that may involve timeframes far exceeding a single human life, which may deal with spatial scales of the very large or small, or with issues that do not fit traditional political polarities of left and right.

Environmental thinking also changes the priorities as to what issues are more significant than others: a small fungus necessary to the life of a tree may be more lastingly decisive than the sensational diaries of a leading politician. Some of the 'radical' posturings of much criticism in the 1980s and 1990s may convey less intellectual and ethical force than the image of a cold plain of scattered boulders on Mars – should it always be left just as it is, or may it be bulldozed one day for human use? The enormity and complexity of environmental issues and their depth of implication in the commonest habits of thought or daily action may also perhaps underlie the intellectual instability of some ecocritical texts, torn as they often are between revisionist insights and lapses, as if on numbed recoil, into outmoded kinds of romanticism or new age rhetoric.

The intellectual pressure exerted by the scope of environmental questions differentiates ecocriticism from other branches of cultural or literary criticism. Mainstream cultural and literary critics have long been dubious of readings that rest on some so-called 'grand narrative', that is, any attempt to interpret the complexity of events through reference to one overarching principle of explanation, such as the 'class struggle', productive forces, or to enlightenment narratives of the progressive human conquest of nature. The moral impetus behind ecocriticism, however, necessarily commits it to take some kind of stance, however implicit, on the huge issue of what relationship human beings should have to the natural world. This is a huge philosophical and even religious demand, and, unsurprisingly, many ecocritical essays fall short of it. Potentially, however, it also makes environmental criticism more exciting even than current work on the literature of post-colonial societies, for it does not write as if human beings were sole occupants of the planet and must open itself to a space in which fundamental questions about the human place in nature are at issue.

A crisis of the 'natural'

Nature writing continues to be used as a term to describe a kind of creative non-fiction associated with usually meditative accounts of natural landscapes and wildlife, but the phrase has a misleadingly cosy feel. Much writing that celebrates wilderness in the mode associated with such nineteenth-century American writers as Thoreau or John Muir may have been slightly anachronistic, even at composition. It is surely out of date now. In some ways *the environment* functions as a term to name what there is once the older term *nature* seems inadequate, sentimental or anachronistic. In the limited sense of places unaffected by human activity there is no 'nature' as such left on the planet, but there are various 'environments', some more pristine than others. Globally, 'the dominant relation with nature has become that of scientific management and a moralizing mode of interpretation'.[10] Timothy W. Luke writes:

> Nature increasingly is no longer a vast realm of unknown, unmanageable, or uncontrollable wild nonhuman activity. After becoming completely ensnared within the megamachinic grids of global production and consumption ... Nature is turning into 'Denature'. Much of the earth is a 'built environment', a 'planned habitat', or 'managed range' as pollution modifies atmospheric chemistry, urbanization restructures weather events, architecture encloses whole biomes in sprawling megacities, and biotechnology reengineers the base codes of existing biomass.[11]

Nature has long been a crucial and perhaps definitive term of western traditions of thought, perhaps the 'most complex word in the [English] language' (Raymond Williams).[12] For an environmental critic, every account of a natural, semi-natural or urban landscape must represent an implicit re-engagement with what 'nature' means or could mean, with the complex power and inheritance of this term and with its various implicit projections what of human identity is in relation to the non-human, with ideas of the wild, of nature as refuge or nature as resource, nature as the space of the outcast, of sin and perversity, nature as a space of metamorphosis or redemption. Ecocriticism usually reads literary and environmental texts with these competing cultural conceptions of nature to the fore. At the same time, a definitive feature of the most challenging work is that it does not take the human cultural sphere as its sole point of reference and context.

The natures of nature

The very term *nature* has several, incompatible meanings whose interrelation can be said already to enact some distinctive environmental quandaries.

At its broadest *nature* is the sum total of the structures, substances and causal powers that are the universe. In this sense, evidently, humanity is part of nature, could never be anything else and even a radioactive waste dump is as 'natural' as a snowdrop or a waterfall.

Figure 2 Roadside reserve (David Carstairs)

A second sense of *nature* is that usually at issue in environmental politics. Here, 'nature' names the non-human world, the non-artificial, considered as an object of human contemplation, exploitation, wonder or terror. In this sense culture and nature are opposed. Being other than or superior to nature in this sense forms a definitive part of many modern conceptions of human identity, and of the enlightenment project of the 'conquest of nature'. At the same time, non-human 'nature' also acquires connotations of the untouched, the pure, the sacral.

Thirdly, *nature* may mean simply the defining characteristic of something, as in the 'nature' of democracy, or the nature of 'nature'.

The phrase 'crisis of the natural' can usefully frame the concerns of this book. David W. Orr contrasts a cornfield in Iowa to the landscape it supplanted: 'An Iowa cornfield is a complicated human contrivance resulting from imported oil, supertankers, pipelines, commodity markets, banks and interest rates, federal agencies, futures markets, machinery, spare parts supply systems, and agribusiness companies that sell seeds, fertilizers, herbicides, and pesticides.'[13]

Boundaries between the natural and the artificial have become porous in relation to projects that involve GM crops or possible manipulations of human biology, as well as the issue of what is 'natural' or not in the planet's landscapes or weather. A neglected roadside verge may sometimes hold more genuine biodiversity than the over-managed 'Nature Reserve' it borders.

In ordinary speech, to say that something is 'natural' or is 'naturally' x or y, is to draw on a word that seems to validate itself as a matter of course, *naturally*. Yet what 'nature' is becomes less self-evident and more contentious by the year. Many appeals to nature seem merely an unjustified dogmatism in disguise, as in prejudices about gay relationships for instance ('it's not natural'). Fantasies of nature as 'unspoiled wilderness' have seen at least 5 million people join the new class of so-called 'conservation refugees', forced to leave their ancestral lands by programmes of conservation funded largely by western charities. Bruno Latour observes that 'never has anyone appealed to nature except to teach a political lesson'.[14]

Michael P. Cohen asks: 'Is "literature and environment" a subdiscipline of literary studies, or an extension out of literary studies into environmental sciences, or a practice largely within the paradigms of the humanities and social sciences?'[15] In fact, Cohen assumes here perhaps too limiting a set of pre-given alternatives, for ecocriticism also reflects a striking feature of the modern crisis of the natural, its challenge to the way human knowledge is organised. Previously accepted demarcations between the natural sciences, the social sciences and the humanities are not just coming under pressure but are effectively being transgressed and disregarded in many environmental issues and controversies. A question such as how much CO_2 an industry should be allowed to emit is at once a matter of politics, economics, climate studies, chemistry, social welfare, intergenerational ethics and even animal rights.

In sum, ecocriticism makes up the arena of an exciting and imponderable intersection of issues, intellectual disciplines and politics. Its potential force is to be not just another subset of literary criticism, situated within its given institutional borders, but work engaged provocatively both with literary analysis and with issues that are simultaneously but obscurely matters of science, morality, politics and aesthetics.

A reading

It may still be needful to stress one thing that environmental criticism is not. It is not affirming 'nature writing' in the lax sense of the following two examples from the prose of Henry Williamson.

The first text is brief and obviously bad, 'The Incoming of Summer'.

> Where by the stream the towers of the wild hyacinth bore their clustered bells, sought by that gold-vestured hunchback the wild bee, the willow wren sang his little melody, pausing awhile to watch the running water.[16]

Such writing offers only a sentimental anthropocentrism. Its cosiness and aestheticism reduce animal life to a set of mobile toys. From the standpoint of natural history, '*the* wild bee' is a nonsensical phrase, with hundreds of different species in Britain alone. This is nature as an adult's fantasy of the toddler's nursery.

The second extract is an account of early autumn.

> One morning in the hollows of the meadow and below the wood lay a silver mist. The sun sweeping upwards in its curve beat this away towards noon, but it was a sign. The fire of autumn was kindled: already the little notched leaves of the hawthorn were tinged with the rust of decay, already a bramble leaf was turning red: soon the flames would mount the mightier trees and fan their pale heat among the willows and ash trees round the lake, lick among the drooping elms and the lacquered oaks, and sweep in abandonment with yawning fire of colour through the old beech forest.[17]

Passages of would-be 'fine writing' of this kind are common in nature writing but often problematic. The natural world is verbalised into a glorious spectacle in the reader's mind, one that implicates the reader only as a kind of detached connoisseur. While Williamson's performance may seem dated, how different is it essentially from the juxtaposed and carefully selected sequences of camera shots and music in a contemporary natural history documentary, such as the BBC's *Planet Earth* (2006)?

A third example is more challenging. The following appears at the end of the introduction of Roger Deakin's *Wildwood: A Journey Through Trees* (2007).

> Once inside a wood, you walk on something very like the seabed, looking up at the canopy of leaves as if it were the surface of the water, filtering the descending shafts of sunlight and dappling everything. Woods have their own rich ecology, and their own people, woodlanders, living and working in and around them. A tree itself is a river of sap: through roots that wave about underwater like sea anemones, the willow pollard at one end of the moat where I swim in Suffolk draws gallons of water in to the leaf-tips of its topmost branches every day; released as vapour into the summer air, this water then rises invisibly to join the clouds, and the falling raindrops ripple out into every tree ring.[18]

Deakin's piece clearly still belongs to a legacy of 'fine writing', but the pejorative force of the phrase may be tempered by other issues. There is the same reference to personal experience and perception as in the Williamson, but also its enframing within a different and non-human sense of scale in time and space. The metaphor in the final sentence is also scientifically informed – for rainwater does influence a tree's annual growth and hence the width of the ring of new material laid down for that year. Deakin is clearly trying to write in a way that is both perceptually accurate, poetically evocative and scientifically precise. The reference to the willow tree brings in processes that are not directly perceived; water rising to the 'leaf-tips of its topmost branches . . . released as vapour into the summer air . . . then [rising] invisibly to join the clouds'. Deakin also seems to be striving to express a loosely ecological sense of the normally hidden interconnectedness of things, unlike, say, the merely surface attention to changing colour in Williamson's evocation of autumn. He exemplifies the attempt in environmentalist writing to inhabit the difficult area between scientific knowledge and immediate perception, between fact and value.

While ecocriticism's concern is far broader than non-fiction of this explicitly environmentalist kind, two features of Deakin's paragraph may represent the more general challenge and interest. The first is its partly non-human focus – human beings are not the exclusive subject. The second is that the passage conveys an implicit commitment that even its metaphorical statements have cognitive value of some ecologically valid kind.

First quandary: climate change

This first quandary may overshadow all the others in this book. Of all environmental issues climate change is acknowledged as the most serious, its horrors bizarrely acquiring already an almost trite familiarity. A study led by former UN Secretary-General Kofi Annan already ascribes to climate change the deaths of 300,000 people a year.[19] Readers of a book such as this will not need reminding of numerous authoritative predictions that, unless something urgent is done to reduce the emission of greenhouse gases, large areas of the planet could even become uninhabitable within the lifetime of people now born.[20] According to the leading atmospheric scientist, James Lovelock, it is already too late, though, here in 2010, this is a minority view.[21]

At first glance, it may seem surprising to find that, while global warming is prominent in contemporary environmental writing, like Gretel Ehrlich's *The Future of Ice* and recent science fiction, literary criticism rarely directly addresses the topic in interpreting literature and culture. It is mostly at issue only obliquely or implicitly. This must be set to change, yet, to date, the only academic article directly on the topic of climate change ever to appear in the leading ecocritical journal *Interdisciplinary Studies in Literature and the Environment* is disarmingly direct about its perplexity. Ken Hiltner compares the contemporary challenge to that of air pollution in early modern London, and how John Evelyn misleadingly scapegoated brewers and dyers for a problem caused by the general population:

> perhaps the most important lesson to be learned from [Evelyn's] *Fumifugium* is that, when confronted with the challenge of representing what neither reader nor writer may wish to acknowledge about their

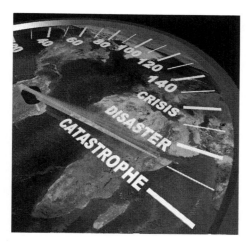

Figure 3 Speeding toward global catastraphe (Iqoncept)

shared practices, the causes of the environmental crisis may be
misrepresented, though perhaps unintentionally . . . it is a real danger
brought about by the challenge of representing a problem that nearly
everyone is causing, but that people are hesitant to confront because
they are unable to stop contributing to it.[22]

Climate change does not appear in the index of Lawrence Buell's *The Future of Environmental Criticism* (2004).

The relative absence in ecocriticism of its most serious issue seems more to do with the novelty and scope of the problem than with personal failing, a measure of how starkly climate change eludes inherited ways of thinking. As a global catastrophe arising from innumerable mostly innocent individual actions, the issue does not present an easily identifiable or clear-cut political antagonist. Its causes are diffuse, partly unpredictable and separated from their effects by huge gaps in space and time. Ecocriticism evolved primarily to address local and easily identifiable outrages and injustices – the destruction of wilderness, the effects of aggressive systems of agriculture on a bioregion and its inhabitants, etc. Climate change thus challenges some green critics with the fact that while they have been inventing ways to think and act in relation to their national cultures and histories, they seem – like almost everyone else – still a long way short of thinking in the way and on the scale demanded by a truly global issue.

Could there be a kind of literary and cultural criticism that reads say T. S. Eliot, Shakespeare or Dante in relation to the shifts in human understanding that climate change may induce? How far would it help? Very few critical interpretations to date address climate change in a direct and sustained way and an introduction like this can still do little more than highlight first directions, challenges and work to be done.

Romantic and anti-romantic

Romantic and 'romantic'

Concern with the environment in the broad sense is necessarily as old as human culture. The initial impetus of modern ecocriticism, however, lies some two centuries in the past, in a broadly romantic tradition of opposition to the destructive tendencies of enlightenment ideals of the conquest of nature, the market-based economy and industrialism. *Romantic* here is meant both in the historical period sense – a complex cultural movement of the late eighteenth and nineteenth centuries – but also, as *romantic* with a small *r*, to name continuing and deeply engrained modes of thought that oppose industrial society with ideas of 'nature' and 'the natural' as modes of secular redemption.

Romanticism in that sense remains a powerful feature of mainstream culture. It is also, since the 1790s, a basis of the numerous forms of countercultural and alternative cultural movements appealing to notions of nature and the natural as norms of health, vitality or beauty and as precisely what commercial/industrial society represses or destroys, both in the human psyche and in the surrounding environment.

Such arguments have been the predominant context for environmental politics. Jonathan Bate writes: 'if one historicizes the idea of an ecological viewpoint – a respect for the earth and a scepticism as to the orthodoxy that economic growth and material production are the be-all and end-all of human society – one finds oneself squarely in the Romantic tradition'.[1]

However, when it comes to what countermeasures to advocate, things become less assured. In this respect, ingrained romantic structures of thought have also been seen as restricting the intellectual scope of ecocriticism. Robert

Kirkham sums up some romantic arguments in danger of becoming stale formulae:

> against mechanism, posit organicism ... against dualism, posit the unity of mind and nature; against the primacy of reason, posit the value of intuition or of feeling; against instrumentalism, posit intrinsic value; against alienation, posit a primordial state of harmony to which we must strive to return. In short, the imperative of relatedness-thinking is to repersonalize, resacralize, and respiritualize the world. This, at least in part, is why we are told from all quarters that we must rethink our 'relationship' with our environment.[2]

Up to the mid 1990s, the terms of such 'relatedness-thinking' would have commanded widespread assent among green literary critics. Since that time, however, such arguments have had to defend and refine themselves against various kinds of criticism. Do some dubious assumptions underlie the supposed desirability of a closer relation to the natural? Thinkers have increasingly come to question deeply ingrained presuppositions that the 'natural', as opposed to the cultural, necessarily names a condition of balance, harmony, stability and health. They argue that what critics and writers in the romantic tradition have often called 'nature' or 'natural' have been insufficiently examined, and that the terms act sometimes as an unacknowledged norm in arguments that belong more properly to openly contentious political debate. Is ecocriticism only 'another version of Romanticism's rage against the machine, a refusal to engage the present moment' (Timothy Morton)?[3]

This section offers a broad overview of the elements of environmental criticism closely connected to traditions of romantic thinking, stressing its key features, and also the way it has increasingly been questioned. Chapters on questions of genre and language introduce in turn some other key issues in debates often framed by romantic assumptions. The philosopher, Martin Heidegger, usually assimilated to the romantic tradition, is also considered here. This subsection of the book ends on the topic of 'post-humanism', with its polemically anti-romantic conceptions of the human and of the natural world.

Overall, environmentalism is now still working through the problem that, even as the issues it addresses have become more pressing, the inherited concepts and language that may engage them have become less assured.

Chapter 1

Old world romanticism

Romantic ecology

Jonathan Bate's *Romantic Ecology* of 1991 forms a leading example of a significant early step in the evolution of ecocriticism, especially in Britain.[1] Bate revived the dominant nineteenth-century perception of the crucial Romantic poet William Wordsworth as a 'poet of nature' whose work forms a coherent protest against the dominant ideologies of 'political economy' and industrialism. Bate's book is subtitled *Wordsworth and the Environmental Tradition.*

A particular target of Bate's was the growing consensus in literary criticism of the 1980s that 'nature' was only a spurious topic in literature, that any account of the natural world in poetry embodied a mode of false consciousness, an evasion of real political issues. He argued that what the Romantic poets called 'the bond with nature' need not be 'forged in a retreat from social commitment . . . a symptom of middle-class escapism, disillusioned apostasy or false consciousness' (164). Bate sensed in such critical views both a blinkered dismissal of the importance of the natural world and an unspoken denigration of poetry itself as not really serious, always in need of justification through relation to a (leftish) politics.

Bate wrote *Romantic Ecology* at an evident turning point in world history, 1989–90, the end of the Cold War and the collapse of the Soviet Union, a time when a politics based on polarities of Left and Right could begin to seem dated compared to new challenges such as the environment. For Bate it was modern 'politicised' critics – in certain narrow conceptions of the political – who were anachronistic. He proposed a 'Romantic ecology', locating the poets Wordsworth and John Clare, the Victorian critic John Ruskin and others at the beginning of a green political movement whose importance few would now question.[2] Modern ecology, the science that studies the complex interrelationships of living things to each other and to their environments, could be read as a retrospective endorsement of Romantic conceptions of nature as a holistic living agent or spirit in which all participate and interact: 'The "Romantic ecology" reverences the green earth because it recognizes that neither physically nor psychologically can we live without green things; it proclaims that there is "one life" within us and abroad, that the earth is a single vast ecosystem which we destabilize at our peril' (40). For Bate and others the insights of modern ecology gave new force of justification to some Romantic writers, to pantheistic claims about the 'one life' in all things.

It might be truer to say, however, that a version of modern ecology was being assimilated into the older tradition of romantic conceptions of nature. Since the mid eighteenth century appeals to nature and the natural world as the other of society, usually as its implicit critique, have taken many politically diverse forms. Nevertheless, the decisive notions at work in such movements have some persistent features, regardless of whether these are used to justify a political programme of the 'right' or the 'left' or even the claims of anarchists. Crucial is a norm of what human nature itself is or should be, one that may be called 'romantic' in a broad sense: that of a lost psychic or cultural *wholeness*, that is, the concept of an originally healthy, fulfilled or unalienated human nature that modern society is understood to have suppressed, divided or distorted and that needs to be restored. In addition, such a condition of psychic wholeness is understood to be 'natural' in the sense of corresponding to the condition of harmony, stability and health that many (but not all) Romantic writers ascribed to the unspoilt natural world.

A recurrent antagonist is the posited fragmentation of the 'whole' person by such phenomena as the division of labour, overvaluation of rationality at the expense of spontaneous bonds of feeling both between people and in relation to the non-human, the growth of cities, loss of oral or folk culture to one of mass print, newspapers and television, and the domination of the market economy as the sole reference for justifying human work or valuing things. These phenomena are interpreted as insidious modes of artificiality and the loss of contact with more balanced natural processes. Thus, in *Romantic Ecology* Bate takes up and reaffirms Wordsworth's proto-ecological, anti-industrial arguments in his *The Guide to the Lakes* (5th edn, 1835), defending the naturalness of the life of local 'estatesmen' (independent small landholders). In poems such as 'Michael', 'Home at Grasmere' and long passages of *The Prelude*, Wordsworth celebrated the unalienated labour of the freeholder as a mode of life that is anti-feudal, inherently republican and more 'natural'. Bate reads Wordsworth's accounts of the life of independent shepherds in the Lake District as an astute revitalisation of the ancient pastoral tradition and its often merely conventional celebration of rural life. Grasmere itself forms an economy largely removed from the market nexus, in a sheltered valley

> Where kindred independence of estate
> Is prevalent, where he who tills the field,
> He, happy man, is master of the field
> And treads the mountain which his father trod.
> Hence, and from other local circumstance,
> In this enclosure many of the old
> Substantial virtues have a firmer tone
> Than in the base and ordinary world.
>
> 'Home at Grasmere', lines 461–8[3]

Bate endorses Wordsworth's understanding of the threats to such a way of life:

> In the *Guide* Wordsworth lamented the decline of cottage industry. He explained that until recently the estatesmen of the Lakes had relied on two sources of income, their flocks and the home manufacture by their women and children of the produce of their flocks. 'But, by the invention and universal application of machinery, this second resource has been cut off' (p. 90f). The whole balance of the economy of the district was thus upset.

As the example of Wordsworth shows, a strong feature of Romantic oppositionalism in the nineteenth century was a profound concern with the nature of *work*, a crucial topic sometimes forgotten by modern environmentalists. Bate recounts how Ruskin saw 'an intimate connection between the conditions in which we work and the way in which we live with nature'.[4] Ruskin argued that suppression of genuine fulfilment through work expressed itself in the brutality of industrial and domestic architecture, so that 'no pleasure anywhere is taken in modern buildings, and we find all men of true feeling delighting to escape out of modern cities into natural scenery: hence . . . that peculiar love of landscape, which is characteristic of the age'.[5] He made radically conservative appeals to a lost and more 'natural' society located in an idealised middle ages, one whose work ethic had found expression in the gothic cathedral, with its sculptural forms reminiscent of foliage and arching woodland. For others, appeals to a more 'natural' state of things and for the replacement of existing modes of production led to left-progressive and even utopian programmes for the reform of institutions such as the family, monogamy and private property.

Modern environmental criticism often continues these older traditions of anti-industrial argument, deploying concepts of 'nature' as a moral and psychic norm. A continuity of Romantic ideas can be traced through elements of the texts of Wordsworth, Henry D. Thoreau, Ruskin and William Morris in the nineteenth century, and, in the twentieth, aspects of the Frankfurt School of Marxism, Lewis Mumford, Murray Bookchin and activist poets such as Judith Wright and Gary Snyder. Lewis Mumford is representative when he writes: 'not the Power Man, not the Profit Man, not the Mechanical man, but the Whole Man, must be the central actor in the new drama of civilization'.[6] Many of the writers listed would also endorse the ideals that, for William Morris, informed a kind of anarchist socialism, a society with 'no consciousness of being governed ... conscious of a wish to keep life simple, to forgo some of the power over nature won by past ages in order to *be more human and less mechanical*' (emphasis added).[7]

For Morris in the later nineteenth century, the Romantic norm of wholeness took the form of celebrating art as that element of human nature suppressed in the modern division of labour, with ideals of liberating the artist in every worker:

> This, then, is the position of art in this epoch. It is helpless and crippled amidst the sea of utilitarian brutality. It cannot perform its most necessary functions: it cannot build a decent house, or ornament a book, or lay out a garden, or prevent the ladies of the time from dressing in a way that caricatures the body and degrades it.[8]

Art, for Morris, was the expression of pleasure in work.

Romantic thinking also informs some ecofeminist arguments against what is seen as the patriarchal over-valuation of calculative rationality, with a counter-celebration of the bodily. This strategy posits a certain idea of the 'feminine' against what are seen as the destructive bases of western thought. The implicit norm again is a romantic one of a recovered wholeness and a harmonious integration of the faculties, more in tune with that equilibrium that is the supposed natural state of the earth itself.

The self-evidence of the natural?

It is possible, however, to be suspicious of the way the terms *nature* and *natural* can work in seemingly self-justifying ways in what are, after all, essentially political arguments. The crucial element of concepts of nature in this romantic tradition is that it expresses a principle of homeostasis, of a psychic and ethical counterbalance. If society seems afflicted by a divisive individualism, then the 'natural' expresses the counterweight of community; if modern society seems dominated by a narrowly calculative rationality, then intuition and feeling are praised as 'natural'; if society seems aggressively instrumentalist and materialist, then the 'natural' may be celebrated in terms of more selfless values.

Arguably, Bate, like Wordsworth, tends to idealise what was under threat in the Lake District. In calling it 'Labour...harmonized with nature' (52) he suggests an unalienated humanity realising itself through a mode of life in tune with the natural world and outside the reifying systems of urban commerce. However, such stress on 'naturalness' could be said to simplify the issues. In endorsing Wordsworth's claim that Lakeland cottages 'may be said rather "to have grown than been erected"' (47), Bate also downplays the way this intensively farmed and managed region is now known to have its origins in the prehistoric destruction of forests to make space for domesticated livestock, its bears and wolves long killed off. Wordsworth's Lake District thus makes a striking contrast to 'the more natural mountain landscapes of Scandinavia, where...upland farms – if they exist at all – form mostly small enclaves within a vast spread of forest land' (Derek Ratcliffe).[9] The cottage industry of freeholders was a specific historical institution, with its own laws of ownership and inheritance and a strong division of labour between the sexes. What Bate and Wordsworth idealise as 'natural' is more accurately described as a mode of relatively non-exploitative and stable *settledness*, a locally focussed pre-capitalist lifestyle that may endure for an indefinite period of time without destroying the resource on which it depends, whatever its original basis in the violence of prehistoric clearances.

Bate's 'Romantic ecology' reaffirms the importance of the natural world as a topic for literary criticism, but at the risk of over-idealising premodern and capitalist ways of life. From the perspective of two decades later, Bate's pioneering work of 1991 may also show some omissions. For instance, the focus on unalienated modes of labour is still an exclusively anthropocentric one, dealing with conceptions of human life alone. In fact, the late eighteenth century had also seen a revolution in attitudes to animals and non-human suffering, something prominent in the work of Robert Burns.[10] In *Romantic Ecology*, however, the claims of the non-human appear primarily as helping to realise forms of a less exploitative, more 'natural' human society.

The inherent greenness of the literary?

Now to another decisive element in the legacy of Romanticism for ecocriticism. This is the fact that conceptions of the creative imagination, of the poetic and literary formed during the Romantic period are still current and widespread, and, as such, still seem to offer an almost ready-made defence of the literary in terms that fit some environmentalist arguments.

This point is best clarified through a specific example. In an essay of 1998, Jim Cheney writes of the challenge of putting into words an ethical demand or appeal felt even in the inanimate:

> Rocks can teach us things by their very presence. Once we give up epistemologies of domination and control, nature's complexity, generosity, its kinship and reciprocity come to mark our epistemological relationship with the earth matrix. Rocks are ancient, enduring presences, the oldest of beings. They are perhaps, 'watchful'. (Here I start using scare quotes. But the use of metaphor here and in what follows is not careless writing. Knowledge moves by metaphor. We must, of course, be careful, critical, and attentive in our use of metaphors – they may reach insightfully into mystery).[11]

Cheney's use of 'watchful' for rocks seems at once both laughable and easy to sympathise with. He is trying to articulate a sense about some rocks that is easy to understand but hard to express in ways that do not transgress accepted knowledge of what they are. His decision to put 'watchful' in scare quotes implicitly acknowledges the problem.

Cheney's answer to the issue of an appropriate language is essentially a romantic one. That is, such figurative or poetic language can be defended as enacting modes of consciousness otherwise rendered illegitimate in a society seen as dominated by instrumental rationality and the managerialist language of economics and technoscience. Talk of the 'watchfulness' of ancient rock is held to express otherwise inarticulate modes of relation to the world that are usually suppressed. Literary or poetic language, in such a reading, is both compensatory and restorative, harking perhaps towards a lost or yet to be integrated 'wholeness' of human nature.

David Kidner draws on similar romantic conceptions in arguing for terms that revitalise 'symbolic embeddedness'.[12] He stresses the way metaphor, mythology, rituals and religion can give voice to 'non-rational' modes of relation between the human and the non-human, so undermining the current paradigm of the person as a detached, rational subject facing an object world. Kidner draws on C. G. Jung's work to describe the lost articulacy of these forgotten 'other layers of selfhood' (73). Just as Cheney resorted to 'scare quotes' to say something both intelligible and usually inadmissible, so Kidner turns to a notion of 'metaphor'. By giving one thing the nature or features of another (e.g., 'an angry sky') metaphorical language can transgress rigid, 'literal' demarcations between one thing and another to suggest levels of intuited interrelation that a more narrowly rationalistic and atomistic mode of perception would block out (e.g., between inert rocks and sentient watchfulness). In effect, literary or poetic language is seen as inherently 'green', 'ecological' in a loose sense. The poetic or mythic offer more holistic modes of language enabling less repressed forms of engagement with things.

Art and the poetic, so understood, can be offered as a therapeutic antidote to psychic alienation and division. Bate's argument in *Romantic Ecology* and *The Song of the Earth* (2000) belongs to this long romantic tradition, with his speculative wager: 'to see what happens when we regard poems as imaginary parks in which we may breathe an air that is not toxic and accommodate ourselves to a mode of dwelling that is not alienated'.[13] For other critics, however, as we shall see in relation to 'post-humanism' (Chapter 6 below), the very ease with which such ecocritical arguments flow down well-worn romantic channels makes them vulnerable to charges of anachronism.

A reading: the case of John Clare

Bate has done more than any other critic to enhance the reputation of the previously minor Romantic poet, John Clare (1793–1864), the working-class, so-called 'peasant' writer who enjoyed a brief cult in the Britain of the 1820s, eventually succumbing to madness and dying in a lunatic asylum. A tragic ecological sensibility lies at the heart of Clare's work, modes of writing aligning him with much modern 'post-pastoral' (Terry Gifford).[14] Clare offers close, even obsessively minute perceptions of local plant, animal and human lives in the context of a lingering peasant economy in the process of being destroyed by the enclosures, the loss of common land to imposed laws of private property.

In his later book, *The Song of the Earth*, Bate moved beyond the anthropocentricism of *Romantic Ecology* to affirm the stance of poems such as Clare's 'The Lament of Swordy Well'. The singer of the lament is the land itself, 'Swordy Well', protesting the violence of the enclosures. Bate ponders the challenge to the western mindset of the poem's attribution to the land of a sorrowing voice (173, 165). Would dismissing this voice as 'mere anthropomorphism' already be an act of violence complicit with what the poem protests?

> Though I'm no man yet any wrong
> Some sort of right may seek
> And I am glad if e'en a song
> Gives me the room to speak.
>
> . . .

> On pity's back I needn't jump
> My looks speak loud alone
> My only tree they've left a stump
> And nought remains my own.[15]

Bate again places his own argument within an avowedly romantic tradition of thought: the poetic or literary is seen to offer a kind of compensatory or restorative experience, a return to a sense of things normally lost to a modern, allegedly alienated self-consciousness. As a space in which the reader hears the land itself singing the poem may suggest to the reader a mode of being 'at one with, not self-reflexively apart from, the world' (154). In other words, 'Through the poetic image, oneness with the world can be experienced directly rather than yearned for elegiacally in nostalgia' (154).

The poetic itself, especially in the self-abnegating form practised by Clare, is seen as a touchstone of both ecological and psychic health, a restorative talisman of the union of mind and nature, of thinking and feeling: 'A human being', Bate writes, 'can do everything except build a bird's nest [old French saying]. What we can do is build an analogue of a bird's nest in a poem' (160).

Setting the issues in these terms, Bate sees the challenge for Clare's readers as lying in how far they can themselves believe or emulate this norm of a lost harmony of mind and world, place and self. 'The Lament of Swordy Well' raises what Bate sees as the crucial Romantic dilemma: that whatever its initial appearance as the musings of a local peasant, with an extraordinarily deep fund of local knowledge and association, Clare's poetry cannot really be seen as communicating an immediate and non-reflective absorption in the natural world, that is, as being 'naïve' in Friedrich Schiller's positive sense of an unalienated union of mind and nature, the condition of some romantic idealisations of the child. As a carefully crafted and printed poem, 'The Lament of Swordy Well' is necessarily 'sentimental' in Schiller's sense of consciously knowing or practising such naïvety, that is, engaged in its loss.

> The poet may, however, aspire to conjure into the reader a knowledge of the Schillerianly naïve. Because we are post-Enlightenment readers, I will never convince you by rational argument that the land sings, that a brook may feel pain, but by reading Clare you might be led to imagine the possibility . . . [that] the poem might re-enchant the world. It can only do so if it is understood as an experiencing of the world, not a description of it.   167

Questions are raised here about the terms of Bate's late romantic argument. Does his central focus on the credibility of states of mind become dangerously close to taking from the poetic any real claim to truth or political force? The poem is said to give us an 'experience' of things, not a description of how they are in fact. The reader is placed in an odd position – not expected to believe that a brook can feel pain, but only to believe an account of believing that a brook can feel pain. The ability of poetry to re-enchant the world is to be cultivated as a kind of salutary fiction or psychic therapy. In sum, a modern romantic ecocriticism of this kind, focussed on the poetic as a supposed vehicle of a change in consciousness or personal attitudes alone, may begin to look inconsequential if divorced from the kind of detailed sociopolitical attention to the nature of work, economics and power that had characterised earlier thinkers.

Assessing such readings of Clare, Timothy Morton observes that Bate is also in danger of repeating the escapist terms in which Clare was idealised as some natural genius or intuitive 'peasant poet' in the brief cult of his work in the 1820s, something Bate has also studied in detail. Perhaps the real question is less the success of ideals of poetry and the poet as talismans of a supposed lost psychic wholeness, than why a continuing function of literary culture in industrial or commercial society seems to be to produce nostalgic ideals of this sort: 'Bate himself observes that the image of an authentic ungrammatical Clare later corrupted by revision is in fact part of a fantasy of ownership in which Clare the primitive becomes an object of consumerism.'[16] We will return to this topic later. The most challenging question for the eco-romantic reading of Clare could be: how far is the celebration of the poetic as a kind of green psychic therapy the wishful illusion of an industrial consumerist society rather than a site of effective opposition to it? The modern Lake District, after all, is now essentially part of the leisure industry.

Deep ecology

In 1972 the Norwegian philosopher Arne Naess founded a movement he called 'deep ecology'. The term *deep* contrasted this movement with the relative shallowness of reform environmentalism and its questionable assumption that environmental issues can be addressed merely by adjusting given economic and political structures.[17] Instead, Naess argued that ecological insight into the complex interdependence of living things entailed a revolution in basic assumptions. Modern people treat the natural world with such brutality because their culture is based on the view that humanity is separate from and superior to it. Deep ecology, on the other hand, affirms an understanding of life in which the thinking of the 'self' must already include other organisms, and all that supports them, as part of one's own identity. Recognition of this 'greater self' must entail an ever-widening circle of identification with other living things. A viable 'self' is not the atomistic individual of liberal capitalism, for which the whole world is a source of possible self-gratification and assertion.[18] A biocentric ethic emerges in the perception that to kill another creature is in some sense an act of violence against oneself.

As a broad social movement, 'deep ecology' names the work of diverse campaigns sharing a broadly biocentric ethic. Naess elaborated his own metaphysical system (called 'ecosophy T') as one possible basis for the movement, but saw no reason why deep ecology could not refer to a variety of belief systems for its basis. In 1984 Naess and George Sessions offered a 'Platform for Deep Ecology', affirming eight basic principles for a revolution in human attitudes.[19] This set out an ethics and politics that respect the inherent value of all life and the wrongness of humanity affecting the diversity and richness of life except for 'vital needs'. Such respect dictates an abandonment of social and economic structures based on aggressive capital accumulation and narrowly materialistic conceptions of self-fulfilment. It also demands a severe reduction in the human population.

There are two reasons why it seems appropriate to treat 'deep ecology' in a broad section on Romanticism. Firstly, to base an expanded ethics on the imaginative act of identification with and participation in a more encompassing 'self' is already a high-romantic argument of the kind found in Wordsworth or P. B. Shelley. For instance, in Shelley's fragment of 1818, 'The Coliseum', a person's circle of identification is imagined expanding to include the very pigeons that fly about the ruined amphitheatre.

> And, with respect to man, his public and his private happiness consists in diminishing the circumference which includes those resembling himself, until they become one with him, and he with them . . . It is therefore that the singing of birds, and the motion of leaves, the sensation of the odorous earth beneath, and the freshness of the living wind around, is sweet.[20]

Secondly, criticisms now made of 'deep ecology' directly recall those made of some romantic arguments. The issue is whether radical social change can ever really result from targeting *personal* attitudes, as opposed to directly addressing the specific political and economic institutions – capitalism, patriarchy, neocolonialism – that determine how people live and think. The emergencies latent in climate change may already make readers impatient with arguments for the spreading of a green version of identity politics in the hope that fundamental material changes will later follow. Timothy Luke writes that without more detailed and practicable ethical or legal thinking, deep ecology 'at best offers the traditional solution, changing the self to change society'.[21]

Chapter 2

New world romanticism

More than with revisionist readings of British Romanticism, ecocriticism as a recognisable school emerged mainly with the study of a distinctive American tradition of non-fictional writing focussed on ideas of the wild, writers such as Henry D. Thoreau, Mary Austin, John Muir, Wendell Berry, Edward Abbey and Annie Dillard. At issue is a tradition of thought that may also be traced through the founding of Yosemite and Yellowstone national parks and into such continuing forces as the Sierra Club and the Nature Conservancy. Even to this day, as the environment has become an urgent public issue, much environmental literary criticism reads as modes of thinking from this broadly romantic tradition working to transform themselves in the face of questions beyond their initial scope.

A fascination with the wild as the acultural or even anti-cultural pervades much environmental non-fiction. 'Wild' nature necessarily offers a space outside given cultural identities and modes of thinking or practice. Gretel Ehrlich's essays on Wyoming, *The Solace of Open Spaces*, memorably quote a ranch hand saying, 'It's all a bunch of nothing – wind and rattlesnakes – and so much of it you can't tell where you're going or where you've been and it don't make much difference.'[1] Throughout history, places such as deserts or forests have been conceived as sites of identity crisis and metamorphosis, as the domains of the monstrous and terrifying, places of religious insight or of rites of passage, as in the biblical 'wilderness'. Such a space of disorientation may attract any number of meanings, hopes or anxieties. Some recuperation of the acultural is inevitable as soon as it enters human discourse. At issue here, however, is again the affirmation of wild nature as a scene of instruction or of the recovery or creation of a supposedly deeper, truer or more authentic identity, whether understood in spiritual, political or often nationalist terms. In the white settler colonies of the United States, Australia and New Zealand, it was, respectively, 'the West' and 'the Bush' that became the stage for such plots, even as the real frontier was also a place of collision between differing conceptions of the natural world and of realities that were often sordid and murderous.

Romantic thinking in Europe sometimes concerned the solitary experience of the natural sublime, as in Wordsworth's account of the Alps. More usual, though, was the tendency to celebrate long settled and 'unimproved' areas or modes of life as embodying some sort of national or regional essence, as in Wordsworth's view of the English Lake District or Ernst Moritz Arndt on the German forests. Wordsworth, Ruskin and Morris, in various ways, drew on ideas of indigenous folk culture for campaigns against unbridled industrialism and urbanisation. By contrast, in Canada, Australia or the United States it was images of wild and seemingly unsettled landscapes that became icons for cultural nationalism or its contestation – the American West, the Canadian North or the Australian Outback. Eric Kaufmann writes: 'Rather than exalt the civilization or familiarization of *settled* nature, this conception inverted the traditional pattern, praising the uncivilized, primeval quality of untamed nature and stressing its regenerative effect upon civilization.'[2] In the US a notion of 'nature' as the space of rebirth, freedom or as (usually masculine) self-creation and assertion became part of that complex and often contradictory myth called 'the West'.

Adrian Franklin writes of the Australian experience, that 'the wilderness aesthetic and movement originated, in its specifically Australian manifestation, from bushwalking and not the other around'.[3] It followed a process of rapacious exploitation and the destruction of huge areas of native life to make way for often unsustainable forms of sheep and cattle farming, creating soil erosion, drought and accidental infestations of introduced species (red foxes, rabbits, cane toads). In North America and Australia colonisation had also involved the cultural and not only cultural genocide of indigenous human populations. The frontier became the site of a destructive one-sided struggle between incompatible conceptions of society, land, religion, food production and property. There was also an 'animal holocaust':

> Once the Indians were out of the way, partly because of the depletion of bison, bluebloods and lowlifes alike, unrestrained by game laws, blasted through the West, bagging or leaving to rot untold myriads of turkeys, elks, ducks, herons, badgers, hawks, antelopes, owls, doves, raccoons, cranes, on and on.   Michael L. Johnson[4]

Alongside and often contesting such aggressive settlement came the 'nationalisation' of some landscapes of the West as American cultural icons, in the form of national parks such as Yosemite or Yellowstone. The associated demands of hiking and recreational hunting fed into nascent environmental movements such as the Sierra Club, cofounded by John Muir in 1892, the Boone and Crockett Club founded by Theodore Roosevelt in 1887, and in 1935 the Wilderness Society associated with Aldo Leopold.[5] Wilderness literature or nature writing thus inhabited or contested a frontier that was as much figurative as literal, whether promulgating the Western myth of great landscapes as touchstones of personal or cultural identity (as with John Muir or Theodore Roosevelt), lamenting their loss, or appropriating them in explicitly countercultural terms, as with the 'anarchist' Edward Abbey ('Mankind will not be free until the last general is strangled with the entrails of the last systems analyst').[6]

Notable texts in the canon of environmental non-fiction in the US are Mary Austin's collection of essays on the high desert of California, *The Land of Little Rain* (1903); John Muir's rhapsodic journal *My First Summer in the Sierra* (1911), or *The Mountains of California* (1894); John C. Van Dyke, *Nature for its Own Sake* (1898) and *The Desert: Further Studies in Natural Appearances* (1901); Enos Mills, *Wild Life on the Rockies* (1909); Roy Bedichek's *Adventures with a Texas Naturalist* (1947); J. Frank Dobie, *The Voice of the Coyote* (1949); Leopold's *A Sand County Almanac* (1949); John Graves's *Goodbye to a River* (1960) on the damning of the Brazos River; various essays and books by Wendell Berry and Edward Abbey; and Annie Dillard's *Pilgrim at Tinker Creek* (1974), an account of one year's observation, and meditations on evolution in a relatively suburban area of Virginia's Blue Ridge Mountains.

A central dynamic of many texts in this tradition has been described as 'the writer's movement from human society towards a state of solitude in nature' (Randall Roorda).[7] The decisive founding text here is taken to be Henry D. Thoreau's *Walden, or Life in the Woods* (1854), rather than, say, the Englishman Gilbert White's more communal text of letters, *The Natural History of Selborne* (1788–9). Lawrence Buell's *The Environmental Imagination* (1995), perhaps the most influential work of modern American ecocriticism, is to a large degree a book about Thoreau and his legacy. Buell's subtitle is *Thoreau, Nature Writing, and the Formation of American Culture*.[8] Thoreau's two-year experiment with a utopia of one is almost too famous to need description. He rejects the life and most of the economy of his home village of Concord, Massachusetts, living alone in a self-made hut near the shore of Walden Pond nearby. He lives there in the woods for two years. It is a rejection of an urban life dominated by commerce, where 'men have become the tools of their tools' (25), a gesture understood as the rediscovery of an alternative identity and a possible freedom.

Walden remains the only work of environmental literary non-fiction (or more truly, semi-fiction) to become part of the mainstream canon of anglophone literature. Buell describes *Walden* as:

a record and model of a western sensibility working with and through the constraints of Eurocentric, androcentric, homocentric culture to arrive at an environmentally responsive vision. Thoreau's career can be understood as a process of self-education in environmental reading, articulation and bonding.   23

In effect, to study Thoreau involves a process of cultural reorientation that matches the shift now associated with radical environmentalism. Buell's intervention, like Bate's, was in reaction against that critical orthodoxy of the 1980s and 1990s that saw 'represented nature [solely] as an ideological screen' (36).

Thoreau also instantiates what came to distinguish this tradition of environmentalist writing, its blend of natural history, spiritual autobiography and travel writing. It may be useful here to compare Vincent Serventy's *Dryandra: The Story of an Australian Forest* (1970),[9] rated by Geoffrey Dutton as one of the hundred great books of Australian literature.[10] Like Dillard, Abbey and others, Serventy offers an almanac – a tracing of the seasons of a West Australian forest, mixing natural history with a broadly environmentalist ethic lamenting the devastation of Australian ecosystems by alien species, and philosophical speculation (Serventy asks, for example, how far a Martian would recognise the difference between human behaviour and that of a wasp [195]). Yet a striking element of work in the US tradition is missing. This is its explicit or implicit focus on the narrating *I* of the text, and the psychic social, cultural and religious insights derived from a personal experience of the wild as a transformation of the self. Focussed on the subjectivity of the writer as the bearer of certain perceptions and feelings in response to the non-human world, writing in this tradition is yet not autobiographical. Neither Thoreau at Walden Pond nor Dillard at Tinker Creek will write about how, say, an experience of solitude helped them to come to terms with some difficult personal relationship. In effect, the 'self' most at question is broadly the socially determined one that has been brought from the town. The focus is outwards on the natural landscape as the agent of the process of psychic transformation, self-realisation and even liberation. The central drama is generalisably philosophical as opposed to idiosyncratically personal. At the same time, this frequent element of US environmentalist writing is necessarily in some tension with its other distinctive feature, an often biocentric focus on the wild as a cultural space of interest in its own right. Is there a danger that the non-human may sometimes be appropriated as simply a function of a human psychic drama or adventure, even as a kind of therapy?

Over the past decade interpreters of this specific literary tradition have become less ready than earlier critics have been to take its psychic drama on its own terms. Recent ecocriticism has argued that the authentic self 'rediscovered' through the wild is just as socially conditioned or determined as the one supposedly left behind. For instance, Thoreau's stress on independence and frugal self-reliance seems an exclusively masculine project.

A case in point is Edward Abbey's self-proclaimed 'anarchism'.[11] Abbey's novel *The Monkey Wrench Gang* (1975) depicted a group of variously motivated eco-saboteurs in the West. Its influence helped give rise to the radical Earth First movement, some of whose principles are definitely anarchist. In Abbey's non-fiction work, however, the stance is more accurately described as an extreme, libertarian individualism. For one thing, Abbey's strong emphasis on the freedom of solitude contrasts strongly with that investment in notions of self-governing community crucial to the anarchist tradition. Abbey's stance can also be called a 'romantic' one (with a small *r*) in that it idealises wild nature as that realm in which the authentic individual can discover itself 'whole', seemingly freed from the institutions of the capitalist state and its conformist morality. In Abbey's case, however, this is not because the natural world embodies some sort of moral order (as in the pantheism of earlier writers such as Muir), but that its very freedom from human meaning aligns it with the grand gesture of rejecting conformist norms:

> Alone in the silence, I understand for a moment the dread which many feel in the presence of primeval desert, the unconscious fear which compels them to tame, alter or destroy what they cannot understand, to reduce the wild and prehuman to human dimensions. Anything, rather than confront directly the ante-human, that *other world* which frightens not through danger or hostility but in something far worse – its implacable indifference.[12]

For Abbey, like a mid-twentieth-century existentialist, the meaninglessness of nature is also the possible realisation of a human freedom. However, his project of meeting 'God or Medusa face to face, even if it means risking everything human in myself' (6) becomes in practice a romantic individualism, affirming an idea of psychic wholeness in the 'rediscovery of our ancient, pre-agricultural, preindustrial freedom' (*Down the River*, 120). This grand gesture of dismissal of what human life became with the advent of agriculture – settled, over-organized, regulated, divided into hierarchies of status and labour – leads Abbey to ascribe enormous cultural significance to what others might dismiss as only leisure or recreational activities: 'At least in America one relic of our ancient and rightful liberty has survived. And that is – a walk in the Big Woods; a journey on foot into the uninhabited interior; a voyage down the river of no return. Hunters, fishermen, hikers, climbers, white-water boatmen, red-rock explorers know what I mean' (*Down the River*, 121). Abbey's cult of individual psychic health can tend towards a strident individualism barely distinguishable from a consumerist ethos of regarding all the things as means for self-cultivation, with the West as 'A place for the free'.[13] The Australian example forms a useful comparison here, for the harshness of the bush produced no idealisation of solitude but a code of 'mateship' and mutual support.[14]

The environmental historian Kathryn Morse exemplifies recent scepticism about the individualistic romanticism in elements of the wilderness literary tradition in the US. Might its 'drama of solitude' (Roorda) or 'aesthetics of relinquishment' (Buell) perhaps obfuscate some realities of environmental history?

> Literature has works such as *Pilgrim at Tinker Creek*; history has smallpox and cholera epidemics, garbage and sewers, imprisoned killer whales, chemical warfare, malls, television, millions of dead birds and kids with cancer.[15]

Morse surely exaggerates here: Abbey's work, for instance, is full, as we saw, of diatribes against 'malls, television, millions of dead birds and kids with cancer'. The deeper and more intractable issue may be that of audience or readership, as with the case of John Clare in Britain. That is: what may be written as a literature of protest is often consumed as a literature of escape.

A reading: retrieving *Walden*

American environmentalism in general often conceives itself in broadly romantic terms, as 'the attempt to regain, restore, or recover our original relationship with nature understood as a "harmony" of interests and needs',[16] and Thoreau has long seemed the archetypal environmentalist. Jane Bennett, however, traces how an anthology of tributes to Thoreau from various US celebrities appropriate him in nationalist terms that his life and work firmly repudiate. He becomes 'an exemplary embodiment of traditional American values',[17] the environmentalist as responsible citizen, one affirming a special place for wild nature in American self-idealisation. Walden Pond, now a site of mass tourism, becomes a shrine to the cult of American exceptionalism.

Nevertheless, for Bennett and others Thoreau emerges, against such appropriation, more as countercultural figure, repudiating notions of identity and property central to American self-definition, the first of a line of writer/activists who strive to make their own daily lifestyle emblematic. Unlike some later writings in the US environmentalist tradition, *Walden* is explicitly about the nature of work and the irrationality of given systems of political economy and property. 'The life which men praise and call successful is one kind' (*Walden*, 19). 'Where is this division of labor to end?' (31). '[T]he laboring man has no leisure for a true integrity day by day... He has no time to be any thing but a machine' (3). *Walden* thus forms a ready answer to accusations that its writing is 'merely aesthetic', but it also bears out Philip Abbot's observation that 'the combination of political radicalism and self-absorption is a common trait in American culture'.[18]

A crude romanticism in parts of American environmentalist culture can be expressed by a play on the term *nature* itself. One goes to 'nature' to recover one's true 'nature' – you really find yourself by going hiking or through a walk in the hills. This basic schema does apply to *Walden* in some ways. The move to the woods is in part the retrieval of an inner core of selfhood supposedly unsullied by society.[19] However, Thoreau's importance is that things are far more questioning than any standard return-to-nature story. If human nature is mirrored in Walden Pond, it is with 'a recognition that nature and the human self in which it is reflected have depths heretofore unplumbed' (Robert Sattelmeyer).[20] Bennett argues that Thoreau anticipated 'postmodern' debates about how far identity is given or socially constructed. This makes Thoreau stand out against the fundamentalism that often mars American environmentalist culture, its 'reactive demand for certainty, for univocal truths, for patriotic self-affirmation'.[21]

Like Thoreau's earlier *A Week on the Concord and Merrimack Rivers* (1849), *Walden* exploits the kind of looseness of form associated with travel literature. The earlier book was a kind of miscellany, interspersing its travel narrative with passages on all kinds of subjects – folklore, an essay on friendship, literary commentaries and jeremiads against American materialism. Likewise, the speaker in *Walden* presents himself directly to the reader as a tour guide, but this time the journey is a figurative one, concerning the experience of living, watching, walking and growing food in the one semi-wild place. While celebrations of American landscapes, flora and fauna fed easily into the literary nationalism strong at this time, Thoreau, by living 'a primitive and frontier life' (*Walden*, 11) in an unremarkable wood in a long colonised eastern state, displaces the expectations of such literature: 'The West of which I speak is but another name for the Wild' ('Walking' [1862]).[22] Both *A Week* and *Walden* are 'extravagant' in Thoreau's etymological sense of wandering beyond the boundaries. Linck C. Johnson writes of the earlier book, it 'seems to defy all boundaries, either spatial or temporal, and... also seems to defy all generic conventions'.[23] *Walden* mixes a kind of acute microvision with the broadest kinds of cosmic speculation. Even the hum of a mosquito at earliest dawn can seem 'cosmical', 'a standing advertisement, till forbidden, of the everlasting vigor and fertility of the world' (60). Thoreau's fear in *Walden* is that 'my expression may not be *extra-vagant* enough, may not wander far enough beyond the narrow limits of my daily experience, so as to be adequate to the truth of which I have been convinced' (216).

Thoreau still called himself a 'transcendentalist' in R. W. Emerson's tradition of reading moral and spiritual guidance in natural forms, yet he had become such an unorthodox one that 'extra-vagant' is the more useful term, the practice of thinking, writing, lecturing and acting '*without* bounds' (*Walden*, 216). Striking in this respect is the way *Walden* slowly changes perspective. The almost exclusively human focus of the long opening chapter, 'Economy', on work, property, money and so on gives way to chapters such as 'The Ponds', 'Baker Farm' and 'Winter Animals', concerned more with the non-human for its own sake. This switch led the critic Leo Marx to accuse Thoreau of drifting into a kind of evasive pastoral retreat, a view criticised by Buell for overlooking a deeper challenge in the shift from anthropocentricism towards a new and still barely recognisable kind of politics.[24]

Sharon Cameron's study of Thoreau's massive posthumously published *Journal* can also foreground what is most challenging in *Walden*. Cameron affirms the very disorganisation and inconclusiveness of the journal's two million words as forming a kind of open drama that affirms the unknowability of nature, the puzzle of how to represent it or what the human relationship to it ought to be. The minute natural phenomena that Thoreau records 'come to life not because of their human significance but because any human significance that could be ascribed to them fails to account for the degree of Thoreau's interest in them'.[25] His so-called transcendentalism, affirming possible analogies between the natural and human worlds, becomes both multiple and opaque. He writes: 'These expansions of the river skim over before the river itself takes on its icy fetters. What is the analogy?' (25 November 1850).[26]

Leonard N. Neufeldt describes the journal as 'a multitext in search of a form'.[27] *Walden*, by contrast, the subject of a process of seven full revisions, is a greater compromise with expectations of order and significance. Thoreau deploys a chronological structure condensing his two years at Walden into one sequence of the seasons. 'The various revisions which culminate in *Walden* illustrate Thoreau's struggle to "represent" nature in the social forms that are receptive to it – the form of the essay, the homily, the didactic instruction.'[28] Even so, Thoreau's assertive and masterful authorial tone deploys such a variety of idiosyncratic modes of perspective that the book as a whole strains against the norms of aesthetic as well as psychological wholeness. It is never finally decidable what it is all meant to be 'about' in a conventional sense.

A short passage can illustrate Thoreau's continuing challenge:

> Our village life would stagnate if it were not for the unexplored forests and meadows which surround it. We need the tonic of wildness, – to wade sometimes in marshes where the bittern and the meadow-hen lurk, and hear the booming of the snipe; to smell the whispering sedge where only some wilder and more solitary fowl builds her nest, and the mink crawls with its belly close the ground. At the same time that we are earnest to explore and learn all things, we require that all things be mysterious and unexplorable, that land and sea be infinitely wild, uncovered and unfathomed by us because unfathomable . . . We need to witness our own limits transgressed, and some life pasturing freely where we never wander.   *Walden*, 211–12

Thoreau does not use the term *wilderness*, which would suggest a large unsettled area implausible for Massachusetts in the 1840s, but *wild*. This suggests a more fluid quality, less localisable and in part a function of human attitudes. This contrasts markedly with, for instance, Abbey's celebration of wilderness in his *Desert Solitaire*. Abbey blends idealisation of wilderness as a 'Paradise' of 'the here and now', of the 'real earth' (167), with a misanthropic stress on the large size and solitude of a wilderness area as the site for his kind of psychic/ spiritual recreation. Thoreau's idea of 'wildness', on the other hand, gives his reader the challenge of a fully acknowledged contradiction: 'we are earnest to explore and learn all things' but 'we require that all things be mysterious and unexplorable'. His is both an ethic of human finitude and limits and a celebration of their continual transcendence in exploration, either in a real or imaginative sense. Nature seems both a realm to be mapped and explored and an elusive agent whose value lies in its inexhaustible heterogeneity, less a stage for human self-realisation than for less predictable metamorphoses.

Wild

The term *wild* has emerged in environmental criticism as a distinctive aesthetic/ ecological and moral category. Take some titles for instance: *Wild Ideas*, an anthology of essays; Gary Snyder's *The Practice of the Wild*; Richard Mabey, *Landlocked: In Pursuit of the Wild*.[29] The term stresses that element of anything that is resistant to human control, prediction or understanding, 'the unmanaged energy of nature' (Mabey)[30] manifest in even the densest cities in weeds that push through small cracks in the pavement or fissures in a wall. For Snyder the wild is a potential in any place but is most realised in genuine wilderness (*Practice of the Wild*, 12). For him, human consciousness, thought and language, especially the poetic, are also essentially 'wild', an argument in part against the excess of claims that thought, language and so on are totally determined by their cultural context.

Again, Thoreau seems a decisive source. Bennett reads 'wildness' in Thoreau as naming 'the remainder that always escapes taxonomies of flora and fauna or inventories of one's character or conscience; it is the difference of the woods that remains no matter how many times one walks in them; it is the distance never bridged between two humans, no matter how well acquainted' (*Thoreau's Nature*, 36). The wild, in the sense of the acultural and the unpredictable, also engages the singularity and the provocative difficulty of Thoreau's writing. He writes: 'In Literature it is only the wild that attracts us. Dullness is but another name for tameness'.[31]

Thoreau's 'wildness' embraces a craving for reality that can celebrate vertiginously the smallest natural object, feature or contingency, even its sheer resistance to human meaning. If, he argues in a bizarre passage, a 'fact' is fronted face to face, 'you will see the sun glimmer on both its surfaces, as if it were a cimiter, and feel its sweet edge dividing you through the heart and marrow, and so you will happily end your mortal career' (*Walden*, 66). Elsewhere, he writes that the true frontier of a culture is not geographical, but 'wherever a man fronts a fact'.[32] The becoming 'wild' of a fact is also its being taken out of its customary frames of reference to evoke possibilities of plural and dissident significance. The very extravagance of Thoreau's writing forms a challenge both to given horizons of making sense, and, in the image of the cimiter, to anthropocentrism itself. In effect, literary writing becomes the making wild of the commonplace, a site of resistance to reading in the mode of armchair consumerism.

It is as if *Walden* were taking to an extreme a feature of environmental writing and criticism already noted: the disorientating but exhilarating speed with which environmental questions touch the limits of received intellectual competence or consensus. Thoreau's transcendentalist striving to relate natural fact and human values opens rifts, perplexities and chastening questions even as it celebrates the natural world in its very illegibility as a scene of moral speculation.

Chapter 3

Genre and the question of non-fiction

Environmental non-fiction in the tradition of Thoreau remains a major if hardly exclusive concern of twenty-first-century ecocriticism. To open any issue of *Interdisciplinary Studies in Literature and the Environment,* the journal of the Association for the Study of Literature and the Environment, is to still find at least as many studies of creative non-fiction as of the novel and poetry. More than in elements of romantic politics, it is in questions of genre that environmental non-fiction challenges the agenda of literary studies. It does not so much 'question the canon' of received literature as address presuppositions that are arguably deeper than choices as to which specific literary texts 'belong in the canon' or not. These concern the hierarchy of genres of writing. Robert L. Root writes:

> For a long time introductory literature courses and creative writing programs have divided literature into three genres – fiction, poetry, and drama. Although nonfiction as a literary form has been around for a very long time, in creative writing communities it is often seen as a vehicle for the discussion of fiction and poetry rather than an equivalent artistic outlet.[1]

Robert Root's suggested name for creative non-fiction, the 'fourth genre' (247), never caught on. The lack of status enjoyed by explicit non-fiction, though a form as old as Herodotus, reflects perhaps the continuing but anachronistic power of the romantic idealisation of creativity in relation to the other genres.

Experimentation with genre characterises environmental writing. It also extends to the mode in which ecocritics may present their work. Ecocritics usually publish in the standard form of the academic article, but some also imitate the travelogue, the essay, the natural historian's notebook or the explorer's diary, or use the experimental form known as 'narrative scholarship' (see Chapter 17 below). Distinctions between the critical and the creative, primary and secondary text, may be unstable. Barry Lopez's *Of Wolves and Men* (1978) is clearly both at once.[2] Terry Tempest Williams's *Desert Quartet: An Erotic Landscape* performs a kind of erotic engagement with desert places, questioning the cerebral mode of the meditative essay.[3]

'You don't make it up'[4]

As we have already seen, a common literary form for environmental or nature writing is the literary essay, often in the form of a first-person meditation.[5] The essay offers freedom from the constraints of stricter kinds of academic or journalistic article, and has sometimes been understood as a kind of 'antigenre'. Theodor W. Adorno saw the essay as an essentially anti-methodical approach to knowledge, one not engaged with 'the game of organized science . . . [or striving] for closed, deductive or inductive, construction'.[6] If genres, including what are sometimes called subgenres or modes, function 'like a code of behaviour established between the author and . . . reader' (Heather Dubrow),[7] then the essay form suits the often perplexingly interdisciplinary nature of environmental issues. Its freedom can embrace material from diverse sources that would not be admitted in a scientific paper or a piece of historical research, taking on the anecdotal, the impressionistic, the polemical and so on. It shares with forms like the journal or travelogue a seeming openness to the contingency of fact, as opposed to the cognitive closure of more 'finished' writing. On the other hand, this very expansiveness can also render the essay rather relaxed or lightweight in impression.

An excellent example of such issues is Barry Lopez's *Of Wolves and Men*. Overall, it is hard to say whether *Of Wolves and Men* is better described as a long essay, a series of essays or a miscellany of mixed genres. Lopez offers readings of human societies and their condition through the test of their attitude to wolves. To offer an overview of western history with the wolf as its focal point is bizarre and provocative, though the essayistic mode can allow the scholarship to be lax at times.[8] Lopez surveys images of the wolf in literature, folklore, fairy-tale, Greek mythology and so forth. At the same time, such familiar historical work is framed by passages of natural history, travelogue

Figure 4 Wolfskin rug (Nicmac)

and by anecdotes of wolf behaviour, some factual and some more speculative. A section on the constellation 'Lupus' (the Latin for wolf) is even a kind of prose poem. In a Japanese context, Ishumure Michiko's *Paradise in the Sea of Sorrow* (1972) is similarly transgressive of genre, engaging the horrific effects of mercury pollution through a mix of non-fiction, mythology, journalism, autobiography and storytelling.[9]

In Lopez one effect of such strategies is that, viewed from such varied perspectives, the term 'wolf' becomes defamiliarized and displaced from its formerly negative cultural senses, with the effect of rendering huge amounts of cultural and historical material the record of western humanity's hatred, terror, vilification and murderous cruelty, all of which cries out for further investigation or even expiation. 'We are forced to a larger question: when a man cocked a rifle and aimed at a wolf's head, what was he trying to kill?' (138) If all human societies define themselves in some basic respects through how they live a human–animal distinction, then Lopez's histories of wolf extermination in America already pose questions for modern American identity. 'Dead wolves were what Manifest Destiny cost' (184). One image – of helpless victims being shot from a helicopter – still resonates as an emblem of US imperialism.

Such environmental non-fiction is usually defined by distinct ethical as well as formal expectations. Crudely speaking, since the text is engaged with the factual in some sense, there is a corresponding ethic of truthfulness. Lynn Bloom also argues:

> Because writers of creative nonfiction are dealing with versions of the truth, they – perhaps more consistently than writers in fictive genres – have a perceptible ethical obligation to question authority, to look deep beneath the surface, and an aesthetic obligation to render their versions of reality with sufficient power to compel readers' belief.[10]

Hence writing like Lopez's will draw authority from modes of discourse taken as more directly representational, such as historical or biographical narrative and, to an increasing degree, scientific papers and reports. The strength of the implicit contract on truth-telling between reader and author emerges when someone breaks it, as in the peculiar controversy that emerged on the ASLE email list when it emerged that some striking details of natural history reported as personal observations in Annie Dillard's *Pilgrim at Tinker Creek* (1974) were actually second-hand, from the reports of others.[11]

Fiction or non-fiction?

As this weird controversy showed, readers of environmentalist non-fiction make a strong ethical investment in the written effect, necessarily carefully produced, of immediate experience. This creates a peculiar uncertainty about the status of literariness and artifice in such work. Roorda traces in the US environmentalist tradition an ambivalence about portraying the act of writing itself or acknowledging that the narrating figure, depicted as out in the wilds, is actually a professional writer. Annie Dillard is unusual here in foregrounding her status. Other writers tend to downplay writing as an implicit intrusion of artifice into the sustained illusion of immediate observation, of something supposedly recorded in a 'cabin', as mere 'sketches' or 'notes' or Wendell Berry's bizarre goal, 'why not write and live at the same time?'[12]

Such difficulties with literariness inform some reactions against too exclusive a critical focus on environmentalist non-fiction. Two issues stand out. The first, to be discussed later, is the association of the major tradition of environmental non-fiction with the specific culture of the (usually) white and privileged. The second is the question of fiction itself, and the cultural and intellectual assumptions inherent in some conceptions of non-fiction. In his *Further Afield in the Study of Nature-Oriented Literature* (2000), Patrick D. Murphy urged ecocritics to move beyond too exclusive a focus on non-fiction. One reason is that the very concept of non-fiction is evidently fragile and even undecidable: how much adding of second-hand material, embellishment, shaping, rewriting and so on will lead people to regard a work as fictional rather than non-fiction? Is not *Walden*, for instance, more honestly called 'fiction', since

Thoreau recast and revised his own experience so much? Such questions, Murphy fears, can only lead into 'a dimly perceived swamp of presuppositions, biases, and unstated agenda'.[13] His major point is that the stress on non-fiction had led many ecocritics to neglect a vast body of 'nature-oriented literature' in other forms. Does not Kiana Davenport's *Shark Dialogues* (1995), for instance, have a great deal to say about the environmental degradation of Hawaii, while also being a fictional novel? Likewise, why neglect science fiction writers like Ursula Le Guin and William Gibson, who invent hypothetic scenarios depicting various 'ecosystems and human interaction with such systems' (41). Murphy concludes, 'the really salient feature of an environmental literary work may be its impact on the reader's point of view, which can be accomplished through fictional stories as well as nonfictional ones' (52).

An aesthetic consumerism

A further question for environmental non-fiction is this. If the pleasure that readers take in a piece of nature writing is not at least partly explicable in terms of some genuine relation to actual things, as opposed to the consumption of a performance of language, then the moral basis for celebrating such texts is compromised. Some argue that the political and ethical engagements of environmentalist writing are indeed negated or overridden by the way it serves its readership as a source of armchair aesthetic consumerism. 'Consumerism' here means not literal ingestion but the basic stance towards experience as a stock of procurable sensations to be tried and savoured, an attitude that arguably emerged in the Romantic period. Timothy Morton writes:

> To be a consumerist, you don't have to consume anything, just contemplate the *idea* of consuming. Consumerism raised to the highest power is free-floating identity, or identity in process. This is a specifically *Romantic consumerism*. Transformative experiences are valued, such as those derived from drugs, or from intense experiences, such as Wordsworth's 'spots of time', traumas that nudge the self out of its circularity and force it to circulate around something new.[14]

Dana Phillips criticises Lopez and others for offering 'evocations' whose main purpose is a dubious escape into a kind of heightened experience.[15] Both Phillips and Morton are replaying here some of the issues of the so-called 'Nature Fakers' controversy of the early twentieth century. John Burroughs, Theodore Roosevelt and others had attacked the sentimental escapism and factual inaccuracy of much of the popular nature writing of the time, its valuing things 'more for the literary effects we can get out of them than for themselves'.[16] The passages of Henry Williamson quoted earlier are obviously consumerism of this kind.

So what kind of writing is this, from *Of Wolves and Men*?

> Wolves are extraordinary animals. In the winter of 1976 an aerial hunter surprised ten gray wolves travelling on a ridge in the Alaska Range. There was nowhere for the animals to escape to and the gunner shot nine quickly. The tenth had broken for the tip of a spur running off the ridge. The hunter knew the spur ended at an abrupt vertical drop of about three hundred feet and he followed, curious to see what the wolf would do. Without hesitation the wolf sailed off the spur, fell the three hundred feet into a snow bank, and came up running in an explosion of powder.   3

The element of aesthetic spectacle is undeniable in such a passage, but it serves a sense of outrage. Critics like Phillips might reply that the new celebration of the wolf is still offering a form of consumerist sublime, a so-called 'great wildlife spectacle' made possible by the long closure of the frontier. In that respect, the cultural space formed for the wolf in Lopez's book would be equivalent to that of a safely controlled national park, like Yellowstone, where grey wolves were controversially reintroduced in 1995. Nature writing, on such a reading, could not help being a symptomatic product of the very situation against which it also protests, the wilderness tamed.

Lopez, however, thinks that a form of nature writing 'will not only one day produce a major and lasting body of American literature, but might provide the foundation for a reorganization of American political life'.[17] These ambitions obviously go a long way beyond the belletrist essay and any implicit consumerism. Lopez's engagement with a plurality of genres may already have the force of an argument here: that there is no privileged genre that can re-present the non-human. Lopez has also chosen to study a creature whose implication in human cultures in the Northern Hemisphere is so forceful as to challenge the possibility of objective study: 'There is no proper name for all this. It is one long haunting story of the human psyche wrestling with the wolf, alternately attracted to it and repelled by it' (206). The human engagement with wolves has always been partly aesthetic, in ways seemingly too overdetermined to be neutralised by the accumulation of more natural historical knowledge. The wolf remains impossible to disengage from an ambivalent animal aesthetic – even a supposedly objective study could be another way of evading the direct challenge conveyed in the stare of a wolf (registered better perhaps in a myth or fairy-tale?). Mixed genre writing here foregrounds both incompatible modes of thinking about wolves and the refusal of the creature itself to be reducible (204): 'No one – not biologists, not Eskimos, not backwoods hunters, not naturalist writers – knows why wolves do what they do . . . To be rigorous about wolves – you might as well expect rigor of clouds' (4). Thus there are many places where Lopez's narratives draw back, qualifying an observer's assumption, for instance, that there is any 'single-minded strategy' in a wolf hunt's driving prey into the deeper snow (61), or questioning that late-capitalist mindset which satisfies itself with seeing everything in wolf behaviours in terms of 'dominance' hierarchies, status and territory (33, 292–3). We have 'analyzed their hunting behavior in human terms, and none of it is worth more than the metaphor it's couched in' (63).

Do other questions about consumerism remain? Consider the evocative/ poetic kind of nature writing practised by Gretel Ehrlich. Ehrlich's ecofeminist writing foregrounds its author's own experience and impressions in a deliberate refusal of the stance of impersonal authority, foregrounding instead a sensuous, bodily interaction with natural forms. Her essay, 'The Solace of Open Spaces' concerns space both literarily, as the sparsely populated expanses of Wyoming, and as the psychological 'space' encountered there. Telling social detail is interspersed with Ehrlich's own version of that risky element of 'fine writing' often found in essays on landscape:

> Spring weather is capricious and mean. It snows, then blisters with heat. There have been tornadoes. They lay their elephant trunks out in the sage until they find houses, then slurp everything up and leave. I've noticed that melting snow banks hiss and rot, then drip into calm pools where ducklings hatch and livestock, being trailed to summer range, drink. With the ice cover gone, rivers churn a milkshake brown, taking culverts and small bridges with them. Water in such an arid place (the average annual rainfall where I live is less than eight inches) is like blood. It festoons drab land with green veins . . .   7

Ehrlich is clearly striving to refresh a certain kind of nature writing with her slightly unusual imagery – snow 'rots' . . . 'elephant trunks', the images of ingestion, 'drink', 'milkshake', 'slurp'. But there is also a quandary implicit here: the greater Ehrlich's success in evoking specific natural effects by surprising language and rhetorical skill, the more the result may risk seeming a virtuoso verbal exercise, 'aesthetic' in a limited sense alone.

Need such foregrounding of language and rhetorical technique in this kind of non-fiction always be liable to seem consumerist, blunting its ethical challenge? Much ecocriticism evades questions of literariness, content with a largely thematic focus on a text's subject matter. Nevertheless, Thoreau's practice of literary language as making 'wild' of the commonplace kept its force by implicating major philosophical and political questions – about identity, property, anthropocentric concepts of what is 'important', the social bond, and so on. Lopez achieves the same effect by juxtaposing various genres and modes of knowledge. Ehrlich's kind of defamiliarisation, however, when without this broader scope, risks sometimes drifting towards the status of a linguistic chocolate box.

A reading: genres and the projection of animal subjectivity

Eileen Crist's study of genre in depictions of animals, *Images of Animals*,[18] demonstrates how prior decisions about modes of language and presentation project totally opposed conceptions of non-human life. In fact, it seems impossible even to begin discussing animal life without already having taken some major decisions simply through one's choice of language or genre. A choice of modes of language can decide in advance issues as momentous as whether killing a non-human animal is akin to murder or more like turning off a switch. Among the kinds of texts Crist studies are those that clearly belong to the genre of natural history and others that belong to classical ethology.

For natural history, Crist uses the example of an early twentieth-century study by George and Elizabeth Peckham on a species of wasp (*Sphex ichneumonea*), the 'golden digger'. This is how they verbalise their observations of a female wasp:

> she came out and walked slowly about in front of her nest and all around it. Then she rose and circled just above it, gradually widening her flight, now going further afield and now flying in and out among the plants and bushes in the immediate vicinity. The detailed survey of every little object near her nest was remarkable; and not until her tour of observation had carried her five times entirely round the spot did she appear satisfied and fly away. All her actions showed that she was studying the locality and getting her bearings before departure.
>
> Crist, 64

The passage forms a narrative. It places the animal, a 'she' not an 'it', within a recognised sequence of events whose coherence is derived from the fact that they are all rendered as purposeful for the wasp – the insect anticipates its need to return to and locate the nest. The function of narrative here may be familiar to literary critics, as in say E. M. Forster's famous contrast of a mere verbal series of events, 'the King died and then the Queen died', with a minimal narrative, 'the King died and then the Queen died of grief'.[19] Through narrative the animal is posited as the author of various actions, engaged in them meaningfully and perhaps consciously, with some minimal sense of anticipation and even planning. The language can also be said to project a 'life world' for the wasp in the sense of a surrounding environment of meanings, dangers and opportunities the insect is able to read.

The Peckhams' use of narrative to make the wasp intelligible has some links that are weaker than others. In another passage the wasp is described as flying off in order – it is supposed – to hunt. Its return without prey is then interpreted to entail not a questioning of the original assumption but the supposed fact that no prey was found (Crist, 66). When the wasp gives only a cursory survey of the nest before flying away, the Peckhams infer an intention to return more quickly. One question is: how far is the use of narrative here – its sequence of goal-oriented action – projecting things upon the insect that might not be there?[20] Roorda surmises that the mere placement of an animal in a narrative already makes it 'human'.[21]

Much literary nature writing often employs narrative in the same way, interpreting animal behaviour as a purposeful whole governed from the first by meaning and foresight. With creatures more complex than the digger wasp, this may seem less problematic. The following passage from Lopez's *Of Wolves and Men* exploits narrative structure by withholding an overall interpretation of what is observed till the very last sentence:

> I recall how one Alaska evening, the sun still bright at 11:30 p.m., we watched three wolves slip over the flanks of a hill in the Brooks Range like rafts dipping over riffles on a river. Sunlight shattered on a melt pond ahead of them. Spotting some pintail ducks there, the wolves quickly flattened out in the blueberries and heather. They squirmed slowly toward the water. At a distance of fifty feet they popped in the air like corks and charged the ducks. The pintails exploded skyward in a brilliant confusion of pounding wings, bounding wolves, and sheets of sunburst water. Breast feathers from their chests hung almost motionless in midair. They got away. The wolves cavorted in the pond, lapped some water, and were gone. It was all a game. 37

The twist in the last sentence is almost like a short story with a 'trick ending'. It imbues the whole scene retrospectively with a 'higher' level of purposive awareness and freedom of choice than any earlier assumption that the wolves must be hunting the ducks.

Crist contrasts her extracts from natural history with passages of prose from classical ethology. They are glaringly different. Here the animal's behaviour is projected as various kinds of physiological event triggered by stimuli in the environment. Crist quotes Nikolaas Tinbergen's study of a species of water beetle:

> The carnivorous water beetle *Dytiscus marginalis*, which has perfectly developed compound eyes... *does not react* at all to visual stimuli when capturing prey, e.g. a tadpole. A moving prey in a glass tube never *releases* nor *guides* any reaction. The beetle's feeding response *is released* by chemical and tactile stimuli exclusively; for instance, a watery meat extract promptly *forces it* to hunt and to capture every solid object it touches.
>
> Crist's emphasis, 109

This beetle is clearly not the agent of a coherent and purposive sequence of actions carried through from start to finish. It is the passive recipient of a series of atomistic stimuli, each separately releasing some instinctual form of behaviour. The insect is not projected as any form of meaning-possessing subjectivity: each stimulus could in principle be directed at a different *Dytiscus marginalis* and produce the same result. There is no need to posit a continuous underling agent 'to whom' these things happen. The behaviour is a series of stimulus response events. Such language, Crist writes, projects a 'mechanomorphic' understanding of animal life, one that sees the creature as essentially a kind of machine. Major, imponderable questions arise. Is such ethology doing violence to the beetle in depriving it of aim and intents, or, contrariwise, might some even claim that the wolves' supposed game with the ducks was wholly or in part a projection of Lopez's mode of language? What *is* the 'literal' language for describing the behaviour of an animal? In sum, far more than modes of language are at issue in the question of where one draws the line between fiction and non-fiction in what Lopez and others write.

Second quandary: fiction or non-fiction?

In the following piece of prose Mark Cocker offers an account of the flower of a variety of Arum (*Arum maculatum*) also known in Britain as the Cuckoo Pint. Two questions suggest themselves, one of which will be left till the end. The first is: in what ways would this passage lose in effect, quality and interest if no such plant existed and Cocker had invented the whole thing?

> This bizarre and gloriously uninhibited bloom consists of two parts. The outer portion, known as the spathe, is like a narrow-waisted vase widening towards the brim, where the upper lip curls in upon itself to form a shallow hood. From within this sheath rises a swollen spike, purplish chocolate in colour, known as the spadix. These two parts have a function that is as complex as their structure. Spring insects are attracted

by the smell of rotting flesh produced by the spadix and tumble into the sheer-sided spathe, where they become trapped by a series of downward-pointing hairs. If they are carrying pollen, then they fertilize the female flowers lying at the base of the structure, and when this takes place the male stamens mature, releasing their own pollen on to the insect, while the imprisoning hairs shrivel to allow its eventual escape.[22]

A second question would be: in what ways would this passage gain in effect, quality and interest if no such plant existed and Cocker had invented the whole thing?

Chapter 4

Language beyond the human?

A pervasive argument in ecocriticism is that language is a decisive human environment and that its currently dominant forms can rightly be called an environmental problem. This refers to such things as the instrumentalist and anthropocentric language of politics and administration or of official documents for regional planning (e.g., assessing the destruction of an ancient wood in terms of 'lost recreational facilities'). More strikingly, it also includes human-centred assumptions about what language is – a mere tool for humans to represent and manipulate the world?

A persistent target of environmental critics, especially in the 1990s, was a view of language which they attributed loosely to 'postmodern', 'deconstructive' or 'post-structuralist' theory. This is the claim that language forms a kind of cultural prison, confining its users to the specific conceptions and presumptions it projects – an argument encountered often in third- or fourth-hand accounts of thinkers such as Jacques Derrida or Jean-François Lyotard, even though their actual arguments are very different.[1] Ecocritics saw themselves as resisting claims that 'no authoritative and definitive expression or conception of reality is possible' and that 'all we can ever perceive about the world are shadows, and that we can never escape our particular biases'.[2] At times this led to what are now acknowledged as ecocritical caricatures of so-called 'poststructuralism'. The relatively uncontroversial argument that human beings cannot know reality absolutely, without some cultural presuppositions, was sometimes taken to be the patently silly one of denying the existence of reality altogether.[3] Nevertheless, reminding people that 'it is not language which has a hole in its ozone layer'[4] also helped critics affirm environmental issues at a time when literary study was dominated by modes of identity politics.

A realist poetics

Refusal of the notion of language as a prison house, a self-enclosed system of cultural projections, led to various alternative conceptions of how language may be open to the natural world.

In 1995 Lawrence Buell offered an influential and controversial defence of the language of environmentalist non-fiction as the practice of 'disciplined extrospection'.[5] He meant by this writing that submits itself to the difficult discipline of inventing language adequate to the endless variety and subtlety of things in nature, such as Thoreau's attempt to verbalise the subtlest gradations of light on the surface of a lake. To illustrate his argument, Buell quoted and approved a detailed prose passage by John Janovy Jr on the underwater life of the larvae of caddis flies – how they build their 'houses' in the rushing water, the use of submerged twigs, their appearance under a microscope and so on. Janovy's detailed account does not pretend objectivity but foregrounds how much is provisional or suppositious in his language, comparing the appearance of the underwater 'houses' to that of 'a colony of cliff swallows'. Such writing is a thoughtful derangement of normal perception (101) in a mode that refuses the normal human scale. Buell's argument also embraced the kind of ecopoetry found in Gary Snyder and Wendell Berry, their opening of language to the ethical and cognitive challenge of the non-human, the acultural (see 'Ecopoetry', Chapter 13).

Buell affirmed such work as forming a 'realist' or mimetic aesthetic against the overwhelming tendency among critics to read references in literature to the natural world solely as a matter of cultural politics between human beings, a view that reinforces, as 'efficiently as air-conditioning' (110), the domination of intellectual life by a narrow urban psyche. Buell's argument was also directed against tendencies towards 'formalism' in literary theory, that is, studying or celebrating a text as a self-contained formal artifact, attentive more to intricacies of structure than to any ethical claim it may make upon its reader.

Buell's 'realism' was primarily a riposte to readings of the American pastoral tradition that interpreted nature solely as an ideological theatre. What Buell terms 'realist' is more strictly the gesture of breaking apart received projections or constructions of natural things in order to affirm their sheer acultural otherness. Critics of Buell's argument do not reject the challenge of the acultural to received modes of language, but they do query whether the best response would necessarily be a 'realist' aesthetic. One issue is the way the term *realism* may carry an unacknowledged bias towards predominantly western, post-enlightenment secular conceptions of what the real 'literally' or 'objectively' is.

For instance, the Martinican novelist and theorist Édouard Glissant argues that 'realism – that is, the logical and rational attitude toward the visible world . . . betrays the true meaning of things'.[6] Faced with the ocean, people from different cultures may see fundamentally different things. The novelist Leslie Marmon Silko argued that for the Pueblo till recently a realistic picture of an elk would have been rejected as too restrictive.[7] Dana Phillips, arguing with Buell in detail, contrasts the relative ecological simplicity of an urban environment with the daunting complexity of many rural ones: 'The upshot of all this may be that ecocriticism should be *more* anti-representational than other forms of criticism, not *less*'.[8]

In sum, Buell's purgative 'realism' could not become a manifesto for eco-criticism generally. A later chapter of his book also affirms in fact mythic or personifying modes of representing the natural world, if only in terms of the human frame of mind they enact (207). Perhaps it does sometimes make more sense to hear in the non-human a speaking voice, as in Clare's 'Lament of Swordy Well'?

The Spell of the Sensuous (1996)

Buell's *The Environmental Imagination* gave detailed attention to the implications of various modes of language as they project or realise variously destructive or benign kinds of relation between the human and the non-human. In a paper on the literature of animal advocacy, however, Rebecca Raglon and Marian Sholtmejer look to the invention of 'a language which will help us extend our sense of family beyond the human'.[9] Against the common claim that language is a uniquely human attribute, David Abram's *The Spell of the Sensuous* (1996) argues that the sources of language lie in a realm in which the distinction of human and non-human does not apply.

The Spell of the Sensuous is a sophisticated example of an essentially eco-romantic argument about language. Abram follows the thinking of the French philosopher Maurice Merleau-Ponty to trace the deeper conditions of language in the way human experience of the world is necessarily a bodily, an incarnate one, and how this always gives us a basic sense of orientation among things. Bodily sentience already structures the 'life world' around any living thing in terms of possibilities of warmth or cold, nourishment or threat. We live in a world already full of incipient 'meaning' and implication:

> The life-world is the world that we count on without necessarily paying it much attention, the world of the clouds overhead and the ground underfoot, of getting out of bed and preparing food and turning on the

tap for water. Easily overlooked, this primordial world is always already there when we begin to reflect or philosophize. It is not a private, but a collective, dimension – the common field of our lives and the other lives with which ours are entwined... the world as we organically experience it in its enigmatic multiplicity and open-endedness, prior to conceptually freezing it into a static space of 'facts'.[10]

Since possession of bodily sentience is a shared feature of all living things, a certain basic common intelligibility exists between creatures. For instance, a fallen tree that looks too high to jump for an adult human being must look similar in that respect to a cow and different again to a bird or a fox. Its perception *signifies*, in multiplicitous but not incoherent ways. 'Too high' is present, however imaged, explicitly verbalised or not, for the cow as well as the person. Even the lichen growing on the tree may signify possibilities of nourishment or support, consciously or otherwise.

Distinctions of temperature, wind and wet all provide, if not a common language, then an underlying *logos* of possible significations. 'Our bodies have formed themselves in delicate reciprocity with the manifold textures, sounds, and shapes of an animate earth' (22). This forms 'a sort of silent conversation that I carry on with things, a continuous dialogue that unfolds far below my verbal awareness' (52). Abram urges a recognition of our 'direct experience', one in which 'we cannot avoid speaking of the phenomenon as an active, animate entity with which we find ourselves engaged' (56, also 69). This partially shared intelligibility of things and the reciprocity of perception is 'the very soil and support of that more conscious exchange we call language' (74).

As we have seen, both Buell and Bate (in relation to Clare's 'Swordy Well') defend the attribution of agency and 'voice' to natural forms as a benign fiction, one expressing an attitude of respect. Abram, however, defends Merleau-Ponty's seemingly animistic language as accurate and justified: 'the sensible "beckons to me"; it "sets a problem for my body to solve"; it "responds" to my summons', etc. (55).[11] Abrams offers another take, in effect, on Jim Cheney's struggle to articulate the quasilinguistic presence of ancient rocks (see above): 'Even boulders and rocks seem to speak their own uncanny languages of gesture and shadow, inviting the body and its bones into silent communication. In contact with the native forms of the earth, one's senses are slowly energized and awakened, combining and recombining in ever-shifting patterns' (63).

Abram sees some kinds of human language as expressing and foregrounding this perceptual proto-language and others as repressing it. Clearly, for instance, to describe a young bull as a 'unit of livestock' is more repressive than evoking a vulnerable social animal with its own needs and perceptions. 'Unit of livestock' also enacts a notion of language solely as a tool of human mastery over the world, denying the dependence of language on that proto-linguistic *logos* shared by living things.

Abram's overall argument is broader, however, and perhaps more fragile, drawing on work in the so-called orality/literacy school associated with Walter J. Ong, Marshall McLuhan and their successors on how different media of communication enable different modes of subjectivity, identity, memory and knowledge. For these thinkers, language is not a mere tool but an environment that shapes the very psyche of those who may delude themselves as simply 'using' it. Mass print literacy and electronic media, for instance, have now come to shape the inner life of modern people in ways far deeper than they usually realise, affecting conceptions of identity, reality, time and history. Abram's contribution is to assimilate such thinking to a recognisably romantic programme of lamenting a lost 'harmony' or 'fusion' with nature, calling for a supposed reconnection to one's truer self. He believes an originary reciprocity with the world known to oral culture was lost in the technologies of print and writing, whose psychic effects divorce the human from its immediate surroundings and reinforce the dangerous illusion that culture is the sole human environment.

Abram sees the loss of orality and the invention of alphabetic writing as the major condition of anthropocentric attitudes. A notion of human uniqueness and superiority fed in turn into a conception of language as an exclusive human property (as opposed to the so-called 'dumb' animal), while language itself became understood solely as a system of conventional signs. Such a conception is in denial of that shared proto-linguistic *logos* that makes any signification possible, our bodily imbrication in the reciprocities of perception. It also overlooks the 'sensuous, evocative dimension of human discourse' (79), the way language is also facial expression, gesture, bodily posture.

The decisive event in human history, for Abram, was the invention of the technologies of writing, but not seen in terms of the freedom of mind such technics enabled. The issue is *animism*, the attribution of agency and spirit to the non-human. The primordial animism of interaction with the perceptual world became the new dubious animism of written language. For writing itself also involves animism, but one now directed exclusively on letters and ciphers, imbuing them with ghostly agencies of meaning and intent (who, for instance, can read these very words without 'hearing' a voice from somewhere?):

> As nonhuman animals, plants, and even 'inanimate' rivers once spoke to our tribal ancestors, so the 'inert' letters on the page now speak to us! *This is a form of animism that we take for granted, but it is animism nonetheless – as mysterious as a talking stone.* 131

With the growing use of writing, the animism inherent to human life became directed upon its own artifacts, and the world of cultural signs became taken as the supreme human environment, whereas, Abram asserts, purely oral languages before the invention of writing and print had formed an unbroken continuity with the common language of bodily sentience:

> The belief that meaningful speech is a purely human property was entirely alien to those oral communities that first evolved our various ways of speaking, and by holding to such a belief today we may well be inhibiting the spontaneous activity of language. By denying that birds and other animals have their own styles of speech, by insisting that the river has no real voice and that the ground itself is mute, we stifle our direct experience.   263

To illustrate what is lost Abram quotes a text – or more strictly, the transcription of an oral performance – showing how, among the Omaha, a rock may be addressed very much in the mode of speech used to a human elder. His point is that this is not mere 'anthropomorphism':

> unmoved
> from time without
> end
> you rest
> there in the midst of the paths
> in the midst of the winds
> you rest
> covered with the droppings of birds
> grass growing from your feet
> your head decked with the down of birds
> you rest
> in the midst of the winds
> you wait
> Aged one.

This kind of language is not *about* the world, making it its object or representation. Words respond to and 'speak *to* the world, and to the expressive presences that, with us, inhabit the world'. The Omaha invocation articulates one way in which human beings may live 'the sensorial affinity' between themselves and the earth (71). Modern people, however, unlike the Omaha, now find themselves locked in a culture for which discourse is seen as exclusively human, and language solely a convention for representation and control.

Abram argues that a different mode of language will enable a change in human attitudes and perception. Our task now is to try 'to respond to the speech of the things themselves' (273), to re-engage animism, as in the various writers to whom Abram refers.[12]

Third quandary: how human-centred is given language?

This quandary concerns what seems the awkwardness of language in science fiction when narrating events way outside the normal human scale, such as depicting the earth from a distance. For instance, take the opening of David Brin's *Earth: A Novel* (1990), imagining the origin of the solar system:

> The virgin sun wore whirling skirts of dust and electricity.
>   Gas and rocks and bits of this and that fell into those pleats, gathering in dim lumps...planets...
>   One tiny worldlet circled in the middle distance. It had a modest set of properties.[13]

The perspective Brin attempts here strains against the fact that intelligible human language necessarily assumes possession and understanding of an earth-bound bodily existence and its attendant dimensions, something inherent to the very intelligibility of such terms as 'tiny', 'middle distance', let alone 'virgin', 'skirts' and 'pleats'. Brin's fantasy overview of the creation of the earth is belied and made perhaps slightly absurd by what seems the already terrestrial measure of human language. Is this why sci-fi phrases such as 'it was just an insignificant blue planet circling an average small star called Sol' so often seem so incongruous?

The issue of the human measure inherent to language is taken up at length in Chapter 19 below.

Some questions arise about how far Abram's focus on developments in language simplifies human history and prehistory. Abram observes that he does 'not wish to imply that writing was the sole factor' (263) in the loss of a natural participatory consciousness, acknowledging the importance of the emergence of agriculture or of the formal notation of mathematics (264). Nevertheless, his argument downplays such issues as changing technologies of food production, urbanisation or the power of natural science, to make language the crucial feature of what is an essentially romantic meta-historical narrative of the artificial being imposed on the natural, and of the natural conceived, familiarly, as a lost cognitive and moral norm. The result can be provocative but also dogmatic. Abram's sweeping notion of 'oral communities', for instance, is a striking instance of how some western ecocritics tend to write as if all non-industrial, premodern societies formed some single interchangeable example of 'ecological' living.

A more flexible argument, comparable to Abram's, is at work in Gary Snyder's poetic practice and his broadened conceptions of human consciousness, thought and language as essentially 'wild', that is, as not ulti-mately a matter of human invention or control. As such they are part of biologically and ecologically determined patterns of signification that are far from exclusively human. Language – oral or written – is 'wild' in the sense of being a self-regulating system or entity, with properties still opaque to human understanding and certainly not a matter of instrumental control.

Snyder and other thinkers complicate the natural–artificial distinction in relation to language by doing, so to speak, the reverse of Abram, that is, not stipulating that an original mode of human language is 'natural' but in devel-oping a conception of the technical that extends it into the realm of the natural, effectively dissociating the notion of the artificial or technical from an exclu-sively human reference.[14] Cary Wolfe endorses Derrida's argument against the seeming self-evidence with which language is reserved as the exclusive prop-erty of the human ('Of course, if one defines language in such a way that it is reserved for what we call man, what is there to say?').[15] Human language is only one of a vast network of signifying possibilities across innumerable species. Thus:

> it is not simply a question of 'giving language back to the animal', but rather of showing how the difference in *kind* between human and animal that humanism constitutes on the site of language may instead be thought as difference in *degree* on a continuum of signifying processes disseminated in a field of materiality, technicity and contingency, of which 'human' 'language' is a specific (albeit highly refined) instance.[16]

Human subjectivity and language are possible only on the basis of deeper structures of signification and communication that have nothing exclusively human about them. For Snyder, as for Abram, such arguments help refute currently dominant views that language, art and myth are exclusively cultural/artificial human tools for the measuring and mastery of the natural world: 'What a final refinement of confusion about the role of myth it is to declare that although they are not to be believed, they are nonetheless aesthetic and psychological constructs which bring order to an otherwise chaotic world.'[17]

'Meaning', 'order', 'significance', as Snyder argues, should not be understood as cultural qualities projected upon things, or 'constructing' our perceptions of them; they are integral to the activities of all living things. In even the simplest example of following a track made by sheep or goats in the hills, signification is written into the world to be read and, literally, followed. The natural world is full of indicators, signs and communications, associated with diverse and (to us) mostly opaque modes of intentionality and reference. Why should the peculiarities of human consciousness be the narrow standard by which other creatures are judged?[18] (Further ramifications of this question are taken in Chapter 19, on anthropomorphism). For Snyder, dance, myth, sculpture, or for that matter a poem, should be read not as the cultural self-assertion of some group or other but as the wildness of human creativity responding to and mediating other modes of meaning and significance in the world. 'It is not nature-as-[supposed]-chaos which threatens us, but the State's presumption that it has created order.'[19]

The views of language and environment surveyed in this chapter, while opposed, share a crucial feature. Both the view of language as emerging from a natural perceptual *logos* or order (Abram) and the view that stresses how coding, signification, technics, the 'artificial' are already inherent to natural systems (Derrida, Snyder, Wolfe) refuse the common view that language is only a kind of human tool, a technology that can be deployed or not as we choose. We cannot choose to step out of language and somehow orient ourselves in the world without it – how in any case would such an experience be conveyed to others? Language is, rather, a kind of decisive environment out of which we define ourselves. This is an environment that, especially in the West, expresses the overwhelming and often oppressive weight of centuries of anthropocentric modes of thought and perception but that still contains hidden resources and inventive possibilities for those writers and thinkers able to discern and exploit them.

Chapter 5

The inherent violence of western thought?

An understanding of language as a decisive human environment also marks the arguments to which we now turn. What if it emerged that general and even commonsense assumptions and language in the West about what it means to understand, know or interpret something – anything – were implicitly violent and in some ways destructive of their object? Such a dysfunction would pervade the workings of thought, speech and practice everywhere and it would obviously form a major element in the current environmental crisis. This seems an extreme claim, but it is one made and defended by the German thinker Martin Heidegger (1889–1976), the one incontestably major philosopher of the twentieth century whose work has been intimately connected with environmental thinking.

Heidegger's claim is that the course of European and increasingly global history has been largely determined as the hitherto unseen working out of utterly basic but unconsidered modes of thinking and being, dating back to ancient Greece. These are now culminating in a global techno-scientific civilisation that Heidegger saw as a threat not just to the earth itself but also to the essence of humanity, for such a 'civilisation' has proved perfectly capable of regarding people as merely another economic resource or even a waste product.

Heidegger traces in European civilisation's basic sense of things since Greece an intensification and hardening of 'theoreticism', that is, the drive towards technical, mathematically formalisable and objectifying modes of knowledge and, with it, the oblivion of premodern traditions of know-how and craftmanship: 'the familiar and well-known has become boundless, and nothing is any longer able to withstand the business of knowing, since technical mastery over things bears itself without limit'.[1] Many intellectual positions often since labelled 'postmodern' inhabit the space opened up by Heidegger's attacks on the absolutism of modernity's drive to know, and his diagnoses of the troubling interconnections between dominant conceptions of what it means to 'know' or 'understand' something and modes of its control, mastery or manipulation.

What, then, is the specific feature of western thought, even two and a half millennia ago, that harbours such latent violence? Michael E. Zimmerman, glossing Heidegger, coins the invaluable phrase 'productionist metaphysics', metaphysics being the study of the nature of things at the most general level, and 'productionist' as relating to an industrial *product*:

> The metaphysical schemes of Plato and Aristotle, Heidegger argued, were based on the view that the structure of all things is akin to the structure of products or artifacts. Aristotle's metaphysics, for example, is 'productionist' insofar as he conceived of all things, including animals, as 'formed matter'. The most obvious example of such 'formed matter' is the work produced by an artisan who gives form to material. Plato and Aristotle seemingly projected onto all entities the structure of artifacts.[2]

Zimmerman's summary highlights Heidegger's basic point: the hidden anthropocentrism of western thought, its unacknowledged projection of instrumentalist or technological modes of thinking upon the cosmos as a whole. While Plato's and Aristotle's thinking still bore traces of older, non-productionist ways of thinking, this was lost as Platonism and Aristotelianism were passed down: namely, all things are held to be intelligible if analysed in terms of notions of basic designs and their copies (Platonism), or in terms of constitutive forms and the material they shape (Aristotelianism). Even medieval Christianity was productionist in its deep assumptions, for it saw the universe in terms of God as maker and the world as his created product.

Heidegger argues that we must free ourselves from 'the technical interpretation of thinking' whose origins 'reach back to Plato and Aristotle',[3] the productionist notion that thinking is a kind of inner toolkit containing 'ideas' to be picked up and employed on 'problems' as occasion requires. Thinking, after Heidegger, cannot be the act of a would-be sovereign consciousness seeking the security and power of an assured and totalising system of watertight concepts. This model of thought is memorably caricatured by Heidegger as the securing of 'booty' from the 'outer' world into the stronghold of the mind.[4] Such a mode of knowledge is linked to the instrumentalist and fundamentally aggressive project of western rationality, now in its globalising phase. Thinking for Heidegger, especially in art, need not mean the conscious positing of various representations of an object world. It must instead be a non-assertive tracing out of the measure and manner of the realm of unconcealment in which it already moves. So it is not a matter of 'grasping', 'securing', 'making certain' and 'mastering' but of 'following', 'hearkening', 'hinting' and 'being guided'.

In a travelogue of his first journey to Greece in 1962, Heidegger saw an objectifying anthropocentrism in action in all the tourist cameras and video recorders at the ancient sites. Yet the ancient Greeks, he argued, had had no sense of 'landscape' or a 'feeling for nature' in any modern sense. For them, instead of everything being referred back to some central human consciousness as a spectator of some kind, the world is not an object but a continual happening, within which alone human consciousness finds itself, has an identity and picks up on things. In the hills and sea around, Greek humanity experienced itself as encompassed by a realm which its own projections or conceptualising could not ground, which thus appeared sacral.[5]

Heidegger offered a genealogy of the term *nature*, tracing its crucial work in helping set up many of the basic terms and culture wars of western history. He traced the term back through the Latin *natura* to the ancient Greek *physis*. *Physis* is often translated as 'nature', but more strictly names, Heidegger argues, *the realm of that which arises of and from itself*, whereas 'nature' tends now to name the natural world only in the assumed mode of objectness.[6] In other words, Heidegger's concept of *physis* is close to that notion of the 'wild' already traced in modern environmentalist writing – that which is not a matter of human control and in which, ultimately, we are completely dependent, embedded, despite fantasies of knowledge and control.

In reducing the concept of *physis* to nature in the sense of objectness, modern thinking, according to Heidegger, enacts dangerous fantasies of human overlordship. A great deal of thinking since the scientific revolutions of the seventeenth century has deployed a conception of the mind as essentially a spectator, an enclosed interiority facing the world in a stance of inherent opposition and appropriation, a 'subject' opposing an 'object'.[7]

Some of the most challenging aspects of Heidegger's work for environmental thinking lie in his notion of the 'earth', which ought to be approached as a kind of technical term, not as just the name of a planet. It relates to *physis* at its most wild, resistant and opaque, to the fact that the inherited nexus of significances, purposes, assumptions and practices that make up a human 'world' does not exhaust the human environment. 'Earth' means not just the physical environment without which no human world would exist, but also the very resistance to understanding and knowledge inherent to the non-human. Heidegger's 'The Origin of the Work of Art' affirmed the reserve and opacity of the earth through a meditation on the nature of rock:

> The stone presses downwards and manifests its heaviness. But while this heaviness weighs down on us, at the same time, it denies any penetration into it. If we attempt such penetration by smashing the rock, then it

shows us its pieces but never anything inward, anything that has been opened up. The stone has instantly withdrawn again into the same dull weight and mass of its fragments. If we try to grasp the stone's heaviness in another way, by placing it on a pair of scales, then we bring its heaviness into the calculable form of thought. This perhaps very precise determination of the stone is a number, but the heaviness of the weight has escaped us. Color shines and wants only to shine. If we try to make it comprehensible by analysing it into numbers of oscillations it is gone. It shows itself only when it remains undisclosed and unexplained.[8]

Heidegger recognised that no facet of the universe, no plant or animal, can even be mentioned without, by that very act, becoming part of the discriminations and significances of a human cultural world: few terms are in fact more scarred by dispute and actual violence than 'nature'. In their beguiling otherness the forms of nature have been engaged to underwrite equally both the most self-deluding egotism or the most chastening piety of thought. Nevertheless, conceived merely in terms of its necessary otherness and resistance to human appropriation, the earth may form a kind of reserve and sometimes refuge from a world constituted by an aggressive anthropocentrism. This is how the earth is engaged in an experimental text of 1947, 'Aus der Erfahrung des Denkens', 'From out of the Experience of Thinking'.[9] This concerns Todtnauberg in southern Germany, site of Heidegger's mountain work hut. It is a place of solitude and the non-human events of time and weather, the sound of a stream at night or of a storm in the building's rafters. In its inexhaustible refusal of human meaning, the earth seems elusively self-secluding.

Heidegger's preference was for places that refused any illusion that the human world rests on foundations of its own positing, places that have – like Delphi and its mountains – the quality of stressing the relative smallness of human objects and dimensions. These are landscapes of a stark horizon in which an explicitly anthropocentric conception of the universe would be almost unimaginable, even if it is also the presence of the human that reveals that very starkness and power. In some ways what captivates Heidegger in such places is not so different from the kind of elemental quality associated with the western United States by writers in the American wilderness tradition. Heidegger's places, however, are all explicitly inhabited – the Black Forest, Athens, Delphi, the shores of the Danube, Provence. The sea, river, mountains in their inhuman grandeur make palpable the 'exocentric' nature of the human inhabitants. In the lectures on Hölderlin's 'The Ister' the path of the river Danube is said to tear 'human beings out of the habitual midst of their lives, so that they may be in a centre outside of themselves, that is, be exocentric'.[10] It is not a matter of some modern, inherently consumerist subjectivity that 'has' experiences but of 'experiences' that 'have' or that open a space for other, less aggressive modes of subjectivity.

The archetypal eco-fascist?

Heidegger's work, directly or more often indirectly, informs that large strain in modern thought suspicious of the deep connections between the drive to represent something in some system of knowledge and the drive to control and master it. Heidegger's difficult readings of the German Romantic poet Friedrich Hölderlin, from the 1930s to 1950s, remain a neglected monument of early ecocritical thinking.[11] Most explicit ecocritical use of Heidegger, how-ever, picks up only the general thrust of his thinking to assimilate him to a broadly romantic reading advocating a more authentic 'dwelling' on the earth, one which lets things be rather than appropriating them in the grid of modern industrial rationality. Bate, for instance, sees Heidegger as offering a mod-ern 'inflection of High Romantic poetics',[12] as affirming 'human dwelling' as distinguished by its 'particularity – by, one might say, its cottageness'.[13]

Such romantic readings highlight the undeniable element of agrarian nos-talgia in Heidegger but this also, as Bate acknowledges, relates to that element of his career that makes Heidegger such an embarrassment to enviromentalists. A *petit bourgeois* concern with 'rootedness' was also part of Heidegger's notorious period of allegiance to the Nazi party in the 1930s. This is the Heidegger who has now become a watchword for the eco-fascism latent in too hasty a rejection of enlightenment ideals of universal rationality in favour of the cultivating of a close, would-be 'authentic' relationship to one's local place, traditions and dialect. Such a stance leads too easily to atavism and even, if not in Heidegger then in others, to racist conceptions of those held not to belong.

How far Heidegger sank in the 1930s is debatable. His disgrace has now become a salutary reminder of the ugly politics that may lurk in romantic ide-alisations of 'closeness to one's native earth', of belonging and non-belonging and so on. At the same time, to reduce Heidegger to an archetype of the eco-fascist is to underplay what is distinctive and challenging about his concept of nature, which he also came to affirm against the totalitarian state. This is his stress on the inherent resistance and opacity of the 'earth', its complete otherness to human constructions and uses of it.

The notion of the 'earth' was coined to displace any notion of 'nature' understood as foundational, that is, as some lost essence or ground of being to which the human ought to correspond, from which it has fallen or from which it can be deduced. Earth is not a ground, it has no meaning, but it 'remains

sheltered in the inapparent law of the possible which it is itself'.[14] So, despite
the tendency to political kitsch in Heidegger's accounts of his home region of
Germany, he cannot coherently advocate a reintegration or recovery of some
lost harmony with such an earth in the way still imagined by some green critics.
The earth has no cultural meaning in itself, however many forms of politics –
romantic, totalitarian, conservative, anarchist – may be projected upon it. To
think the 'earth' in Heidegger's sense becomes no kind of 'return' to nature,
but an emptying out of given concepts against the element of a chastening
opacity and refusal. 'Is there a measure on earth? There is none' (Hölderlin).[15]

The forest

At this point we turn to Robert Pogue Harrison's *Forests* (1992),[16] one of the
outstanding works of ecocriticism to date. Harrison offers a broad historical,
philosophical and literary study of forests as marking the 'edge of Western
civilization, in the literal as well as imaginative domains' (247). This project
rests in part on a Heideggerian argument at odds with any idealisation of
agrarian rootedness.[17] Harrison's study as a whole may also show how false it
would be simply to identify 'Heideggerian' and 'eco-fascist'.

The force of Harrison's study lies in its focus on something that is an empirical part of the natural world – the forest – and yet has also been constitutive
for human self-understanding, historically, culturally and imaginatively. Harrison's subject is 'the forest' as it relates to a whole historical series of different
ways of conceiving and inhabiting the opposition between the human and the
wild. Here 'history does not mean the grand events of the past but rather the
human appropriation of the earth as a place of dwelling' (208). Harrison's is
thus a kind of transcendental '"poetic history" [of the forest] which has its
basis in empirical and cultural history but which cannot be reduced to either'
(93).

Harrison is not writing as a disciple of Heidegger. Nevertheless, his thought
becomes explicitly Heideggerian towards the end. Put crudely, the issue is the
working of the culture–nature distinction, of how human meaning emerges
amid the realm of natural givenness, a 'world' from out of the opaque self-
affirmation of 'the earth'. The argument can be illustrated by the simplest
logical point. What happens when a line is drawn transecting an otherwise
undifferentiated space, like, say, a path across a forest? The mere line at once
makes possible a 'this side' and a 'that side', a 'here' as opposed to a 'there',
known against unknown, domesticated space against surrounding wilderness
and so on. With the securing of the human space as a form of clearing, there

also emerges the projection of the possibility of narrative, linear time, paths of memory and tradition, as against the non-human circular time of the forest, the undifferentiated eventhood of natural forms, the endless cycles of decay and growth.

The border between the human clearing and the forest is both an empirical one – the boundary of inhabited land – and also a mark of conceptual differentiation and definition. At different times in various ways (traced by Harrison in detail) it is implicated in such distinctions as civilised–wild, controlled–unpredictable, known–unknown, useful–useless, human–animal, legal–outlaw, secular–magical and so on.

A simple but powerful logical point differentiates this mode of thinking from green arguments in the tradition of romantic oppositionalism. For Harrison (as for Heidegger) the distinction between the human and nature is not posed as one that can or should be 'overcome'. The gap between the human and its others is constitutive of the human: abolish it, erase the line, and the human disappears. 'We dwell not in nature but in the relation to nature. We do not inhabit the earth but inhabit our excess of the earth. We dwell not in the forest but in an exteriority with regard to its closure' (201).[18]

In the last stages of the book Heidegger's presence becomes most legible, if unacknowledged. Harrison is at his most Heideggerian in the refusal of notions of the human that look to some supposed lost unity with the natural world, neutralising or evading the definitive separateness of human beings. The least crossable border with the forest is that of human language as the space of human desire and 'making sense'. The very fact that we feel so drawn to natural things to ask questions of their and our own significance 'means that we have already left nature's closure behind . . . We long for meaning's closure, but only in our longing does the human world make any "sense"' (230).

Harrison's 'poetic history' is partially indebted to another of Heidegger's major arguments. This is the understanding of art and literature as a privileged site in which fundamental assumptions about or definitions of the human and non-human and their relationship may become newly perceptible or at issue, as in Ovid's versions of classical myths of the forest as a space of metamorphosis, where distinctions made by custom, language, sanction or law may even break down. Actaeon, transformed into a stag by the Goddess Artemis, whom he has glimpsed naked in the forest, is torn to pieces by his own hunting hounds. Pentheus is killed by his own mother, who mistakes him, under the influence of Dionysos, for a lion. Harrison writes of Actaeon's fate:

> The story has an unmistakable psychological effect upon the reader, for while Actaeon is literally de-anthropomorphized, the stag that he turns

> into becomes humanized. Now that Actaeon has become a stag we are
> able to suffer its fate as if it were a human being. The distinctions
> collapse. Like Actaeon, we are made to see that the forms of the world
> are transient, illusory and reversible.   26

A history of ways of conceiving and treating the forest is thus one of different conceptions of being human. The forests form 'an opaque mirror of the civilization that exists in relation to them'. Harrison writes of how the enlightenment and modern 'reduction of the forests to the status of a material resource in need of management' (120) also projects, as its very shadow, conceptions of the forest as the embodiment of anti-modern values, so giving thought access to 'the shadow of Enlightenment ideology' (108). This shadow Harrison reads in emerging ideas of the forest as both the space of the non-rational and as sanctuary, in the writings of Jean-Jacques Rousseau, for instance, or, conversely, of 'the humanist's terror of a world that transcends human grounding' (147), as in the famous close description of the gnarled bark of a tree in Jean-Paul Sartre's *Nausea* (1938).

To trace the shifting demarcations of the line between human and nonhuman shows how those conceptions of nature that people have inhabited possess no absolute status but 'are given by historicity' (163). This point is central to Harrison's ironic reading of William Wordsworth's sonnet 'The world is too much with us' and his poem 'Lines Written in Early Spring'. Harrison shows how even this definitive 'nature poet' already enacts an essentially urban consciousness. For it is Wordsworth's sense of 'what man has made of man' that both 'divorces the poet from nature but at the same time lies at the source of his nostalgia for origins, [drawing] nature into its presence, allowing its "thousand blended notes" to sound their harmony' (163). Such idealisations find their determining condition in what they are opposed to.

Harrison's Heideggerian reading of Thoreau's *Walden* also refuses the commonplaces of self-discovery through a return to nature, finding instead an anti-romantic romantic. *Walden* is about dis-location, literal, cultural and psychic, about the uncanniness of self-consciousness. Harrison homes in on the passage in which Thoreau turns his house, so to speak, inside out, moving all chairs, bed and bedstead out of doors so he can clean the floor. Such estrangement of the normal boundaries of dwelling enacts an anti-romantic view of nature as 'where we go to get lost', finding in ourselves only the truth of that estrangement. '[N]ature . . . teaches us that it cannot assume responsibility for human existence' (227).

Chapter 6

Post-humanism and the 'end of nature'?

Would someone from five hundred years ago actually recognise many modern people as human beings at all?[1] Jacques Derrida's question may introduce the extraordinary arena of debate, fantasy and politics known as 'post-humanism'. This concerns the way recent scientific and technical developments challenge inherited concepts of what the 'human' is or means. We live at a time when the question 'what is man?' no longer allows the leisure of theological and philosophical speculation, but may take on 'a terribly concrete and urgent form'. Derrida, for instance, writes of the fear that some future manipulation of the human genome could become a 'crime against humanity', something 'against the essence-itself of humanity, against an idea, an essence, a figure of the human race, represented this time by a countless number of beings and generations to come'.[2]

Other debates concern nano-technology, genetic modification of plants and animals, gene therapy, biometrics, cloning, stem cell research, artificial life, artificial intelligence and new reproductive technologies. All challenge given demarcations as to what is 'natural' and what is not. Slavoj Žižek writes: 'nature is no longer "natural", the reliable "dense" background of our lives; it now appears as a fragile mechanism which, at any point, can explode in a catastrophic manner.'[3] Some modern technical and scientific developments no longer merely aim to dominate nature, but actually to supplant it.

Catherine Waldby follows N. Katherine Hayles and others in defining post-humanism as 'a general critical space in which the technocultural forces which both produce and undermine the stability of the categories of the "human" and "nonhuman" can be investigated'.[4] It is also necessary, however, to make some crucial distinctions. Post-humanism in a critical sense is not what is sometimes called 'trans-humanism', that is those relatively naïve, technologically inspired narratives about humanity transcending itself in a supposed process of ever more powerful self-construction. The hype sometimes produced by biotechnology companies and their supporters merely continues the modern-age assumption that humanity should oversee, control and mould nature to its own ends. Able to manipulate and produce more and more of their own biology, human beings may, it is claimed, acquire almost limitless power, as with a brain supplemented by an embedded microchip, bionic limbs and so on, defeating natural finitude and perhaps even attaining immortality. Such rhetoric intensifies rather than questions inherited mind–body and culture–nature dualisms. In this way new technologies have all too often fed outmoded types of humanism, exalting the human as essentially mind, reason or some other essence. Teresa Heffernan writes of modern biotechnologies:

> Pig valves in transplant patients or tissues grown with the aid of a cow egg or hamster eggs fertilized with human sperm to test fertility or pigs spliced with human genes are all acceptable hybrids in the construction of the new post-Enlightenment body of science because, in the process of the assimilation of the 'non-human', the hierarchical divide between it and humanity is sustained. The owning, controlling, patenting, and manipulation of what is understood as nature (as excluding humanity but in its service) is left unchallenged . . . [5]

The fallacy in such hyper-humanism is to assume that technology is only a tool, the servant of certain presupposed human features and faculties that are somehow always unchanged – reason, progress, a certain egalitarianism and progressivism, self-improvement and so on. Even if the human is seen as being altered through new technologies, this is nevertheless understood to happen in the service of some core 'human' values, assumed to remain self-evident and unchanged.

The limits of the view of technology as essentially only a tool have been known for a long time. Technologies have always defined and changed the human – consider only the prehistoric inventions of clothing, fire and the conventions of sign-making. Other arguments stress the centrality of the invention of writing and later printing as conditions for the emergence of modern interiorised subjectivity, modern systems of politics and institutions of science. To be human is from the first a matter of engagement with technics and such prosthetics as systems of signification and externalised memory. Consider, for instance, the blow to human conceit implicit in the revolutions of thought made possible merely by a change in conventions of recording numbers – try multiplying CLVII by DCV and compare that with the relative ease of doing the same thing as 157×605.

Decades ago, Gregory Bateson wrote of the old but still exciting question, 'can machines think?':

Now let us consider for a moment the question of whether a computer thinks. I would state that it does not. What 'thinks' and engages in 'trial and error' is the man *plus* the computer *plus* the environment. And the lines between man, computer and environment are purely artificial, fictitious lines.[6]

Bateson homes in here on the way human thinking is mediated and made possible by elements outside the brain. The thinking 'mind' is located in the interactive and continuously shifting feedback loop between computer screen and brain. The fact that Bateson's point applies just as well to someone working with pen and paper, or just using language, reinforces the basic view of human thinking that has emerged out of cybernetics and systems theory. Human thoughts are relational parts of an open system whose other components would include physical media and shared codes of understanding.

For many, then, the human has always been 'post human'. Post-humanism, strictly understood, challenges dominant conceptions of the human even apart from the implications of new technologies. Here, environmentalist arguments touch on that most immediate and seemingly apolitical issue, my immediate sense of myself as an 'I'.

At stake is the now dominant liberal humanist conception of the human self, that of a seemingly pre-given, personal, unique identity, a realm of unshakeable privacy, centre of its own world of values, perceptions, beliefs, commitments and feelings. Such a conception of the 'I' now seems self-evident to many people. It is crucial to that possessive individualism pervading modern culture and markets: one's 'self' becomes something to be more truly 'discovered', cultivated, developed and protected, so that life becomes a kind of project of self-creation and enhancement, and so forth. The fact that such language already begins to resonate with the terms of advertising hints at the deep connection between liberal humanist concepts of subjectivity and the workings of consumerism and late capitalism, with their creation of ever new markets of needs and desires or lifestyle choices and so on. The self as the ongoing project of a unique 'me' is already the self as consumer.

A distinguishing feature of post-humanism is its rejection of images of the natural as some lost condition to which the self should return or be restored. For the philosopher Bernard Stiegler the human has always been a construct of its own tools, which of course can no longer be understood simply as 'tools', for they are more than the instruments of their supposed users but help make those users the creature they are.[7] John Lechte sums up: 'Were there no *what* (external material support in general, including tools and all forms of technology), there would be no *who* (humanity as subject, actor, community, person, self, consciousness, interiority)'.[8] In Donna Haraway's influential phrase, human beings are 'cyborgs'.[9]

Post-human arguments, in sum, are anti-romantic, refusing claims that there is some original human nature suppressed by the artificial, from which it must be retrieved.[10] Instead, the 'self' is understood as 'local, fluid, contingent, and as contesting and rending the hierarchal binaries of nature/culture, self/other, male/female, human/nonhuman' (Heffernan, 'Bovine Anxieties', 118). A post-humanist would query, for instance, David Abram's eco-romantic commitment to the notion of a determinate pre-given human nature, one which some media supposedly express fully (e.g., primitive orality) but others suppress or distort (e.g., print literacy). Study of the various psychic and social effects of different media of communication could lead to equally reasonable conclusions that what a human being actually is is malleable, a partial construct of its own communication technologies and social structures. There is no pristine but now suppressed human nature, but a general mix of malleability and resistance, together producing differing effects of disposition and capability according to context and conditions. Provocatively, it is increasingly recognised that this is the status also of many non-human species, so blurring not only the distinction of human and mechanical but of human and animal.

A reading: *Frankenstein*

Mary Shelley's famous novel of 1818, and its various film versions, are frequently mentioned in relation to experiments with genetics, the modification of crops or new reproductive techniques. The power of Shelley's myth is such that some scientists even attribute much of people's suspicion of biotechnologies to its influence, the horror of so-called 'Frankenstein' foods.[10] Often, such resistance seems evidently just, as in efforts to resist corporations like Monsanto patenting their seeds and adding a terminator gene to their products, so forcing farmers to buy them anew each year. At other times, the repugnance felt for biotechnology seems rather a matter of rational prudence – given the incalculable complexity of natural forms, who knows what might ensue? At other times still, however, it seems more of a knee-jerk reaction, part of an idealisation of the 'natural' as pure or even sacrosanct in some sense.

Can humanity manipulate the natural world without, in the process, altering itself? *Frankenstein* seems to hover between two continuing extreme positions, not really endorsing either, both as powerful today as they were in 1818. The first is that humanity can potentially control nature and mould it to its will; the second is that nature totally defines the human and sets up a moral norm that

Figure 5 GM protest (Spinka2)

should not be transgressed. Morton suggests that '*Frankenstein* is an ecological novel precisely *not* because it compels us to care for a pre-existing notion of nature, but because it questions the very idea of nature'.[11] In creating a pseudo-human being and then rejecting it in horror, Victor Frankenstein has been held to anticipate major and opposite reactions to modern biotechnology. The first is a sense of enhanced power and control over the forces of nature. Before the creature actually becomes alive Victor indulges a self-image as a scientist who has broken the bonds of nature: 'Life and earth appeared to me ideal [i.e. imaginary] bounds, which I should first break through, and pour a torrent of light into our dark world. A new species would bless me as its creator and source . . .'[12] Like Victor, some advocates of gene manipulation see themselves as potential beneficiaries of mankind, committed to the inexorable increase of human control over nature, a defiance of natural limits. Biotechnology, on this view, becomes another enactment of the fantasy that humankind is not part of nature, but its overlord, and that the human mission is to render more and more of the natural world part of a usable technics – as if, somehow, the environment of a whole planet could be exploited for immediate use without this having further consequences for its inhabitants. Just as the surrounding air, water and food become altered by human activity, so the very fantasy of being above and apart from nature 'paradoxically produces us as increasingly hybrid, as increasingly part of and produced by that other' (Teresa Heffernan).[13]

Frankenstein anticipates here modern novels about the denaturation of life, focussed on waste, pollution and the effects of living in an overwhelmingly synthetic environment of simulacra. Reading Don De Lillo's *White Noise* (1985) and John Updike's *Rabbit at Rest* (1990), Cynthia Deitering writes that 'toxic waste seems to function in recent fiction both as a cultural metaphor for a

Figure 6 Child with gas mask (Earth First!)

society's general fears about its collective future and as an expression of an ontological rupture in its perception of the real'.[14] In Christa Wolf's novel *Accident: A Day's News* (1997) the daily routine of a middle-aged writer during a beautiful spring day in a village in (then) East Germany is pervaded by news of the nuclear accident at Chernobyl. Anxieties about predicted fall-out drastically alter perception of the radiance of the sun; there is a sense of the collapse of normally defining geographies, the distinction between the familiar and consoling and the far away and dangerous. Can the nature poetry of the past ever be read in the same way? Who will again write so innocently of a 'cloud' or 'white cloud' (wandering lonely or otherwise)? The garden must be weeded wearing rubber gloves.[15]

In rejecting the creature in horror when it comes alive, Victor instantiates another common contemporary attitude, that spontaneous horror of the 'unnatural' which is so strong a feature in modern reactions to biotechnology. As a result of Victor's repulsion, his experiment causes a series of disasters and moral failures that invoke a sense of crisis as to what a human being and nature actually are. Unlike all those horror plots in which to confront the monstrous serves finally to police and strengthen the division between human and non-human, in *Frankenstein* distinctions between creator and creature become uncertain, the one doubling the other. Victor's horror at his own creation can also be seen as that of someone who, investigating the secrets of life in assembling putrid fragments of dead bodies and putting them together, discovers that, as with modern researchers on the genome, there is no 'secret' as such, that the biological is itself the material horror that can seem entirely to constitute us, a fluid and manipulable biological machine.

In *The End of Nature* (2003) Bill McKibben argues that nature, in the sense of that which is defined by lack of human interference, no longer exists on earth.[16] *Frankenstein*, however, also contrasts with such protests on behalf of a lost nature. It raises the more disturbing question of whether the current transgressions of all kinds of divides (cultural–natural, animal–human, synthetic–biological) are not instead a revelation of the very fragility and permeability of categories that were never as secure as people may once have imagined. Slavoj Žižek writes: 'there is . . . no *Nature qua* balanced order of self-reproduction whose homeostasis is disturbed, nudged off course, by unbalanced human intervention'.[17] With Žižek's point in mind, one turns to *Frankenstein* with a new sceptical understanding of Victor's need, when telling his history, to vehemently moralise his action in retrospect as a terrible transgression that could only lead to disaster. Such moralism recoils from the more uncomfortable possibility that there may be no natural moral order to transgress.

Ecology without nature?

The project of Morton's *Ecology without Nature* (2007) is clear from its title. In discussing what sort of relationship people should have to their environments, why not drop the term 'nature' altogether, as a frequent source of confusion, obfuscation and moral dogmatism?

Morton observes, like many others, how various ideas of nature and the natural have functioned to legitimate corresponding ideas of community and nation. 'Different images of the environment suit different kinds of society' (17). Some examples have already been cited: under the heading of relating to 'nature', Jonathan Bate idealises a sedentary rural economy; Edward Abbey celebrates landscapes of the western United States in terms that re-enact American liberalism's basic myth, the self-realisation of the individual against artificial convention. Other people find that living in what they must now call a 'developing' country also means having their livelihood disrupted by the requirements of the supposedly unspoilt 'wilderness' in which they have always worked. The appeal to a certain kind of behaviour, place or entity as 'natural' often still has the force of a magic word: 'natural' often really means 'in no need of further justification'. Hence the danger of the term as a means of policing human norms ('this behaviour is not natural', etc.).

'[I]t is in art that the fantasies we have about nature take shape' (11). Morton argues that ecocriticism too often endorses modes of regressive fantasy in its commitment to an underexamined notion of 'nature' as that which is sacred, pure, untouchable and overendowed with an aura of moral authority and wisdom: 'Putting something called Nature on a pedestal and admiring it from afar does for the environment what patriarchy does for the figure of Woman. It is a paradoxical act of sadistical admiration . . . transformation into . . . fetish object[ ]' (5).

Morton argues that some ecocriticism, in projecting such an image of pure nature as a source of authentic experience, forms a kind of spiritual consumerism, one whose terms perpetuate strict divisions between the human and nature that a more genuinely ecological insight would refute. This is not the natural world known to biological research. Morton urges instead a new organicism, one that recognises the mechanical and algorithmic in the natural (190ff). In a reverse of the sacralisations of deep ecology, such a new organicism would affirm the need to love what may seem revolting, pointless or mechanistic, crossing the boundaries of both human and animal and human and machine. With reference to the Ridley Scott's film *Blade Runner* (1982), for instance, it would be a matter of loving the replicant human being as a replicant and not as a fantasy human, or, in another revisionist reading of a high Romantic text, Coleridge's 'The Ancient Mariner', a matter of the mariner's sense of kinship with the slimy water snakes (158–9). An ecology without 'nature' would mean refusing to deploy ideas of the natural and authentic as hidden ways of policing unexamined moral and aesthetic norms. Nature is already us, in mixed, uncomfortable and sometimes even disgusting ways, not something 'out there'.

Evidently, Morton's rejection of 'nature' is nothing like the sweeping claim that nature is only a social construct, rather the reverse. It is an affirmation of something wild, contingent yet also often disconcertingly mechanistic that constitutes us. So, despite his title, it is not finally a matter of thinking ecologically 'without nature', but only 'without "nature"' as a touchstone of intellectual certainty and moral purity or guidance.

Morton also refers to Shelley's novel:

> The augury of *Frankenstein* is the reverse of deep ecology. The task becomes to love the disgusting, inert, and meaningless. Ecological politics must constantly and ruthlessly reframe our view of the ecological: what was 'outside' yesterday will be 'inside' today. We identify with the monstrous thing. We ourselves are 'tackily' made of bits and pieces of stuff. The most ethical act is to love the other precisely in their artificiality, rather than seeking to prove their naturalness and authenticity.   195

The immediate impact of post-humanist thinking in environmental criticism may be to highlight the sometimes hidden ethical–political decisions inherent each time someone refers to 'nature' or 'the natural' as a source of moral authority. It is no longer self-evident, in all cases, what 'natural' means. Adrian Franklin writes, at the end of a book on animals and what he terms eco-nationalism in Australia:

> Globally, we are entering a period of intense biopolitics, a new field of politics that contests our 'proper' relation to the biological or, more exactly, to life itself . . . this politics can never be based on the sensible debating of, and drawing the right conclusion from, *the scientific facts*. This is partly because there is no proper, correct or authentic nature in the first place: models of ecological balance and stability are romantic and unrealistic, particularly when it comes to understanding where humans fit. Human history, but also nature, is essentially about *disturbance* and change.[18]

Franklin's argument is perhaps drifting here towards a dangerous overconfidence that 'nature' is a matter of human decision. This would be to lose that salutary sense of the daunting 'wildness' of the universe and of the finitude of human perceptions and abilities found in Thoreau and others. In relation to a distant galaxy, the sense of nature as that which arises without human agency seems unassailable. In relation, however, to many things happening now on the surface of the earth, 'nature' – in the romantic sense, as the seeming other of 'culture' and a norm of psychic health and moral guidance – will seem far more problematic and in need of further clarification.

The boundaries of the political

Fourth quandary: the crisis of legitimation *74*

This section offers an overview of various critical arguments and methods engaged with conceptions of environmental justice. The environment emerges here as a peculiarly challenging topic. In one sense, it seems limited, the focus of single issue campaigns. In another, environmental issues refuse to be contained within given political structures. After all, the environment is, in a sense, everything.

Environmental questions challenge inherited conceptions of politics and effect a crisis in their criteria of legitimacy. At times, green attacks on existing society are accompanied by calls for new kinds of thinking and practice so extreme that they amount to a dismissal of given political institutions altogether. A search for alternative political traditions has ranged from idealisations of various premodern cultures or of indigenous peoples, to new age religiosity ('respect for Gaia', etc.) and a fascination with some eastern religious traditions. One unfortunate result of the intellectual instability and the huge complexity of environmental issues is that green attitudes often recoil into an easier kind of personal moralism. Bob Pepperman Taylor writes:

> the search for new ethical and political traditions . . . tends to
> reduce questions of environmental ethics to issues of personal
> consciousness . . . it appears that concern for political reform almost
> falls away altogether in the search for an appropriate individual
> consciousness and lifestyle . . . [1]

This section engages such political and meta-political issues as: the tensions between reform environmentalism and radical environmentalism (can environmental questions be adequately engaged within existing democratic structures?); the world-wide environmental justice movement and its challenge to some forms of environmentalism and ecocriticism; the latent conflict between environmental questions and those liberal traditions of politics focussed on issues of individual human liberty; ecofeminist arguments that connect the oppression of women with that of the natural world; and efforts to 'green' post-colonial criticism by aligning environmental issues with the interests of colonised or indigenous people.

As this thumbnail survey suggests, criticism in relation to environmental justice works largely by extending to environmental questions modes of thought, equity and judgement already practised in thinking geared towards conceptions of justice amid human beings. Thus, for example, if the liberal tradition sees itself as developing and expanding conceptions of human 'right', some environmental thinkers ask if these may now be extended further to embrace the non-human.

The identification of broadly left-progressive conceptions of social justice with the supposed interests of the natural world seems in part a response to one obvious danger – *eco-fascism*. This is the all too plausible counterargument that protection of the natural world, justice for future generations and for the non-human can only be achieved by authoritarian governments prepared severely to regulate current modes of life. An unqualified biocentric ethic is especially vulnerable to accusations of latent eco-fascism. After all – to take this to an extreme – from the viewpoint of most inhabitants of the earth the most 'eco-friendly' policy could well be the extermination of most of the human species.

Overall – and overriding some significant differences – the general stance of radical environmental criticism at the end of the century's first decade is this: biocentric ideals of an equal flourishing of all life remain an inspiration and ultimate goal. In practice, however, the immediate orientation of twenty-first-century environmental criticism is on the destructive effects of human systems of hierarchy and inequality. Nevertheless, some environmental issues, notably overpopulation and climate change, still seem inadequately addressed by an ecocriticism adapting modes of oppositional politics developed in relation to human beings. The challenge to received ways of thinking remains.

Fourth quandary: the crisis of legitimation

The issue of climate change again throws into alarming relief the crisis of legitimacy inseparable from environmental politics. To hold in one's head both the uncertainty and yet terror of the futures at stake is to produce an irresolution, even a derangement, in given criteria of decision. Bearing in mind such issues as the mass extinction of non-human life and the probable deaths of many millions of people, how honestly certain is it which of the following two statements is finally the more responsible:

> Climate change is now acknowledged as a legitimate and serious concern and the government will continue to support measures to improve the fuel efficiency of motor vehicles.

> The only defensible relationship to have with any car is with a well-aimed brick.

Chapter 7

Thinking like a mountain?

Anyone familiar with radical environmentalist thinking who begins work in a local campaign is soon confronted by a quandary. The only way in which you will realistically prevent an airport from being expanded or a road or nuclear power station from being built is to appeal to the policies, values and criteria of those with the power to make the decision. To campaign about more fundamental issues such as the evils of 'anthropocentrism', 'the arrogance of humanism' or the stupidity of an endless pursuit of economic growth would be merely to alienate many allies. In order to be heard at all, campaigners must speak in terms accepted within existing structures of governance and economics, the very things they may consider ultimately responsible for environmental degradation in the first place. This is a recognised syndrome in environmental politics: radical environmentalism in theory often turns into merely reform environmentalism in practice.

This quandary can be traced in two of the most influential examples of modern environmental writing, Aldo Leopold's *A Sand County Almanac* (1949) and Rachel Carson's *Silent Spring* (1962). Leopold's book has been described as 'the first self-conscious, sustained, and systematic attempt in modern Western literature to develop an ethical theory which would include the whole of terrestrial nature and terrestrial nature *as a whole* within the purview of morals' (J. Baird Callicott).[1] Carson's detailed polemic about the evils of mass pesticide and herbicide use was the landmark book from which the modern environmental movement is often dated. We turn to Leopold first.

Leopold offered his readers the challenge of 'thinking like a mountain'. This striking phrase has since become a biocentric motto, representing at once much that is most problematic and yet most exciting about environmental politics. Leopold's overall proposal needs to be quoted in full:

> All ethics so far evolved rest upon a single premise: that the individual is a member of a community of interdependent parts. His instincts prompt him to compete for his place in that community, but his ethics prompt him also to co-operate (perhaps in order that there may be a place to compete for). The land ethic simply enlarges the boundaries of the community to include soils, waters, plants, and animals, or collectively: the land.
>
> This sounds simple: do we not already sing our love for and obligation to the land of the free and the home of the brave? Yes, but just what and whom do we love? Certainly not the soil, which we are sending helter-skelter down river. Certainly not the waters, which we assume have no function except to turn turbines, float barges and carry off sewage. Certainly not the plants, of which we exterminate whole communities without batting an eyelid. Certainly not the animals, of which we have already extirpated many of the largest and most beautiful species. A land ethic of course cannot prevent the alteration, management and use of these 'resources', but it does affirm their right to continued existence, and, at least in spots, their continued existence in a natural state.
>
> In short, a land ethic changes the role of *Homo Sapiens* from conqueror of the land community to plain member and citizen of it. It implies respect for his fellow members and also respect for the community as such.   203–4

'Thinking like a Mountain' is the title of one essay in the middle section of the *Almanac*. What Leopold himself meant by it is fairly simple. For a mid-twentieth-century ecologist 'to think like a mountain' means to take an holistic view of an environment and its often hidden networks of interdependence; to see, for instance, that shooting all the wolves with the aim of increasing the deer population for hunters may lead ultimately to overgrazing and ecosystem collapse: 'The cowman who cleans his range of wolves does not realize that he is taking over the wolf's job of trimming the local herd to fit the range. He has not learned to think like a mountain. Hence we have dustbowls, and rivers washing the future to the sea' (132).

The phrase highlights the finite scope of human thought, its limitation, for instance, to stretches of time that would seem minuscule to a mountain. Leopold is held to have anticipated the biocentric philosophy of the 'deep ecology' movement that emerged with Arne Naess in the 1970s.[2] 'Thinking like a mountain' may also include a perception of things encompassing one's own death, either as literal extinction or, say, as the self-negation practised in Peter Matthiessen's *The Snow Leopard* (1978) as a kind of Buddhist meditation exercise.[3] Leopold's strictly nonsensical phrase again highlights how environmental issues push against the limits of inherited language and concepts.

How to enact so unusual a perspective in a rhetorically effective way? If Leopold had highlighted the politics first, would the book have had any readership or even a publisher? His strategy was to introduce something as novel as the land ethic to a mid-century US readership in a deceptively ano-dyne popular form. Letters to possible publishers show him worrying over how to achieve a 'literary effect'. He also wrote that he wanted to maintain the book's 'home-made' aspect.[4]

Leopold was primarily a scientist and a practical forester. As a writer he takes the major strategic decision to present a potentially radical political argument in the mode of an apparently lightweight literary form, a series of often personal nature essays, illustrated by homely drawings. Essay-like individual chapters move through three sections in various minor genres. The first is the almanac itself, an essay for each month of the year, giving detailed attention to the area around the Leopold family's 'shack' (a converted cowshed) in one of the so-called sand counties of central Wisconsin. The title 'sand county almanac' was later chosen posthumously for the whole collection. These essays are written in a sometimes dated mode of 'literary' nature writing, rendering the lives of an individual chickadee or grouse in a slightly anthropomorphic way that may reinforce rather than challenge the cultural associations of animal characters with the infantilised or childish. Then follows the more inventive section, 'Sketches Here and There', recollections of various regions and ecosystems visited or studied by Leopold, and finally 'The Upshot', bold expository writing on the aesthetics and ethics of land communities. The book thus has the underlying structure of an inductive argument, moving from specific observations to more generally applicable conclusions, especially in the form given the book by Leopold's executors, who placed the crucial statement, 'The Land Ethic', last of all.[5]

Seemingly light nature writing draws the reader into deeper and broader perspectives in space and time and across the species barrier, an opening out of given modes of perception whose force takes focus in the strictly impossible phrase. One issue is to challenge received ideas of the aesthetic. Western appre-ciation of nature, then as now, followed canons of taste and composition that are essentially eighteenth century, that is, a preference for well-composed visual spectacles and 'views' or 'scenery', such as those three-dimensional monuments to the 'picturesque' or the 'sublime' preserved in national parks. Leopold chal-lenged 'the idea that wild landscape must be "pretty" to have value'.[6] He works towards an aesthetic of natural forms that would not be derivative from art ('that under-aged brand of aesthetics which limits the definition of "scenery" to lakes and pine forests') towards modes of seeing informed by scientific ecology and a realisation of evolutionary processes that have taken an unimaginably long time. This informed aesthetic of the 'wild' contrasts with the kinds of landscape aesthetic that were available to a frontiersman like Daniel Boone:

> Ecological science has wrought a change in the mental eye. It has disclosed origins and functions for what to Boone were only facts. It has disclosed mechanisms for what to Boone were only attributes. We have no yardstick to measure this change, but we may safely say that, as compared with the competent ecologist of the present day, Boone saw only the surface of things. The incredible intricacies of the plant and animal community . . . were . . . invisible and incomprehensible to Daniel Boone.   174

To add a temporal dimension of almost bottomless depth to the spectacle of a marsh and its noisy geese or to an empty grassland transforms them drastically. Leopold's small essays on the ecology of marshlands or on seemingly boring plants such as the Bur Oak or the Draba ('the smallest flower that blows' [26]), work towards a new sense of beauty expressive of the overall health of an ecosystem, 'beauty, in the broadest ecological sense of that word'.[7] For Leopold, watching the endangered sand hill crane, a knowledge of evolution ('our untameable past . . . that incredible sweep of millennia' [96]) enhances the sense that 'The ultimate value in these marshes is wildness, and the crane is wildness incarnate' (101).

The aesthetic

Is it a problem that much popular environmentalism is primarily or 'merely' aesthetic in motivation, the defence of pretty woodland from new housing, or of a charismatic animal from extinction? The limiting association of environmental politics with the 'merely aesthetic' is reinforced by ever more beautifully filmed nature programmes based on the old scenic categories of the *beautiful, sublime* or *picturesque*.

J. Baird Callicott, following Leopold's *Almanac* (191), sees such canons of perception, however psychologically therapeutic, as limited, anthropocentric and ultimately 'trivial'.[8] This view finds support in the fact that, in the West, it was only with the attainment of a certain level of material comfort and security that the natural world began commonly to appear as other than a mixed threat, obstacle and resource. Walter J. Ong argues of the romantic idealisation of wild landscapes that 'Romanticism and technology . . . are mirror images of each other, being both products of man's dominance over nature'.[9] 'Scenery', after all, is a term originally from theatre, now usually expressive of a kind of visual consumption by people who live and work elsewhere.

Figure 7 *Sand County Almanac* (Oxford University Press)

Gernot Böhme's work offers a very different argument.[10] Böhme makes a case for a new aesthetics of the natural world. He argues that natural beauty is not our projection of art-derived modes of seeing, but that aesthetic qualities are out there, objective presences registered by the human body as itself part of nature. It makes as much sense to call a particular valley 'serene' as it does to call it 'green' or 'steep'. For proof, consider that someone in a completely different state of mind, say grief-stricken, can still recognise the valley as having 'serene' qualities, even if these are currently blocked out. The serenity is an objective quality of the place for human perceivers. Böhme also refers to the art of landscape gardening, which gives objective methods of producing moods or atmospheres in nature that are recognised by anyone.

Böhme argues that traditional aesthetics has been modelled solely on the issue of appreciating works of art. Modes of thinking from that limited context have then been transferred to perceptions of nature, something evident most of all, perhaps, in the eighteenth-century cult of the 'picturesque'. This is to reduce the beauty of natural forms to one human use of nature in competition with others. Böhme's aesthetics of nature on the other hand would also eschew the intellectualism of traditional aesthetics, with its narrow focus on the artwork and cultural communication, that is, the assumption that an artwork 'says' something other than itself, a mode of thinking broadly inapplicable to natural forms.

The aesthetic for Böhme is a basic part of everyday experience, of which traditional art-directed aesthetics is only a small subdivision. Aesthetic atmospheres are inseparable from the fact that the human body, as a part of nature, participates in the showing and letting-be-felt of things in their multiplicity and varied tonalities. The dismissal of some environmentalist concerns as 'merely aesthetic' implicitly denigrates this definitive element of human existence.

What then of specific and immediate political implications? Both the *Almanac* and Carson's *Silent Spring* have been as successful as any book can really expect to be. Amidst sexist vilification and denial, Carson received wide attention in the US media and testified on toxins to a committee of Congress, helping lead to significant changes in legislation across the world after her early death from breast cancer. Leopold's *Almanac* became an indispensable reference for environmentalists and a practical guide to principles of land conservation in the United States and elsewhere – the focus now tends to be on the whole biota of a region, not just on one or two favoured species. Both Carson and Leopold strengthened the idea that environmental protection should be part of the rationale of the modern state.[11]

Nevertheless, such achievements in the realm of reform environmentalism do not fully eclipse elements of environmental issues that arguably exceed and potentially subvert inherited systems of government and economics. Leopold's ambition of changing the conception of land from being a 'commodity' to being a 'community' has social and political ramifications far in excess of those he seemed to envisage. Wallace Stegner extrapolates some: 'They smack of socialism and the public good. They impose limits and restraints. They are anti-Progress. They dampen American initiative. They fly in the face of the faith that land is a commodity, the very foundation-stone of American opportunity.'[12] In the *Almanac*, however, Leopold's explicit antagonists remain only the vaguely named 'progress' and 'the economist'. Leopold still assumes as normal the recreational hunting, fishing and eating of animals he practises himself. Although his topic cries out for it, Leopold does not question the institution of private property itself beyond arguments about instilling a sense of ethical obligation 'on the part of the private owner' (214) and expanding the notion of 'public interest' to embrace land health. For Leopold, 'our present problem is one of attitudes and implements' (225–6). Thinkers influenced by ecofeminism and social ecology might see in such statements an evasion of the ultimate sources of environmental degradation in oppressive social and economic structures and of the drastic political reform that would be necessary to give the 'land ethic' any chance of broad implementation. After all, one possible logical chain of inference could lead straight from the land ethic to the abolition of the United States, or at the very least its reform beyond recognition.

'Great Possessions', one of the weaker essays (though apparently Leopold's favourite), shows up a gulf between some ramifications of the land ethic and many of the social and political assumptions at work in his modes of thought and presentation. The essay concerns the sense of boundlessness that comes to the narrator when walking beyond the environs of his farm in the very earliest morning. The recurrent trope is that of ownership and possession:

> One hundred and twenty acres, according to the County Clerk, is the extent of my worldly domain . . . Books or no books, it is a fact patent to both my dog and myself, that at daybreak I am the sole owner of all the acres I can walk over. It is not only the boundaries that disappear, but also the thought of being bounded. Expanses unknown to deed or map are known to every dawn . . .   41

The institution of ownership is even projected on to animals, not as fellow owners, as the land ethic might suggest, but as tenants. 'Like other great landowners, I have tenants. They are negligent about rents, but very punctilious about tenures' (41). The dawn walk becomes a kind of inspection of this animal domain of property disputes, 'before my title runs out' (43). As often in the book, each animal is depicted as preoccupied, whether comically or valiantly, with its own narrow circle of concerns. The birds are depicted as each loudly proclaiming its own claim to space. For instance:

> the robin in the big elm warbles loudly his claim to the crotch where the ice storm tore off a limb, and all appurtenances pertaining thereto . . . The robin's insistent caroling awakens the oriole, who now tells the world of orioles that the pendant branch of the elm belongs to him.   42

By implication, perhaps, such solipsism might be applied also to the human narrator's fantasy of the wide dawn landscape as his own commodity, but such irony seems absent. The essay ends with a reaffirmation of the breakdown of property boundaries, but again only through the fantasy of owning it all: 'A tractor roars warning me my neighbor is astir. The world has shrunk to those mean dimensions known to county clerks' (44). 'Great Possessions' was Leopold's own preferred title for the whole book. A later essay refers tellingly to birds on the farm as 'My pleated woodpeckers', 'My barred owls' (76), 'My wood ducks' (77). Whatever the ramifications of the land ethic, some of the first section of the *Almanac* about 'our farm' would not even be out of place in a property magazine.

Proposals that actually call for a drastic and unprecedented shift in human self-understanding are not seen as implicating given social and political institutions beyond some reforms in planning law and in the attitudes of landowners. Even Stegner, hailing Leopold's book as 'the utterance of an American Isaiah', finds hope not in changed economic and political structures but in the implausible narrative of 'a change of heart and mind, a personal conversion, a reversal of individual and communal carelessness, which might lead to changes in public policy'.[13]

A similar issue has been studied in relation to Carson's *The Silent Spring* (1962), the book that first made the environment a significant force in popular politics. Carson repeatedly sidesteps considered discussion of the sources of environmental pollution by toxins in an agriculture dominated by the values and demands of corporate capitalism. Instead, her strategy is to foreground emotionally powerful but politically evasive images of its effects, the silent spring, ruined pastoral landscapes, all playing on Cold War fears of the deadly hazards at work in invisible materials (i.e., pesticides, but also, of course, radiation). Yaakov Garb's study of Carson's carefully judged rhetorical strategies concludes:

> The relation to nature that Carson proposes is one of cautious 'guidance' (p. 243, p. 261), 'reasonable accommodation' (p. 261), sensitive 'management' (p. 80), and an ethic of 'sharing' (p. 261) rather than 'brute force' (p. 80). These are valuable orientations in themselves, but less so when they function as vague substitutes for attention to the relations of human groups to one another.[14]

An important point affecting environmental writing generally is at work here. Committed to actual change with a sense of urgency, environmentalist writing must aim to be popular. It makes sometimes considerable compromises to increase its chances of being read by more than a few specialists.[15]

A major question for environmental politics has been: can environmental problems, which many argue demand a restructuring of all political, social and economic life, be satisfactorily addressed within given democratic and legal structures? Carson and Leopold, in writing books aimed to transform public opinion, are committed to the hope that they can. At the same time, the very cases they detail raise far deeper questions about modern society and capitalism than they publicly engage. Andrew Dobson observes in green politics generally a 'tension between the radical nature of the social and political change that it seeks, and the reliance on traditional liberal-democratic means of bringing it

HARVEST

Figure 8 Eco-sabotage (Earth First!)

about'.[16] Few people are as direct as the vehement essayist Chen Yu-feng, who, living on the increasingly trashed island of Taiwan, develops ecological ideas into an open advocacy of eco-sabotage.[17]

Other people have taken up the task of affirming the land ethic beyond the remit of merely reform environmentalism. A 1987 information handout from the Earth First! movement states two of the movement's 'deep ecological' principles. The first is that 'all natural things have intrinsic value, intrinsic worth . . . They exist for their own sake'.[18] The second quotes Leopold's slogan-like summary of the land ethic: 'A thing is right when it tends to preserve the integrity, stability, and beauty of the biotic community. It is wrong when it tends otherwise' (224–5). However, the Earth First! movement itself also reads as a practical critique of the blind spots of *A Sand County Almanac*. The movement follows the logic of the land ethic to a conclusion in an active engagement with property law and the market economy, peaceful protest, vegetarianism, direct non-governmental action, the sabotage of construction machinery and other forms of countercultural resistance.

Fifth quandary: what isn't an environmental issue?

Leopold's farm almanac also shows how problematic an 'environmental issue' can be politically. Because the environment is, strictly, everything, environmental questions can enact a bewildering or disconcerting explosion of the political, especially now in relation to carbon emissions.

For instance, Leopold does not see some basic social institutions as an ecological matter in the way they could be. There are several reasons why the nuclear family should be an environmental issue. Many modern needs in transportation and infrastructure are actually driven by the atomistic nature of contemporary society and the nuclear family. The Leopold family has one weekend shack, while another drives to a shack further down the road. The nuclear family is the principal site of consumerism, with each individual household accumulating the same consumer goods, washing machines, televisions, cars, heating systems and so forth, a wasteful duplication compared to more communal ways of life. Divorce also becomes an environmental issue if it creates two households instead of one.

At the same time, as these examples suggest, do environmentalist concerns, refusing either to fit given understandings of the political or yet adequately to transform them, threaten to become only a new kind of personal moralism in the smallest affairs of day-to-day life?

Chapter 8

Environmental justice and the move 'beyond nature writing'

From the texts covered so far in this book a reader might not guess one of the most distinctive features of the environmental crisis. All across the world groups of people have come together outside the normal frameworks of politics to protest local outrages or environmental threats. The Indigenous Environmental Network, for instance, is 'A network of Indigenous Peoples empowering Indigenous Nations and communities towards sustainable livelihoods, demanding environmental justice and maintaining the Sacred Fire of our traditions.'[1] Together with the proliferation of various non-governmental bodies, such movements now form a kind of cosmopolitan politics, its actions and concerns unconfined to the boundaries of the nation state.

The environmental crisis, Ulrich Beck argues, is itself inherently a delegitimation of traditional political structures:

> In terms of social politics . . . the ecological crisis involves a *systematic violation of basic rights*, a crisis of basic rights whose long-term effect in weakening society can scarcely be underestimated. For dangers are being produced by industry, externalized by economics, individualized by the legal system, legitimized by the natural sciences and made to appear harmless by politics. That this is breaking down the power and credibility of institutions only becomes clear when the system is put on the spot, as Greenpeace, for example, has tried to do.[2]

In such a context, it is no wonder that critics concerned with the US wilderness tradition have sometimes come to look like defenders of outdoor leisure pursuits. Purist notions of the environment as pristine wilderness may seem complicit with an essentially contemplative privileged attitude to the natural world – after all, by such a definition, wilderness is not where anyone actually lives. Even the notion of 'purity' can have uncomfortable social overtones. Cinder Hypki, an urban environmental activist, recalls: 'It suddenly became very clear to me that the real purist notion of environment – that it is just the natural world – just can't work in today's world. It doesn't work for peasants in Costa Rica, and it sure doesn't work for people living in inner-city Baltimore.'[3]

The injustice of such things as locating a waste plant near people too poor to oppose it is evident. There may also be elements of racism. To associate some people with filth or the unclean has been a recurrent feature of social bigotry: issues of communal hygiene may merge with notions of a more figurative purity that cast some people as supposedly polluting presences. To work in the field of ecojustice is to question the boundaries between recognised environmental issues, matters of public health and social discrimination.

Responding to criticisms of its implicit cultural politics has profoundly affected twenty-first-century ecocriticism. Firstly, there have been continuing attempts to expand the scope of ecocritical readings. Can ecocriticism 'be usefully applied to texts beyond the study of nature writing – to the novels, say, of Henry James?'[4] Secondly, there has been a striking turn to issues of environmental justice. This is instantiated in work collected in *The Environmental Justice Reader* (2002): 'We define environmental justice as the right of all people to share equally in the benefits bestowed by a healthy environment. We define the environment, in turn, as the places in which we live, work, play, and worship.'[5]

Environmental justice primarily names a social movement, plural and engaged in the urgency of local campaign work. In relation to literary and cultural criticism, its effect has been a proliferation of thought on just how varied and culturally complex ideas of nature have been. What links the turn to issues of ecojustice to efforts to expand ecocriticism beyond nature writing is that both usually focus on how conceptions of human identity relate to or vary with environmental contexts, rural or urban. For instance, answering their own question about reading Henry James, Armbruster and Wallace argue:

> Think of some of his more well-known works, such as 'Daisy Miller' and *The Portrait of a Lady*, that focus on young, female American expatriates who find themselves in environments where they are distinctly out of place. In our ecocritical analysis we would trace the connections between this lack of grounding in physical and cultural place and the misunderstanding, objectification, and alienation these young women experience.[6]

Concern with ecojustice and cultural difference tends to align ecocritical arguments with the kind of left-progressive political stance that now passes almost as the norm in the humanities. Greg Garrard describes a general tendency towards the stances of 'social ecology' in recent criticism: that is, arguments that human violence against the natural world is ultimately a product of oppressive structures of hierarchy among human beings.[7] Nevertheless, while 'social ecology' is clearly relevant, the method of much twenty-first-century ecocriticism is effectively simply that of mainstream cultural criticism, that is, to map out the cultural politics of some issue or concern, usually from an implicitly liberal/progressive viewpoint. The distinction of ecocriticism becomes simply that it is concepts of nature that are so studied, delineating the different cultural contexts, presuppositions and exclusions of varying ideas of nature, or tracing how different conceptions of identity are enmeshed in varying notions of the environment. Such well-used procedures of reading usually treat fiction and non-fiction in the same way, as the arena of competing cultural representations and identity claims.

Social ecology

This is a term largely associated with the work of Murray Bookchin, and, more loosely, with arguments that violence against the natural world has its origins in human social and economic institutions based on oppressive systems of hierarchy and élitism. In books such as *The Ecology of Freedom* (1985) and *Post Scarcity Anarchism* (1971)[8] Bookchin argued that 'The objectification of people as mere instruments of production fostered the objectification of nature as mere "natural resources"' (*Ecology of Freedom*, 240). Bookchin sometimes argues by means of a broad historical overview of human development since prehistory, tracing the loss of small organic communities without hierarchies of power, the gradual change of communal relationships into market relationships, effectively converting people into commodities. The loss of conditions of wholeness and freedom in society led simultaneously to people regarding all natural entities in the same acquisitive and instrumentalising way.

Bookchin argues – dubiously some think – that a wild, unaltered ecosystem is itself 'libertarian', 'an image', that is, 'of unity in diversity, spontaneity and complementary relationships, free of all hierarchy and domination' (453). An organic human society, for Bookchin, would thus be one in harmony with nature as a space of 'symbiosis and mutualism' (460). The modern 'seemingly autonomous ego' that now serves as the ideal self in western society would be replaced by a more 'natural' one, an 'individual whose very completeness as an ego was possible because he or she was rooted in a fairly rounded and complete community' (211).

Questions arise here of whether a certain romantic-anarchist political ideal is not being projected on to nature and this model of 'nature' then used supposedly to ground or validate that specific political programme.[9]

Take, for instance, a reading of *The Narrative of the Life of Frederick Douglass, an American Slave* (1845) from the collection *Beyond Nature Writing* (2001). Just as mainstream critics concerned with issues of social justice and representations of identity might analyse how, for example, concepts of manhood play out in Douglass's writing, relating it to issues of racial identity and the authority of authorship, so a concern with environmental justice leads Michael Bennett to subject the idea of nature in *The Narrative* to a similar kind of scrutiny. The association of rural landscapes with the hated cotton plantations is seen to inform an element of anti-pastoral in African American writing: 'The definition of the slave as property makes it difficult for Douglass to have a positive relationship with the Southern landscape since he is legally part of that landscape.'[10] Inverting idealisations of wilderness, it was the city that offered a space of freedom and self-realisation.

A reading: *A River Runs Through It* (1976)

The best way to explore how environmental justice issues can inflect literary criticism may be through staging a specific reading. The stakes can be further highlighted by choosing one of the classics of US western writing, Norman Maclean's *A River Runs Through It*.

This lucid and poignant novella of 1976 was a favourite of the first generation of ecocritics in the United States. It is a semi-autobiographical account of the Macleans, a family of Scots descent living in early twentieth-century Montana. The men in this family, whose head is a Presbyterian minister, have a kind of private cult of fly fishing. The text is formed from the memories of the older brother Norman, whose narrative as an old man focusses on his younger brother Paul, a man who made fly fishing an art but whose obscure life as a gambler and heavy drinking journalist led to a violent death. Norman's attempt to understand his lost brother, become now the epitome of a vanished way of life, has the poignancy of recognised failure: 'Now nearly all those I loved and did not understand when I was young are dead, but I still reach out to them.'[11]

A River Runs Through It adds itself to that distinctive minor tradition of literature that idealises fishing as a blend of the contemplative and active lives. Fishing becomes an art form almost, combining the suspense and skill of hunting with the meditative intensity of a religious exercise. In Maclean's novella fly fishing has a role that some have ascribed to the aesthetic in modern society more generally: to go fishing is to open a temporary utopian space that is at once a form of escapism from daily society and its implicit if limited critique.

The most challenging scenarios of environmental justice lie in the neocolonialism that still structures relations of North and South, the topic of a later chapter. However, questions of environmental justice already bear on Maclean's idealisation of fly fishing. First, it is solely the reserve of male members of the Maclean family, Norman's mother, mother-in-law and wife all being cast in the role of admirers and supporters. An intense misogyny even emerges in the way the brothers mistreat the figure of 'Old Rawhide', a prostitute that Norman's clueless brother-in-law (a mere bait fisherman) brings fishing with the Maclean brothers. The place of fishing as an exclusively masculine ritual also informs the stress on Paul Maclean's toughness and his conformity to a certain recognisable 'western' outdoor type, self-reliant (even to the point of self-destructiveness), taciturn, but committed absolutely to his own particular code of honour.[12] Fishing forms a space for values outside the shady realms of journalism, gambling and alcohol abuse that eventually destroy him. Paul's half-Indian girlfriend, whom the narrator had romanticised as 'Mo-nah-se-tah' but who is otherwise unnamed, shows a similar kind of displacement. Her life of tawdry bars and inciting men to fight for her finds a redemptive outlet in dancing: 'She was as beautiful a dancer as he was a fly caster' (26). The elegy for Paul as symbol of a lost frontier ethos aligns *A River Runs Through It* with many elements of the wilderness tradition. At the same time, the novella's restriction of the place of the frontier ethos to a symbolic re-enactment in a leisure pursuit already shows its fragility as a cultural legacy.

Another aspect of an environmental justice reading would relate more directly to the Montana environment as one of the last parts of the West to be colonised by Europeans. At issue here is a stereotyping, not of the Indians but the Scottish immigrants or rather their American descendants, on whom are foisted a great many supposedly typical 'Scottish' characteristics. The reason, perhaps, this seems unmarked by readers is that the stereotyping is applied to Maclean's own family and is no sort of vilification but rather a fondly indulged practice, even a kind of boasting. This kind of minoritarian narcissism is very common, especially in countries that result from settler colonisation, such as the US and Australia. This widely indulged kind of atavism celebrates supposedly ancient cultural roots, but, in this case, as part of an aged Norman's intense nostalgia for a recently conquered and occupied part of North America, it may seem a striking kind of self-legitimating double-think, projecting a long-imagined settled ancestry into a landscape whose settlement was very different. Robert Redford's 1992 film of the novella, starring Craig Scheffer and Brad Pitt, even includes the scene of a man in a kilt playing the bagpipes while looking out over the mountains of Montana as a kind of ultra-Scotland. Of Norman's mother-in-law, also 'Scottish', we read: 'More than most mothers,

Scottish mothers have had to accustom themselves to migration and sin, and to them all sons are prodigal and welcome home. Scotsmen, however, are much more reserved about welcoming returning male relatives, and do so largely under the powerful influence of their women' (11).[13]

The crudeness of Norman's generalisations about Scottishness is a mark of their fragility: who would dare speak that way in Scotland itself? However, an untold story may lurk in the reference to the trials of migration, though there is no overt sign of it in the novella beyond a reference to 'the original family home on the Isle of Mull in the southern Hebrides' (27). This story is that of the brutal 'clearances' of the eighteenth and nineteenth centuries that dispossessed so many Highland families to make room for sheep, driving thousands of people across the Atlantic. The brittleness of the Macleans' vaunted Scottishness seems in any case a mark of displacement and insecurity. The act of clinging to an increasingly self-caricaturing 'Scottish' identity suggests the same kind of inner fragility as Paul's code of a masculine self-reliance, a code that succeeds only in the realm of sport. Even the novella's assurance about trout and trout fishing is fragile, with the narrator at one point making what seems an elementary mistake about the natural history of the fish.[14]

A kind of cultural displacement applies even to the trout. There is a hierarchy of species of trout in the novella. To catch a Rainbow Trout is admirable, the Eastern Brook Trout is mentioned (39) but the real prize is the Brown Trout. This fish is 'mythological'. '[S]ome of those Brown monsters' are what Norman feels he must catch if he wants to equal his brother (40; also 45). It is presumably this species Paul catches dramatically in his final fishing trip with his father and brother. The phrases 'mythological Brown Trout' and 'mythological fish' are repeated in Norman's reveries while fishing (40–1) and suggest some kind of timeless spirit of the landscape. In fact, however, like the people themselves, the Brown Trout is an introduction, a fish native to Europe and Asia but not to North America, as the Rainbow and Brook Trout are. Montana received its first Brown Trout in 1889.[15] A similar story applied in nineteenth-century Australia, where many animals (such as the red fox) were introduced to enable colonising Europeans to continue with inherited customs of hunting and fishing. People even lined the harbour in Hobart, Tasmania, to welcome the first successful shipment of salmon ova.[16] Issues of environmental justice clearly arise in the effect of such introductions on the native animals and their place in the culture of the indigenous people. The Brown Trout, in fact, is a predator that has done untold damage to the river ecosystems where it has been introduced.[17]

The issues of introduced species and 'Scottishness', then, may inform an ecojustice reading of Maclean's novella, attentive to the social and psychic effects of both literal and cultural displacement. What might seem in some ways merely reactionary in Norman Maclean's nostalgia for a Montana of the frontier, crystallised in the elegy for a lost brother, also re-enacts the personal and familial defensiveness of a settler society, its self-image and self-evasions.

Environmental criticism as cultural history?

What might this example show? Firstly, perhaps, that the procedures of this kind of reading differ quite strongly from those of the ecocriticism covered so far. In a nutshell, a previously dominant *realist* paradigm, that is, reading a text in relation to the ethical and cognitive challenge of its rendering of the natural world, is being displaced by a *culturalist* one, that is, reading a text's stances in terms of the various kinds of cultural identity projected or at issue. Thus the Montana rivers and their fish are seen in relation to kinds of identity claim focussed in displaced conceptions of Scottishness and frontier authenticity. The question of whether fiction or non-fiction is at issue is now made irrelevant by the fact that either mode can be studied in terms of the kinds of cultural identity it projects.

Some questions may also be raised about such an approach. One issue is less that many ecojustice readings differ not at all in method from a conventional critic's mapping out of the cultural politics of a concept, image or narrative, but that this method may itself be complicit with a destructive preconception of the human relation to the natural world. There may be a risk of reducing environmental debate to a function of competing identity and justice claims – for instance, the immigrant 'Scottish' idealisation of Montana's rivers as set against the places known to earlier inhabitants or against the littered venue of recreational tourism they have in part become; or Douglass's conception of the rural as imprisonment as contrasted to white idealisations, and so on. The natural world, in this kind of criticism, gets treated as a function of the various claims and conceptions of different and competing human groups. However, can environmental criticism, previously concerned with the ethical challenge of the non-human, be limited to the matter of an equitable sharing out of the earth's spoils or 'the right of all people to share equally in the benefits bestowed by a healthy environment'? After all, one of ecocriticism's founding gestures was to reject the adequacy of reading 'nature' as no more than a function of cultural politics. The work of an older generation of ecocritics, celebrating Wordsworth, Clare or Thoreau and the US wilderness tradition, is now in turn being attacked as constructing nature in partial or contestable ways. Does this, however, totally neutralise arguments against reducing the natural world to an ideological theatre?

Maclean's novella may also bear out reservations about too instrumentalist and anthropocentric an ecojustice approach. An exclusive focus on the book's constructions of identity, ethnicity and gender would foreclose attention to places and animals other than in relation to a human-centred cultural politics. The book is, after all, partly a celebration of the Big Blackfoot River itself, something whose understanding is a matter of long study and practice, what fishermen call 'reading the river' (63). If the novella celebrates the world of fly fisherman, it does so not only in terms of social ideas of manhood, status, ethnicity, but also in terms of skill, perceptiveness and habits of mind induced by hours in a complex non-human environment. It is also about the chastening discipline of learning to anticipate the perception and actions of a wary animal. Fishermen, one can argue, are subject to a process of identity formation in which the place is itself as much an agent as any social role, the rivers making their own obscure challenge to any overly human-centred sense of reality.

Sixth quandary: the antinomy of environmental criticism

Overall, ecocriticism often presents the scene of an interplay – or sometimes stand-off – between work that stresses the cultural aspects of various concepts of nature, as in the reading of Maclean given above, and work that stresses the element of the natural within culture, as what culture overlooks, takes dangerously for granted or destroys. Thus, on the one side a large body of US wilderness writing becomes itself understood as the implicit self-assertion of the values and interests of a predominantly white élite. On the other side, defenders of Abbey, Leopold, Austin, Maclean and others will reaffirm the importance of trying to project in literature the intrinsic value of the natural world.

Any specific ecocritical reading could be situated in the space between the poles of a culturalist and a realist reading, in what might perhaps be called the *antinomy of environmentalist criticism*:

What any writer calls 'nature' can always be read as a cultural/political construction.
  But
culture always depends on and is encompassed by actual nature, which requires recognition.
  But
that 'nature' can always be read as a cultural/political construction.
  But
  etc.

For instance, Terry Gifford describes *Cave Birds* (1978) by Ted Hughes in a similar zigzag fashion, as 'making a myth about the essence of material nature with awareness that nature is mediated by culture. He is also using this myth to reconnect us to the nature in ourselves, knowing that culture is nature . . . [so healing] our alienation from nature and from ourselves.'[18] This interplay could itself be continued by observing how culturally specific Gifford's own romanticism is here, with its familiar plot of alienation from and reunification with 'nature' as our true selves – yet in turn . . .

Chapter 9

Two readings

European ecojustice

In Europe a sustained concern with protecting the environment has often been associated with a simplistically conservative or sometimes nationalist politics, defending some place or way of life as an icon of a cultural identity or as an image of once traditional ways of life. 'Green' critics have accordingly also felt a need to highlight issues of justice in terms of the politics of nostalgia. Comparison between two recent arguments, one on an English novelist and one on a German novelist of the 1880s, shows a striking convergence of concerns.

Wilhelm Raabe's *Pfister's Mill* (1884) has been called Germany's first 'eco-novel'.[1] Its basic story is simple enough, that of an honest miller and later tavern keeper who is forced out of business by the effluent from a nearby sugar beet refinery. This first clogs up the mill-stream and later ruins the mill's second life as a picturesque tavern because of its pervasive stink. The miller fights a court case against the refinery, aided by the figure of Adam Asche, a chemist and tutor of the miller's son Ebert. The case is won, but the business is doomed anyway. Ironically, Asche later uses his scientific expertise to run a dry-cleaning business in Berlin, which also pollutes its local river. The main story is told in retrospect by Ebert, now a teacher and an inhabitant of Berlin, who has chosen to spend a summer holiday with his young wife at the mill, shortly before it is to be demolished and the land further developed. During the holiday, Ebert engages in both talk and writing that romantically celebrate and idealise the old place.

This short novel eschews suspense, any very striking plot or simple moral stance. It is not a green parable. The story seems partly based on cases of industrial pollution in the Duchy of Brunschweig, where Raaabe lived, and which would see the collapse of the local water supply not long after the novel appeared.[2] Yet the tone is curiously undramatic and non-judgemental, certainly compared to contemporary novels of environmental outrage. Its distinctiveness is its subtle use of the device of the limited narrator, the rather ordinary and slightly shallow Eberhard (or Ebert) Pfister, son of the last miller. Ebert's account sometimes idealises the tavern as a paradise it could never actually have been. Raabe's novel becomes a sympathetic but anti-romantic staging of the cultural politics of nostalgia, especially as it related to the rapid industrialisation in Germany after 1870. The subtitle, *Ein Sommerferienheft*, 'a summer holiday note book', already tinges the story of the lost rural idyll with the escapism of the holiday-maker, like some modern-day tourists in 'Hardy's Dorset'.

An essay by Berbeli Wanning focusses on that part of the history of the mill when it had been converted to a picturesque tavern, before the stench from the effluent drove custom away. The place had thrived by setting itself off from the society on which it yet depended, seeming to offer an aestheticised touchstone for supposedly 'timeless' preindustrial modes of life. For a time the Pfisters lived off this idyll, in effect, marketing it: 'the constructed idyll draws in people from the nearby town in search of relaxation and conviviality'.[3] As if obeying an old cultural script, customers had been drawn to the mill/tavern as to some archetypal pastoral image. Eventually, like some contemporary 'cottage' guesthouse situated on the edge of a national park where a new road is planned, the tavern's contradictory relation to its social context collapses as pollution of the river intensifies.

Wanning traces two strands in the novel. The first she calls the 'Text as Medium'. This simply conveys the facts of the destruction of the local river system through industrialisation and pollution. The destruction of the mill marks the end of a traditional relation to nature, dooming a whole way of life. Raabe's novel could also be related to the way many controversies in environmental justice concern the iniquities of treating water as just another commodity or waste product rather than as communal value and resource.[4] As in George Eliot's *The Mill on the Floss* (1860), the mill is not just a means of economic support but a defining element of family identity. The illness that takes the elder Pfister seems partly psychosomatic, inseparable from the death of place.

Wanning's second strand of reading, 'the text as [Ebert's] project' (199), complicates any familiar reaffirmation of preindustrial conceptions of nature. Ebert's narrative is that of someone striving to make sense of and crystallise the significance of the lost mill of his childhood. Wanning traces how Ebert's narrative, despite itself, is that of someone who no longer really believes the image of the mill as a lost natural paradise. For one thing, that image, ostensibly defended, is also undermined, especially by the form of the narrating itself. This jumps between past and present in short sections, gradually moving towards recounting Ebert's life after the mill as a Latin teacher in Berlin, contented citizen and dependent of a now industrialised Germany. Ebert's inability in writing to connect his Arcadian rural ideal to any currently credible social or economic reality demonstrates one of Raabe's most powerful points: the transformation in Germany is necessarily also a change in the subjective, inner life of its inhabitants. Nature is in fact no longer credible as a site in which a human being can project an image of unalienated consciousness. That image is now only a 'literary construction'.[5] Wanning's phrase might also link an idealised nature to a character in the novel she does not mention, the aged romantic poet, Felix Lippoldes, once famous but now a drunkard who embarrasses others with his garbled performances. All Ebert too can do is offer various images without a coherent ordering. He asks repeatedly, 'Where do all the images go?' This strand of the novel denies the reader any simple moral stance on the mill's destruction. In any case, the idealised scenes of childhood that possess Ebert's memory are of the mill as a lively tavern and beer garden, already, that is, as a space of semi-rural escapism in the economy of the nearby town. In Ebert's failure cogently to defend the images of his childhood past, he begins to confront the inevitability of what his wife calls 'our actual existence now on this earth'.[6] A later passage in the book depicts pleasure boats moving on the polluted river Spree in Berlin as if nothing had happened to it.

Wanning sums up the conflict between the 'text as medium' and the 'text as project'. The issue is not just an idyll lost, but a fatal compromising of its very credibility. The book's 'landscape idylls, the obvious expression of this supposed harmony [of human and nature] contradict in their form what they think to present in their content'.[7] The image of the mill in newly industrialised Germany offers an icon of a lost way of life, but the subtler, more insidious point is that change has also fatally undermined that icon's credibility as the mark of a social alternative. So the mill becomes, temporarily, a place of tourist fantasy or a 'literary construction' only. Wanning's point that Ebert's ideal can only now exist in a 'psycho tope limited to the aesthetic realm' questions the political efficacy of that romantic strand of ecocriticism that takes poems 'as imaginary parks in which we may breathe an air that is not toxic and accommodate ourselves to a mode of dwelling that is not alienated' (Bate).[8]

Richard Kerridge's 'Ecological Hardy' is an essay in the *Beyond Nature Writing* anthology (126–42). As with Wanning on Raabe, one issue is the viability of icons of romantic nostalgia, especially their problematic status as commercial commodities, even among Thomas Hardy's own readership. Kerridge quotes the following passage from *The Woodlanders* (1887) on the characters of the rural workers Giles Winterbourne and Marty South:

> From the light lashing of the twigs upon their faces when brushing through them in the dark either could pronounce upon the species of the tree whence they stretched; from the quality of the wind's murmur through a bough either could in like manner name its sort far off. They

knew by glance at a trunk if its heart were sound, or tainted with incipient decay; and by the state of its upper twigs the stratum that has been reached by its roots.[9]

Kerridge's concern here is the narrator of this passage, whose attitude is also that of many of Hardy's mainly urban readers, then and since. 'To this narrator, [Marty's and Giles's] work, hard as it is, possesses the undividedness of mind and body, self and environment, that is the object of so much romantic longing' (137). Kerridge's interest is the implicit opposition of rural character and disembodied urban spectator/reader – the reader stands outside the book, but Giles and Marty inhabit the woods. This issue in turn raises questions of environmental ethics and historical change, the growing penetration of the market economy into more areas of Wessex life. The novel's very tribute to Wessex culture can seem aligned with Hardy's general practice of 'commodifying the scenes of his rural childhood for a mainly urban and middle-class readership' (127). It is perhaps as if Ebert Pfister had found a publisher for his memories of the mill.

Building on Wanning and Kerridge here, one could suggest a broader reading of a whole strand of British literature since the eighteenth century. For a great many people, the social function of literature has been to provide a cultural space analogous to Pfister's mill. Ask in Britain about the immediate associations of the phrase 'English Literature' and many people will answer 'being on holiday'. The primary association of a well-known writer is now with scenic places to visit, with no less than three buildings in the Lake District associated with Wordsworth alone. There has emerged what might be named the 'heritage school' of pseudo-criticism, the idea – to put it satirically – that no one can discuss a text who has not traipsed through its author's house and garden and had a drink at the local pub.

Literary culture has long been an active part of the syndrome of celebrating some element or site of traditional or preindustrial society in a mode yet complicit with its demise and commodification. A founding instance of the syndrome could well be *Ossian*, that influential and mostly fake late eighteenth-century poem pretending to be the product of an ancient Celtic bard.[10] This lament for the Gaelic culture of the Highlands made a fortune for its author James Macpherson at the time of that culture's actual destruction and assimilation into growing commercial networks, including tourism. The textual idealisation of a way of life is also its conversion into a more fluidly symbolic commodity, ready to circulate in the markets of the society that has either destroyed or threatens the original. This is a crucial and recurrent syndrome of nineteenth- and twentieth-century literature, though surprisingly little studied.[11] Kerridge reminds us how Hardy himself encouraged this 'heritage' reception. His General Preface of 1912 presents the Wessex novels as a whole in topographical/realist terms, bolstering the reality of Wessex with maps that match fictional places and names with the real counterparts.

Kerridge's concern, nevertheless, is to disassociate Hardy from any stance of simplistic or opportunistic nostalgia. He draws on Donna Haraway's critique of the supposed stance of neutral spectatorship in scientific work, a stance criticised for enacting fantasies of an impartial overview often belied by the actual cultural prejudices at work in science. A writer's stance too, Kerridge argues, must be sensitive to its own cultural situatedness, qualifying any claim to final authority. Kerridge argues that Hardy's idiosyncratic narrators are 'situated' in that sense. The novels deploy the familiar convention of the narrator as omniscient spectator, but they also highlight clashes of perspectives. Thus in *The Return of the Native* (1878), a passage about the figure of Clym Yeobright cutting the furze on Egdon Heath depicts, at the same time, both an educated man returned from Paris and 'a brown spot in a midst of an expanse of olive-green gorse and nothing more'.[12] Such jumps can have a meta-contextual dimension: to see the passions of human life as if from an astronomical distance. Kerridge also relates Hardy to Lawrence Buell's advocacy of an 'ecocentric vision' that would seek 'not only to assert the value of [non-human] perspectives but also somehow to accommodate them in the human sphere in "plot"' ('Ecological Hardy', 135). Other critics have traced how *The Woodlanders* blends incongruously elements of Darwinism and Romanticism, of both nostalgia and its demystification.[13] Such changes in perspective, Kerridge argues, form a kind of 'narrative mobility . . . incompatible with a simply conservative attitude to change' (137).

Kerridge celebrates the proliferation in Hardy of different ways of seeing the same things, affirming the loosely 'ecological' sense of interconnection and plurality this induces. His argument is a green version of the kind of postmodern reading of Hardy instantiated by Linda Shires on *Tess of the d'Urbervilles* (1891):

> At the narrative level . . . Hardy relies on multiplicity and incongruity. He adopts these strategies within a general structure of tragic and ironic ambiguity. In doing so, Hardy questions the very foundations of traditional representation and belief. He wants the reader to become conditioned into thinking simultaneously in terms that are multiple and even contradictory.[14]

In calling such a sense of multiple viewpoints 'ecological', Kerridge distances himself from the relativistic view that all perspectives are of equal value as cultural options. Their very plurality is, rather, an insight into the greater objective reality of the interconnections in which any one event or character is suspended.

Kerridge also counteracts the kind of rural heritage nostalgia associated with Hardy by taking up the novelist's multiplicity of vision to speculate upon the lifestyle of a hypothetical future Winterbourne, that is, a figure who would both work in the woods, be supported by the National Health Service, have access to the Internet and would not, as in the novel, find himself homeless because of a feudal property regulation. This image, however, must remain wistfully inaccessible without detailed and protracted political work of a kind Kerridge does not describe.

In these readings of Raabe and Hardy the tensions at work in social and industrial modernisation are read as both producing and undermining forms of simplistic nostalgia, even while a sense of real destruction and loss remains unplaced and unfixed. They are inarticulate wrongs still seeking a language. Currently, if either Winterbourne or South were somehow to find themselves in a twenty-first-century Little Hintock, one certainty is that they could not afford to live there. Madeleine Bunting writes:

> The hijacking of the countryside by the middle class, who used both conservationist and environmentalist arguments to defend their self-interest, is an untold story of the past century. They have used the planning system, and, latterly, the housing market to create the kind of picture-book zones that cover large areas of Hampshire, Sussex, Gloucestershire and Wiltshire. They have become gated communities in all but name.[15]

The most immediate impact of Wanning and Kerridge's arguments, however, may be their challenge to elements of the culture of environmentalists themselves. By not simplifying the issues in moralistic ways and by implicating the narrators and their readers in the stakes of environmental destruction, they resist what Morton calls the culture of the 'beautiful soul' in some green circles, that off-putting stance of righteous indignation and blame, blind to the depth of its own complicity in what is happening to the world.[16]

Chapter 10

Liberalism and green moralism

It might seem strange at first that an introduction to literature and the environment should have a chapter on liberalism, a topic only sometimes discussed in green literary criticism, though prominent in other discussions of environmentalism. Liberalism, in the broad sense of that political tradition focussed on individual liberty as the supreme aim of politics, remains nevertheless a dominant political context for ecocriticism and marks it decisively.

Kerridge sets out one of the basic problems:

> unlike feminism, with which it otherwise has points in common, environmentalism has difficulty in being a politics of personal liberation or social mobility . . . environmentalism has a political weakness in comparison with feminism: it is much harder for environmentalists to make the connection between global threats and individual lives.[1]

Modes of reading geared to the affirmation of individual liberty and the policing of individual rights and their infringement have become the bread and butter of mainstream literary criticism. Ecocritics largely see themselves as part of this progressive enlightenment tradition, with its aims of human self-liberation through the overcoming of prejudice and injustice. This is why the turn to issues of ecojustice proved so easy to make. It is often in fact the values of a progressive liberalism that form the unacknowledged reference when green critics endorse alternative religious traditions or new age ideas.

At the same time, environmentalist thinkers dissociate themselves from unqualified endorsement of another defining aspect of the enlightenment tradition. They must divorce the project of human liberation from that of the exploitative conquest of nature that mars mainstream conceptions of 'progress' and 'modernisation'.

Can the two strands of enlightenment heritage be coherently separated? Bob Pepperman Taylor writes starkly of the clash between ecological limits and the pursuit of universal individual prosperity: 'the ecological facts of life threaten to challenge our most dearly held political values: justice, freedom, and democracy'.[2]

A striking point of contention has been the language of political rights. A great deal of modern work in the humanities has concerned itself with questions of justice and social exclusion in which notions of rights and infringed right are a crucial reference. Such criticism is 'political' in the sense of being sensitive to issues of prejudice and iniquity as a mode of infringed right. Unsurprisingly, therefore, some environmentalist thinkers and critics advocate extending the notion of rights to some or all animals and, in some cases, plants or even inanimate landscapes. For Roderick Frazier Nash in *The Rights of Nature* (1989), environmentalism forms no major break in the traditions of western thought but is a logical expansion of its doctrines of liberalism. Just as it once may have seemed absurd to some to accord certain rights to slaves or to women, so now the seeming absurdity of according rights to natural creatures and forms is beginning to be eroded. Animals and places become simply the latest entities to be embraced by the ever-expanding frontier of the liberal tradition. Environmentalism, as a biocentric ethic, becomes for Nash 'both the end and a new beginning of the American liberal tradition'.[3]

There is, however, a simple logical problem with Nash's proposal. In Bob P. Taylor's words: 'as the extensions of rights to non-humans becomes progressively more inclusive, the concept is progressively reduced to meaninglessness. Bearers of rights have *special* claims that take precedence over the claims of others. If all things in the natural universe have equal rights, all rights are equally meaningless.'[4] Another challenge to Nash's ugly US-centric rhetoric of ever-onward moral progress lies in the nature of the liberal tradition itself. Wilson Carey McWilliams's *Idea of Fraternity in America* (1973)[5] observes that the foundational assumption of liberal thought is that a human being is an essentially private, atomistic and apolitical individual. Politics arises because the relative scarcity of natural resources compels such individuals to form compacts of mutual recognition and respect, *rights*, in order not to come into conflict. In other words, the liberal political tradition looking back to Thomas Hobbes and John Locke in the seventeenth century, stresses right as individual self-interest and sees politics as essentially a kind of compact between individuals for the better mastery of nature and free use of individual property. Locke wrote, 'The earth and all that is therein is given to men for the support and comfort of their being. And though all the fruits it naturally produces, and beasts it feeds, belong to mankind in common' these yet become the individual property and exclusive right of whoever first invests his labour in them.[6]

Michael Zimmerman is especially severe on the provenance of notions of right in western conceptions of property, ownership and identity that are already deeply implicated in environmental crisis. Rights doctrine is

> *androcentric* because its conception of persons is based on masculinist experience that excludes (and implicitly negates) female experience; *hierarchical* because it gives precedence to male experience, and also because it portrays humans as radically more important than anything else; *dualistic* because of its distinction between humans (rational, intrinsically valuable, rights-possessing) and non-humans (non-rational, instrumental, lacking in rights); *atomistic* because it portrays humans as isolated social units; and *abstract* because conflicts about rights are settled by rationalistic impersonal debates that ignore both feelings and the particular needs/traits of the individuals involved.[7]

In other words, environmentalism could not easily be seen as an extension of the liberal tradition that now dominates conceptions of politics. Catherine L. Albanese concludes: 'the checks and balances of [the American] constitutional system become, for liberals, part of a competitive process conceived as the best means to subdue nature while yet controlling human combat'.[8] This simple observation has drastic implications. The need to find notions of right and value outside the individualistic liberal rights tradition, to affirm, say, the intrinsic value of a creature or place, is at odds with the intellectual and constitutional bases of the US and other modern nation states. Is it any wonder that environmentalist politics so often shifts from a reformist agenda towards a more revolutionary and anarchist one?

Under the current model of liberal democracy the environment has political force mainly as an 'interest' that some individuals assert, to be weighed against 'interests' asserted by other individuals. In the place of such 'liberal democracy' Robyn Eckersley's *The Green State: Rethinking Democracy and Sovereignty* (2004) advocates the development of what she calls an 'ecological' democracy. Decisions in such a state would not emerge from the aggressive market-like model of competing interests but from a process of informed deliberation in which all the parties who stand to be affected would be represented in some way, including parties outside the territorial borders of the state. The group of the potentially affected greatly blurs and extends the normal boundaries of political representation:

> ecological democracy may be best understood not so much as a democracy *of* the affected but a democracy *for* the affected, since the class of beings entitled to have their interests considered in democratic

deliberation and decision making (whether young children, the infirm, the yet to be born, or nonhuman species) will invariably be wider than the class of actual deliberators and decision makers.[9]

Non-human species, for instance, might be represented by scientists or other advocates, somewhat in the way that representatives already work on behalf of other people.

The limits of liberal criticism

Is there, then, an intellectual clash between the many demands of the environmental crisis and the overwhelmingly liberal political tradition in which most literary and cultural criticism operates? Work in the humanities often concerns itself with questions of justice and social exclusion for which notions of rights and infringed right are a crucial assumption. Even where the foreground arguments are more sophisticated the rhetoric of liberalism pervades literary criticism ('free ourselves from x', 'hemmed in by y', 'imprisoned by z', 'resists its marginalisation', 'strives for autonomy', etc.). Romantic assumptions about self-discovery, of asserting one's true nature and so forth, also lie close to the liberal tradition, a point that makes some people uncomfortable with the implicit individualism of much of the US wilderness tradition.

If, as Andrew Vincent concludes, 'it is the very values and practices of liberalism which now constitute the supreme environmental danger', then the liberal norm itself is a justified issue in ecocriticism. Firstly, as Vincent writes, 'it would appear, even from the mildest environmental perspective, that value extends beyond human agency. If liberal justice theory is tied closely to a *strong* anthropocentric position, then it is not easily adaptable for environmental issues.'[10] Secondly, as the human population expands, the case grows stronger that the liberal property-and-rights-holding citizen can no longer function as a justifiable political or social norm because its condition was an era of colonial expansion and commercial exploitation that assumed a boundless externality. 'Locke's theory [of exclusive individual property] depends upon the existence of a New World with an endless supply of space and resources ripe for colonization and plunder' (Robert Frodeman).[11]

Environmental criticism resembles some forms of feminism in being often circumspect of readings whose implicit or explicit principle is essentially that the status of an individualistic property-and-rights-holding subject should simply become applicable to all. The political theorist Wendy Brown argues that contemporary work on kinds of contestation for cultural power and recognition is too often 'tethered to a formulation of justice that reinscribes a

Figure 9 Road rage (Earth First!)

bourgeois (masculinist) ideal as its measure'.[12] Worse, it reinforces the liberal norm by way of protestation of exclusion from it. As we saw, one of the failings of some work in the field of environmental justice is that it sometimes still turns on the issue of inclusion–exclusion in relation to this norm, focussed more on moral outrage than with engaging 'post-materialist' values or the defence of alternative modes of life. There have been no convincing rebuttals of the maxim that for everyone to have the material standard of living of the average American would require the additional resources of three more planets the size of the earth.[13] Does this not also mean that readings of modern literature and social exclusion that implicitly endorse a just world as one in which everyone could, for example, own a car, are not cogent, for such a world would have already consumed its own future?

A third difficulty with the liberal rights tradition is this. Liberalism depends at some point on a demarcation of the public and the private. Beyond the boundary of what is considered 'private' the state is held to have no right to interfere. However, it is a distinctive feature of the environmental crisis to break down received distinctions of the political and non-political in ways that currently find no outlet in the categories of cultural or literary criticism. Ulrich Beck writes:

> Class conflicts or revolutions change power relations and exchange élites, but they hold fast to the goals of techno-economic progress and clash over mutually recognized civil rights. The double face of

'self-annihilating progress', however, produces conflicts that cast doubt
on the social basis of rationality – science, law, democracy. In that way,
society is placed under permanent pressure to negotiate foundations
without a foundation. It experiences an institutional destabilization, in
which all decisions – from local government policy on speed limits and
'parking lots' to the manufacturing details of industrial goods to the
fundamental issues of energy supply, law, and technological
development – can suddenly be sucked into fundamental political
conflicts.[14]

The fact that a critic's being a motorist, flying to conferences, eating beef-
steak or even buying a particular kind of banana may ultimately be of more
real environmental significance than his or her professed political stance must
destabilise modern criticism in bizarre and uncomfortable ways. It is symptomatic of this issue that writers such as Snyder or Lopez or Roger Deakin
(in Britain) or Judith Wright (in Australia) also strive to be known for their
different modes of life and environmental activism as well as for their writing.
On the whole, however, a green criticism of literature and culture is still struggling to find ways of dealing with that imponderable 'politics' inherent in often
undiscussed assumptions about personal affluence and lifestyle, conceptions
of professional success and mobility, distinctions between the public and the
private and so on. At present, however, there seem few ways of conceptualising
issues such as excessive affluence that do not slide towards being an off-putting
kind of green moralism. One effect of modern society's championing of individualistic ideas of freedom has been to give environmentalists the image of
interfering prigs.

Richard Kerridge has studied this mismatch of environmental issues and
the individualism dominant in contemporary culture in relation to some environmental eco-thrillers and films. He argues that films such as *Jurassic Park*
(1993) or *Water World* (1995) or Paul Watkins's novel *Archangel* 1995) (on a
forest finally saved by an industrialist's sudden change of heart) really evade
the imponderable complexities of environmental issues. They resort instead
to traditional plots of individual heroism pitted again simplistically immoral
antagonists.[15] Such dramas are still a long way from, say, Bill McKibben's brief
vision, concerning depletion of the ozone layer by CFCs, of a nation consigning
itself to oblivion with underarm deodorants.[16] A Hollywood film like *The Day
After Tomorrow* (2004), compressing climate change into an implausibly swift
but filmic disaster, would also be vulnerable to readings showing how the kind
of macho individualistic heroism and sentimentality it pivots on is actually
complicit with the industrial capitalism whose disastrous results it portrays.

A reading: William and Dorothy Wordsworth

The heritage of liberal conceptions of personhood is of concern in an article by Scott Hess. His 'Three "Natures": Teaching Romantic Ecology in the Poetry of William Wordsworth, Dorothy Wordsworth, and John Clare'[17] focusses specifically on notions of nature as they relate to different conceptions of human identity. Hence the three 'natures' of his title.

Hess takes up Wordsworth's famous daffodils poem, citing the shorter three-stanza version of 1804. He contrasts the poem to the entry in Dorothy Wordsworth's journal for 15 April 1802, which narrates the initial incident out of which the poem arose, and, later, to a text by John Clare. Various points emerge relating Wordsworth's poem to conceptions of authorship, identity, literary form, the aesthetic and their relation to differing assumptions about 'nature'. Crucially, for William, the encounter with the flowers is seen to form part of 'the construction of an autonomous identity' (9):

> I wandered lonely as a cloud
> That floats on high o'er vales and hills,
> When all at once I saw a crowd,
> A host, of golden daffodils;
> Beside the lake, beneath the trees,
> Fluttering and dancing in the breeze.
>
> The waves beside them danced;
> But they out-did the sparkling waves in glee:
> A poet could not but be gay,
> In such a jocund company:
> I gazed – and gazed – but little thought
> What wealth the show to me had brought:
>
> For oft, when on my couch I lie
> In vacant or in pensive mood,
> They flash upon that inward eye
> Which is the bliss of solitude;
> And then my heart with pleasure fills,
> And dances with the daffodils.

The key pronoun in William's poem, Hess observes, is *I*: the encounter with the daffodils is – or becomes – a solitary experience. His text is a celebration of how a chance encounter fed into a purposeful dynamic of individual growth. The poem ends indoors, with the poet once more in solitude and enjoying the inward image of the daffodils. Hess sees this as a kind of appropriation – 'what wealth the show to me had brought'. The basic stance is one in which the solitary mind encounters nature-as-spectacle, an event known 'in exclusively visual terms seen from the outside' (8). It even resembles a landscape painting whose features are arranged for a kind of consumption. 'Even as he defines himself through his relation to the daffodils, the narrator of the poem stresses his superiority and radical separation from them, in terms of elevation, detachment, and mobility, including his ability to internalize and carry them with him in memory' (7).

Comparing this poem to the related extract in Dorothy's Grasmere journal, Hess traces by contrast how Dorothy's writing is attentive to the differences and individuality of the flowers, with some seeming to rest their heads on the rocks, others 'stragglers a few yards higher up'. Her general sense of things is not that of an observer consciousness engaged in solitude with an object world, but with the landscape as a place of work ('We got over into a field to avoid some cows – people working') and interrelationships. Such prose contrasts with the more egocentric movement of her brother's lyric and its exclusive focus on individual experience, its meaning for him. Hess writes that Dorothy 'constructs a non-hierarchical and relational model of difference' (7) while William uses the daffodils as fodder for his model of creative imagination and solitary individualism (8).[18]

The broader point to be made here is this. Unlike in much politicised literary criticism, the liberal ideal of the 'free' or autonomous self as instantiated by William is not being used as the implicit norm for criticising the deprivations of the less privileged. It is itself being criticised for its reductive and exploitative notions both of nature and of personal identity. Hess writes:

> [The] version of environment in Wordsworth's poem . . . authorizes a society of individual bourgeois writers and readers, claiming autonomy from one another while at the same time producing their identities and social relationships through this shared symbolic internalization of nature, apart from any specific local environment. Dorothy Wordsworth's journal entry, in contrast, supports a relational model of identity, produced through immersion in a specific environment and complex overlapping networks of human and non-human relationship – an identity which cannot be easily abstracted from its contexts. 11

Hess shows in unusual detail how the institutions of private property and its attendant values form or deform the basic moves and assumptions of a famous poem, even linking it to such injustices as the enclosures and, by implication, to the contemporary devastation wrought by neoliberal capitalism and its institutions. Aspects of Hess's reading might well be disputed (see Ninth Quandary).[19] Nevertheless, his argument shows in detail how the assumptions and culture of individualist liberalism may be at stake in the reading of a famous poem.[20]

Seventh quandary: the rights of the yet-to-be-born

One of the most significant features of the early twentieth-first century has been a growing awareness of a deep and systematic injustice in the workings of contemporary government, political thinking, and many modes of thought and analysis in both intellectual and daily life. The injustice is incalculable in its extent, possibly catastrophic, but also so foreign to currently dominant modes of thought and practice as to seem bizarre or even nonsensical when first described. This injustice is the lack of political representation of future generations.

At no time before has the future condition of the physical world been so assiduously studied and mapped out, especially in relation to climate change, to the point, ironically, of neutralising the horror of the probable scenarios. Despite this, the yet-to-be-born remain unrepresented in governments that enact laws and pursue policies already well understood as set to degrade or even ruin their lives. Anthony Giddens writes:

> The classical liberal view of the rights and responsibilities of individuals . . . is that every individual should be free to pursue whatever lifestyle he or she chooses, so long as those choices do not harm others. However, the liberal state has not been accustomed to extending that principle to environmental goods, or to the avoidance of harm to future generations; both now have become absolutely central.[21]

At present, the person yet to be born has a peculiar hovering status, between being an evident non-issue – someone who does not exist can obviously have no rights – and being the latest and strangest form of the victim, being utterly without power.

Kristian Ekeli proposes that measures to safeguard the claims of future generations be incorporated into the constitutional bases of states. Thus 'courts should have the competence to appoint guardians for future people, and these guardians should be empowered to initiate legal proceedings on behalf of posterity'.[22] Alan Carter, however, argues that the injustice to future generations, as well as many non-human lives, is now so serious and the environmentally destructive syndromes of world politics and economics so deeply entrenched that civil disobedience is a duty: 'the environmental crises are so pressing that we do not have time to wait.'[23]

The issue of injustice to future people is implicit in many scenarios in science fiction. As yet, however, no recognised method of reading the literary and cultural archive corresponds to this massive structural injustice.[24]

Chapter 11

Ecofeminism

The term *ecofeminism* has been widely used since the late 1980s to name a growing political, cultural and intellectual movement, both activist and academic. Ynestra King has named it 'the third wave of the women's movement'.[1] Its defining claim is that the destruction of the environment and the historical oppression of women are deeply linked.

Ecofeminist thinkers come to environmental issues expert in controversies about distinctions between sex ('natural') and gender ('cultural'), questions of whether the category 'woman' or 'women' has any clear natural referent or is not, in fact, an unstable product of social conditions. This helps render ecofeminism perhaps the most sophisticated and intellectually developed branch of environmental criticism.[2] It is especially sensitive to the environmental implications of differing conceptions of human personhood. Nevertheless, as Glynis Carr writes, 'While ecofeminist philosophy and politics are relatively well developed, ecofeminist literary theory and criticism are not',[3] a discrepancy that arguably applies to ecocriticism generally.

The following statement by Donna Haraway would now command almost universal consent among ecofeminists and the majority of ecocritics:

> certain dualisms have been persistent in Western traditions; they have all been systemic to the logics and practices of domination of women, people of color, nature, workers, animals – in short, domination of all constituted as *others*, whose task is to mirror the self. Chief among these troubling dualisms are self/other, mind/body, culture/nature, male/female, civilized/primitive, reality/appearance, whole/part, agent/resource, maker/made, active/passive, right/wrong, truth/illusion, total/partial, God/man.[4]

The point being made about these dualisms ('man/woman', 'culture/nature', etc.) is that the first term of each pair has often been defined in opposition to and with implicit superiority over the other. Environmental critics refer often to such hierarchical dualisms, though there are various different ways of engaging them. As often in this field, one can draw a crude but workable distinction between romantic/essentialist arguments and broadly post-human ones. For the first, the critic's task becomes simply to take up the more denigrated term and affirm it. Ecofeminism of this kind is a variety of identity politics, affirming, that is, woman as a given identity crossing distinctions of nationality, religion or political allegiance. For others, like Haraway herself, the fact the two terms (man–woman, etc.) have been mutually defining – 'woman' being understood by her relation to man and vice versa – must mean that simply affirming the supposedly lesser term is inadequate. The whole set-up or opposition and its complex implication in a related set of hierarchies needs to be rethought *in its totality*. Such ecofeminism cannot, then, remain an identity politics, simply affirming a given 'woman' or 'nature'. It gives itself the challenge of unravelling whole networks of assumptions and practices in cultures across the globe. Even a seemingly trivial item in a novel, poem or report that draws on assumptions about sexual difference may then ramify into huge social and political questions.

A characteristic ecofeminist gesture has already been encountered in Scott Hess's reading of the Wordsworths. Criticising the liberal conceptions of personhood implicit in William's text, Hess contrasted it to the very different conception instantiated in Dorothy's journal. Dorothy 'constructs a non-hierarchical and relational model of difference' (7) attentive to the flowers as living things beyond their status as aesthetic spectacle, part of a working landscape of human and non-human relationships of which any observer is a part.

Rachel Stein considers the poet Adrienne Rich as a different kind of nature writer and makes similar points about the rejection of implicitly masculinist and exclusively heterosexual conceptions of personhood and agency. Rich gives no credit to finding 'solutions to societal problems by exiling herself in the wilderness'[5] or the use of nature as a means to self-cultivation. Crucial here is the rejection of that tradition of thought and writing that would project the illusion of being a detached spectator or observer, either as a kind of consumer of experiences or in the fantasy of an unimplicated objectivity. Stein endorses the way in which Rich writes from out of an affirmation of her own specific and particular situation, identity and history, 'as a white middle-class woman, an assimilated Jew searching for meaningful traditions, a lesbian, a teacher, a North American, and a person suffering with an aging and increasingly ill body' (198).

Masculinist conceptions of identity and personhood are held to involve a simultaneous denigration and fear of the bodily, associated with the 'natural' as opposed to the 'cultural', and the 'woman' as opposed to the 'man'. Against this Rich thinks through her own painful experience of arthritis. The intellectual as well as physical unease of immediate participation in nature undoes any fantasy of detached human spectatorship:

> The problem is
> to connect, without hysteria, the pain
> of any one's body with the pain of the body's world
> For it is the body's world
> They are trying to destroy forever
>   'Contradictions: Tracking Poems'[6]

Rich's affirmation of the bodily nature of human identity is not an essentialist affirmation of the body simply *as* nature. Stein sees it as an endorsement of the argument that '"the body is neither – while also being both – . . . self or other, natural or cultural, psychical or social. This indeterminate position enables it to be used as a particularly powerful strategic term to upset the frameworks by which these binary pairs are constructed"' (Elizabeth Groz).[7] Thus, Rich's poem presents bodily pain as itself a refusal of the very nature–culture split at work in much other nature writing.

In Gretel Ehrlich's *The Future of Ice* (2004) an affirmation of bodily experience also serves as a kind of identification with the physical earth. Ehrlich's is a kind of hybrid writing, blending personal narrative with historical anecdote and snippets of popular science. To experience oneself as a physical body, acted on by other material bodies, is seen to challenge 'the myth of objectivity',[8] crucial to the authority of science when used as an ideology and in the cultures of global managerialism. Ehrlich's prose is accordingly full of images that are bodily and erotic, involving taste, touch and smell as well the more mediated senses of sight and hearing.

Ehrlich makes frequent reference to the frightening scientific consensus on climate change: 'I would write a book about winter and climate change, about what would happen if we became "deseasoned," if winter disappeared as a result of global warming' (xi). Clearly, her alternative sensuous modes of interacting with nature are not tantamount to the accusation that those of the sciences have no validity. The issue is that they need not also delegitimise other valuable kinds of engagement with the world, non-dualistic, sensuous and non-hierarchical. Elsewhere she writes:

> To separate out thought into islands is the peculiar way we humans have of knowing something, of locating ourselves on the planet and in society. We string events into temporal sequences like pearls or

archipelagos. While waiting out winter, I listen to my mind switch from logic to intuition, from tree to net, the one unbalancing the other so no dictatorships can stay.[9]

Throughout *The Future of Ice* the background threat of climate change produces all kinds of cognitive, rhetorical and emotional shifts, altering even mundane events and sights. These suggest with an alarming ease bigger implications in the sight of a glacier whose 'forehead has been torn open and is posed to fall' (46). In an earlier passage Ehrlich sees the side of a mountain that has been churned up by tourists as 'a fresh wound, a whole shoulder torn, with a watery ooze and a hole that's getting bigger . . . As I walk I see how the wound grows, where backpackers have climbed farther up to avoid the mud but, in so doing, have torn the Earth's skin more' (30).

An *écriture ecofemine*?

Ecofeminist criticism is especially strong on the implications of various notions of human personhood. Rich's affirmation of women's 'weak ego boundaries' is reminiscent of a point made about the science of ecology by Neil Everden: that its tracing of energy and nutrient flows disregards the boundaries between one creature and another, dissolving hierarchical subject–object dichotomies: 'Is there even a boundary between you and the non-living world, or will the atoms in this page be part of your body tomorrow?'[10] A major contemporary challenge for ecofeminism could be stated as being to maintain the critique of liberal and neoliberal conceptions of the person without forfeiting the moral or political force usually identified with that rights-based tradition.

An ecofeminist essay affirming alternative models of personhood and agency is L. Elizabeth Waller's 'Writing the Real: Virginia Woolf and an Ecology of Language'.[11] Waller focusses on the innovative and experimental style and narrative forms of Woolf's *The Waves* (1931) and other texts. *The Waves* consists of multiple narratives moving through various natural cycles (spring to autumn, day to night), each with its various non-human protagonists. The six human characters are presented in what critics usually take to be 'stream of consciousness' modes. Waller, however, challenges the mainstream view of this text as 'an exploration of the workings of the minds of the six named characters within the text . . . interspersed with depersonalized prose which describes constantly shifting patterns of light and water' (Kate Flint).[12] Consider the following passage:

'Now they have all gone', said Louis. 'I am alone. They have gone into the
house for breakfast, and I am left standing by the wall of flowers. It is
very early, before lessons. Flower after flower is specked on the depths of
greens. The petals are harlequins. Stalks rise from the black hollows
beneath. The flowers swim like fish made of light upon dark, green
waters. I hold a stalk in my hand. I am the stalk. My roots go down to
the depths of the world, through earth dry with brick, and damp earth,
through veins of lead and silver. I am all fibre. All tremors shake me, and
the weight of the earth is pressed to my ribs. Up here my eyes are green
leaves, unseeing. I am a boy in green flannels with a belt fastened by a
brass snake up here. Down there my eyes are the lidless eyes of a stone
figure in the desert by the Nile. I see women passing with red pitchers to
the river; I see camels swaying and me in turbans. I hear tramplings,
tremblings, stirrings around me.'[13]

The term 'stream of consciousness' is disputed here. It already sets up the
multiple non-human agencies as peripheral, as images only for the 'inner' life
of the human beings. Waller objects: 'Are only human characters "named"?
Is Woolf's prose "depersonalized" when it comes to nonhuman characters?'
(147). It is false, she argues, to submit Woolf's prose to a hierarchical presupposition that the so-called 'depersonalised' passages exist only to serve the purpose
of human characterisation. It is rather a matter of a less exclusive conception
of character and identity: 'Does human identity exist outside the context of
nature – ever?' (148).[14] The 'depersonalised' passages should be acknowledged
as granting a genuine agency to the non-human, as describing that vaster field
of agency in which human thought, perception and identity are enmeshed ('My
roots go down to the depths of the world, through earth dry with brick . . . ').
   The effect of reading the non-human action as 'foreground' at least as much
as the human is a drastic jump that highlights how far received notions of characterisation in a novel assume, as an unexamined presupposition, a severance
and privileging of human action as against everything else. By comparison with
The Waves, most other novels may come to seem like enormous and unjustified acts of selection and abstraction. A whole tradition of the realist novel and
'commonsense' Western assumptions about human life are defamiliarised.
   What other critics simplify as an exclusively human 'inner' meditation or
stream of consciousness emerges instead as a kind of plural dialogue of multiple
agencies and 'subjects'. Waller quotes Ronnie Zoe Hopkins: 'attempting to
limit "discourse" . . . broadly construed, to an activity that only a single species
practices . . . seems quite uninformed biologically, just as restricting the sphere
of what can be said to be "known" to the domain of human representation
would seem to consign us to a kind of species-wide solipsism'.[15]

Woolf's experiment anticipates modern ecofeminist practice and theory in celebrating the sensuous and even the erotic as non-appropriative ways of knowing the natural world, a form of knowledge that is not at once also a kind of power but is open to the agency of others.

Other aspects of Waller's argument seem more dubious. She reads Woolf's provocative experiment in compositional method as a letting speak of that part of the natural world that is her own body, with its organic rhythms and correspondences. Thus, Woolf is said to let 'the flow and flux of ecocentric reality voice the language to describe' a real world supposedly lost to merely anthropocentric conceptions of discourse (138). This focus on physiology, however, drifts towards a more questionable romantic metaphysic. Woolf's compositional method is seen to open a usually blocked path to a supposedly lost and unalienated human nature, located in the female body. A loss of an original 'discourse' of human and non-human agents thus becomes the more conventional story of the human fall from a lost state of nature/childhood, here politicised as a fall into the divisive categories of patriarchy:

> As days, seasons, and years pass, the human characters each struggle to unite culture and nature in language as they did as children, while earth continues conversing with or without them. We read their process of separation, isolated in individualism, and saturation into androcentric culture as the novel progresses. In many ways, what is illustrated in *The Waves* is exactly what happened in the course of five thousand years of patriarchy.   150–1

Waller hypothesises a fall from an Edenic condition that did not sever 'culture from nature, internal environment from external environment, human from nonhuman' (151). It is here, however, that she touches on claims that other ecofeminists would wish to qualify. Others see such myths of some lost matriarchal paradise more as foci and incentives for contemporary struggles than as the topic of a speculative and dubious prehistory. Michael Zimmerman writes:

> Many cultural ecofeminists share aspects of the goal of early romantic poets: to overcome social fragmentation and alienation by developing a new myth that is compatible with reason. Political activists who ignore this spiritual yearning in favor of secular rationalism fail to see that societies founded on such rationalism often lack legitimacy precisely because they do not satisfy the meaning-seeking aspect of human experience.[16]

For others, however, new age idealisations of the Great Mother or 'Gaia' are damaging simplifications of what nature is, personifications made from given stereotypes of the feminine. Catriona Sandilands writes:

> Nature was viewed as the obverse of all that is wrong with civilization. As patriarchal culture was individuated, nature was interconnected. As androcentric institutions emphasized rationality, nature was mysterious. As capitalism was inherently crisis-driven and unsustainable, nature was inherently stable, balanced, and sustaining. Nature was defined in terms of stereotypical femininity because contemporary culture was the manifestation of all that is quintessentially male.[17]

Sandilands might be writing here of this aspect of Waller's work on Woolf. Waller's essay contrasts in this respect with Louise Westling's otherwise comparable reading of Woolf as developing a practice of writing at odds with masculinist notions of personhood (this time in *Between the Acts*). Westling, like Waller, relates Woolf's prose to modern critiques of dualisms of human and animal, mind and nature, but not as harking back to dubious idealisations of a lost human essence. Instead her writing forms a new, iconoclastic practice opening new channels of communication and insight. Woolf's techniques help us 'recognize how literature can help bring those many voices into presence for a posthumanist future'. Human culture in Woolf is shown as enmeshed in and dependent on multiple non-human agencies, 'a reality beyond human comprehension and sense of time'.[18]

Finally, both Waller's and Westling's readings of Woolf's experiments suggest a challenging rereading of Dominic Head's account of the mismatch between any would-be ecological perspective and the kind of focus and timescale dominant in the tradition of the realist novel, with its focus on individual personal development in an exclusively social context.[19] Might the mismatch now suggest not that ecocriticism has unrealistic or utopian expectations, but rather the alarming extent to which dubious and destructive assumptions about humanity have passed as almost self-evident in literature for centuries?

'Nature provides us with few givens' (Lealle Ruhl)[20]

Much modern feminism sits squarely within the liberal tradition. It can be summarised as working to affirm for women individualist norms of autonomy and right against old, reductive identifications of women with passive 'nature' or prejudices that women are 'naturally' x or y. In this context ecofeminism has sometimes looked anomalous. Might the two elements 'eco' and 'feminism' pull in different directions?

Contemporary ecofeminism usually now differentiates itself from that strand which Sandilands has nicknamed 'motherhood environmentalism'.[21] This took up stereotypical associations of women under patriarchy not to oppose them directly but to affirm them as environmental countervalues. Thus women were endorsed as somehow 'closer to nature' than men, usually through their connection with motherhood and nurturing. The association of women and the domestic sphere could be reaffirmed as their greater sense of respect for nature as a sort of home ('ecology' being from the Greek 'science of the household'). Few ecofeminists would now agree with such simple assertions. Rather, 'It's not that women are actually closer to nature than men . . . but throughout history, men have chosen to set themselves apart, usually "over and above" nature and women.'[22]

Ecofeminism nevertheless remains a flashpoint for the clash between the ideals of modern liberalism and environmental questions. Are calls for women to 'think like a mountain' a 'blatant slap in the face' (Janet Biehl) for struggles towards individual selfhood and independence?[23] Such questions also underlie arguments between second-wave, liberal, rights-based feminism and so-called 'natural law' feminists who resist the intrusion of the state, the market economy and various reproductive technologies in what they take to be women's natural association with conception, gestation, childbirth and mothering. Lealle Ruhl, on the other hand, criticises this 'natural law' position for its tendency to project 'the natural' as a social and moral imperative.[24] 'Instead', she argues, 'of trying to determine the boundaries of the natural, it is perhaps more useful to enquire into the placement of the boundaries of the natural, how these boundaries appear where they do, and why.'[25]

The poetry of Rich may also show the strain between some ecofeminist projects and liberalism as the now dominant mode of political self-assertion. Rich writes, 'We are attempting to . . . break down that fragmentation of inner and outer in every possible realm.'[26] This does not mean the familiar romantic programme of the retrieval of some supposedly lost personal essence through engagement with nature. It is, rather, to recognise that the inner–outer dichotomy is already a patriarchal fiction, a stance of would-be transcendence of the bodily and the natural world. She continues: 'The psyche and the world out there are being acted on and interacting intensely all the time. There is no such thing as the private psyche, whether you're a woman – or a man, for that matter.'[27] Such an assertion is directly at odds with modern neoliberalism and its focus on the atomistic individual and its 'rights'. Margaret Thatcher's notorious statement in this respect, 'there is no such thing as society', seems the very inverse of Rich's 'There is no such thing as the private psyche.'

In practice, however, Rich's politics and poetics remain far closer to a liberal kind of feminism than her observations of the fragility of the ego's borders would suggest. The strident assertiveness of her work, affirming the rights of a given identity, often conflicts with her simultaneous affirmation of women's 'weak ego boundaries'.[28] The poetry seems divided between perceptions of modes of fluid identification and dissolution of the personal ego on the one hand, and the creation, on the other, of a political identity whose voice could be recognised within given models of politics. This issue of voice in Rich exemplifies again that problem that bedevils environmental politics: how to make one's case heard in a society whose ears are attuned to respond only to the kinds of argument and assumption one also wishes to question?

Chapter 12

'Post-colonial' ecojustice

'[T]here is no rush by African literary and cultural critics to adopt ecocriticism or the literature of the environment as they are promulgated from many of the world's metropolitan centers' (William Slaymaker). Even writers 'for whom "environmental" issues are central, such as the Nigerian poet Niyi Osundare, are still valued more in relation to more familiar social political issues'.[1] A history often of war, dispossession, and colonial and neocolonial exploitation offers little space for an ecocriticism that has sometimes looked like the professionalised hobby of a western leisure class.

Nevertheless, it is in the so-called developing world that environmental disputes are at their most intense, most fraught with political, ethical and religious overtones and even violence. In contexts where international capitalism pits itself directly against traditional land use or where people may find themselves in the way of their own government's infrastructure schemes, fundamental questions are often immediately at issue about modes of life, human identity and social justice.

Environmentalism as neocolonialism?

In the encounter between 'post-colonial' thinking and ecocriticism to date, it is ecocriticism that first seems the more in need of revision. For, to many people, modern environmentalism can look like another form of colonialism. Critics will often now distance themselves in uneasy ways from the way reform environmentalism has become part of a system of global managerialism, closely related to institutions like the IMF or the World Bank, with its Global Environmental Facility. For example, the setting aside of a large area as a 'national park' may be part of the deal for reducing a country's debt, one also requiring the 'liberalising' of internal markets, that is, their increased penetration by international capitalism, forcing people into the money economy, with the effect of replacing small rural communities by urban shanty towns. This is the story of the Batwa of south-western Uganda, expelled from the dense montane forests where their ancestors had lived unobtrusively for thousands of years and often now living in shacks on the Bwindi park border. 'In one more generation their forest-based culture – songs, rituals, traditions and stories – will be gone.'[2]

Big international non-governmental environmental organisations (BINGOs) have become objects of suspicion. Mark Dowie gives a sample of their appropriating jargon:

> The rationale for 'internal displacements', as these evictions are officially called, usually involves a perceived threat to the biological diversity of a large geographical area, variously designated by one or more of the BINGOs as an 'ecological hotspot', an 'ecoregion', a 'vulnerable ecosystem', a 'biological corridor', or a 'living landscape'.[3]

Such criticisms have led to an increased recognition among non-governmental organisations themselves that the boundaries between conservation, colonialism and the depredations of international capitalism may often be uncomfortably blurred and uncertain.

Environmental debate is nevertheless part of the faltering creation of a planetary public sphere. Since the 1980s, for instance, the world has witnessed a weird alliance between first-world environmentalists and fourth-world people fighting to defend their indigenous way of life. Celebrities such as the pop star Sting are filmed flying into the Amazon region to meet representatives of native Indian tribes. The Indians even become a kind of icon, circulating in all sorts of commercial images.

This seeming convergence of interests between northern urban environmentalists and southern indigenous Indians has worked to the benefit of both. Environmentalists gain new legitimacy by presenting themselves as defenders of indigenous rights, while the Indians, in the word of a Rainforest Foundation spokesperson, have discovered that 'the rainforest card is stronger than the indigenous card'.[4] The Indians exploit the symbolic capital inherent in their identity, or, to be more precise, the idealised image of that identity circulating in affluent societies.

Such alliances form a kind of 'middle ground' in Richard White's sense:

> Diverse peoples adjust their differences through what amounts to a process of creative, and often exceeding, misunderstandings. People try to persuade others who are different from themselves by appealing to what they perceive to be the values and practices of those others. They often misinterpret and distort both the values and practices of those they deal with, but from those misunderstandings arise new meanings and through them new practices – the shared meanings and practices of the middle ground.[5]

In North America, a well-known figure of such 'middle ground' is the so-called 'ecological Indian': people of indigenous American descent assert their own cultural distinctiveness in the very terms in which they have been idealised by some western environmentalists.[6] The public recognition thus achieved may be offset, however, by the way that the cultural pronouncements of a Native American poet such as the Muscogee Creek Joy Harjo can end up sounding disconcertingly similar to the standard romantic line in environmental diagnosis in the developed world, with the blame falling on 'alienation' from the land and the compartmentalising reductiveness of western rationality.[7]

Is there yet a specifically environmental post-colonial criticism?

How to adapt ecocritical arguments to post-colonial questions? This question has had the effect of highlighting elements in given ecocriticism that are not so universal as they once seemed. Post-colonial critics question the way some environmental thinkers refer simply to 'humanity' as the antagonist of the natural world, a view that ignores vast differences between human groups and with a sometimes 'peremptory conviction . . . that global ethical considerations should override local cultural concerns'.[8] Yet the implicit demands being made on a future environmental criticism are also enormous here – to be able to engage in any culture across the world in relation to such already difficult issues as the ethics of relating to the non-human, environmental justice, the nature and limits of anthropocentrism, duties towards future generations and so on.

At the moment ecocritics generally make headway simply by affirming a common interest between defending the natural world and defending the cultures of local or indigenous peoples. Patrick D. Murphy, for instance, endorses the work and often non-realist technique of numerous non-western writers, each engaged with tracing the encroachments of industrialism and commodification on their part of the planet. Whether the topic is Ishumure Michiko on an old Japanese fishing village, Linda Hogan on the Osage in Oklahoma, Edna Esacamill on a Chicano community in southern Arizona, or Karen Tei Yamashita on contemporary Brazilian forest people, Murphy traces in each text a disruption to old traditions rooted in the local or regional, where identity was based on communal values rather than an possessive individualism, and on respect for the natural world as opposed to capitalist exploitation.[9] If globalisation and neocolonialism often serve up recognisably familiar antagonists in different cultures across the world, then such environmental criticism feeds into an emerging, international countersphere.

However, recent thinking also uncomfortably highlights not just the familiar antagonism between conservation and capitalism, but 'a separate conflict between conservation and human rights' (Robert Cribb),[10] one that is becoming more acute. Is the frequently made identification of local interests and green politics a 'middle ground' disguising as many differences as it reconciles?

Colonialism as the 'Conquest of nature'

An environmentally informed reading can both enhance and question the work of a post-colonial reading. To give a brief example, in his *Beginning Postcolonialism* John McLeod offers a post-colonial reading of Rudyard Kipling's 'The Overland Mail (foot-service to the hills)', a poem depicting an Indian runner taking the imperial mail from the coast up to the summer headquarters of the British Raj in the foothills of the Himalayas, where the administrators moved to escape some of the heat of the season. The Indian landscape, McLeod observes, is described as a place of 'Lords of the Jungle', tigers and robbers but otherwise curiously depopulated except as a 'wilderness of obstacles' for the intrepid to overcome, 'dark, menacing, and dangerous; full of tempests and floods where even the roads are vulnerable'.[11] McLeod reads the landscape as a metaphor of colonial human relationships: the unnamed runner climbs toward his rulers and a more benign landscape of 'rose-oak' and 'fir' trees. He is depicted as a personification of the irresistibility of an imperial duty, though with undertones of compulsion that blur slightly the implicit contrast between him and the 'robber' who retreats from his path. Kipling's final stanza depicts the arrival of the post in the hills:

> There's a speck on the hillside, a dot on the road –
> A jingle of bells on the footpath below –
> There's a scuffle above in the monkey's abode –
> The world is awake and the clouds are aglow.
> For the Great Sun himself must attend to the hail: –
> 'In the Name of the Empress, the Overland Mail!'

How does one read the last line but one, the claim, unbalanced even if tongue-in-cheek, that the sun is subservient to Queen Victoria, empress of India?

McLeod's reading overlooks this line entirely, but the poem surely becomes more puzzling here. For the poem's co-opting of the sun contradicts the whole logic of its metaphorised landscape, its tracing of a gradual welcome ascent from the sultry jungle into the cooler, pleasanter 'British' hills where 'we exiles' have retreated precisely to escape the sun's heat. '[T]he Great Sun himself must attend to the hail' is a statement whose complacency throws a different light over the whole text. For a post-colonial critic to overlook a line of such literal absurdity could be taken as symptomatic of McLeod's own mode of reading: this shares with Kipling's poem the strategy of reading landscape entirely as an expression of human relationships, even if it sees those relationships differently.[12]

However, colonialism was and neocolonialism is, primarily a matter of the 'conquest of nature', the appropriation of local resources. Is it not the perversity of this that becomes legible in the poem's nonsensical landscape and climate images? 'One interpretation of the current environmental crisis is that it represents nature's backlash – its counterinsurgency – against the forces of human colonization' (Eric Katz).[13]

Mayumi Toyosato's reading of Kiana Davenport's Hawaiian saga, *Shark Dialogues* (1995) is an example of how far identification with local interests and peoples also offers critics a stance of explicitly environmental opposition. The novel traces the modern history of Hawaii and its colonisation and eventual annexation by the United States. Its central character, Pono, already of no longer purely Hawaiian descent, is a kind of seer and embodiment of indigenous values and beliefs as these come to adapt themselves and change through the twentieth century. Davenport's saga traces the various characters' responses to environmental injustice as the islands turn into a destination for mass tourism and are damaged through various agricultural, energy, military and infrastructure projects. In this process the native population suffers social collapse, 'unemployment, alcoholism, crime, suicide',[14] and large immigrant communities of plantation workers suffer similarly. Toyosato's concern in reading the novel is to trace a shift 'from race-oriented identity to cultural identity'.[15] The issue finds focus in Pono's close but difficult relationship with her four granddaughters, long after their four separate mothers have died or become alienated. The fact that each of the granddaughters is only partly Hawaiian by blood, and an adopted grandson, Toru, a Vietnam veteran, not ethnically Hawaiian at all, proves no impediment to the identification with place and the characters' practice of the native values of *aloha 'āina* ('love of the land') and *'ohana* ('extended family'). Extended family means, in Pono's case, a lifetime of living with, helping and forming alliances with immigrant communities from China, the Philippines and Japan. Toyosato affirms the novel as tracing the emergence of a new and viable oppositional Hawaiian identity, based on identification with the land rather than ethnic origins. In this way, her reading offers itself as both post-colonial and environmentalist at the same time: 'The novel . . . reveals how resistance against the destruction of the environment means resistance against the social/political marginalization, especially for nondominant cultural groups'.[16] Localism and resistance to international capitalism are taken to be inherently green. In fact, a simple identification of this kind informs most criticism striving to unify post-colonial and ecocritical stances.[17]

Ecological or environmentalist language also acts as a 'middle ground' for writers in various post-colonial contexts. Bessie Head's novels, *When Rain Clouds Gather* (1968) and *A Question of Power* (1973), explore ideas that correspond to what would later be called a bioregional project of 'reinhabitation' (see Chapter 13). Head imagines communities in Botswana who combine a revival of traditional wisdom with modern science in order to disengage themselves from the ideologies of modernisation transforming the larger environment. Such projects of imaginative reinhabitation may also take the form of a rejection of models of personhood associated with modernity and the hegemony of the West (individualism, rootlessness, pursuit of personal success, etc.).[18] Leslie Marmon Silko's *Ceremony* (1977), still the novel most frequently studied in relation to environmental post-colonialism, depicts the return to his native Navaho community of a soldier traumatised by the Second World War, and his gradual recovery through native ritual, understanding of place and a reconfiguration of the terms of personal identity.[19]

Richard White's 'middle ground', however, was defined as a space of compromise, of partial or even illusory identifications of interests as much as of encounter and agreement. Two broad points seem relevant to this. Firstly, when a modern ecocritic endorses some traditional religious practice or the use of non-realist rhetorical or narrative techniques in representing ritual, as in *Ceremony* or the scene of Pono's transformation into a shark in *Shark Dialogues*,[20] it is invariably modern secular environmentalism that acts as the decisive if inconspicuous frame within which the value of indigenous beliefs and their modes of presentation are being celebrated. The cultural authority accorded indigenous practices is actually second-hand.[21]

A further issue is that, in taking over their methods of argument from kinds of oppositional politics, ecocritics have yet to evolve modes of argument able fully to engage those crucial environmental problems in which *all* the individual agents involved are benign or innocent – issues such as the millions of formerly impoverished people in India or China saving to buy a first car. As more people aspire to western kinds of prosperity, problems are arising for which it is not primarily a matter of opposing oppressive structures of power, for which there are few criteria of judgement and few recognised or accepted modes of political arbitration. In such cases, it is clearly insufficient to address environmentalist arguments only by pointing out the neocolonial overtones of some policies or actions, or by admonishing readers to factor 'cultural difference into both the historical and contemporary ecological and bioethical debates'.[22] Major environmental problems can fall outside the schemas of oppositional post-colonial thinking altogether.

A reading: Amitav Ghosh, *The Hungry Tide* (2004)

As yet little work exists that addresses such tensions. An exception is discussion of Amitav Ghosh's recent novel, *The Hungry Tide* (2004), set in the Sundarbans, the vast archipelago of islands in the delta of the Ganges in Bengal, on India's border with Bangladesh. The area is internationally renowned as a protected wetland, and is especially famous as a preserve for the threatened Bengal tiger. Rajender Kaur maps out the social-political co-ordinates of the various characters.[23] These are, principally, Piya, a visiting American biologist of Bengali descent, a woman travelling alone whose concern is primarily with the native river dolphins of the Ganges delta; Fokir, a native fisherman, maintaining his livelihood amid the policed restrictions of a national park; Nilima, a local activist who has independently built up a thriving health centre, and Kanai, her nephew and visitor, a prosperous middle-class businessman from New Delhi whose money comes from running translation agencies. In some ways the novel appears to be a kind of political parable, ending with the American biologist deciding to stay, teaming up with the local health activist to make dolphin conservation a grass-roots activity, one sensitive to the needs of the local community. This is after her having been saved from death in a typhoon by the self-sacrificing figure of the fisherman whose martyrdom, problematically, seems somehow necessary to the final reconciliation of global environmentalism and local politics. Piya comes to learn, 'As for myself I know that I don't want to do the kind of work that places the burden of conservation on those who can least afford it. If I was to take on a project here I'd want it to be done in consultation with the fishermen who live in these parts.'[24] A possible marriage is even on the cards between the biologist Piya and Kanai.

Graham Huggan and Helen Tiffin sum up the problem with the green parable so far described:

Piya's astute decision at the end to become a 'rooted cosmopolitan' rather than a 'footloose expert' is only possible because the local people have no particular problem with dolphins. The much more intractable problem of the tiger (and its sanctuary) on which the novel is premised is displaced by the relatively easy dolphin 'solution', and neither a practical nor a philosophical management of the problem is offered.[25]

The Bengal tiger is unusually aggressive and kills 20–80 people in the Sundarbans each year.[26] Kaur's reading is that the tiger reservation, established by Indira Gandhi to win international prestige for India, remains an example of the insensitivity of neocolonial environmental schemes that override the concerns of local people. The novel also focusses on the violent removal from the reserve in the 1970s of refugees from the war which led to the foundation of Bangladesh. Kaur sees Ghosh's novel overall as looking to 'a new ecocritical paradigm where global entrepreneur and cetologist can become conscientious collaborators with local underclasses towards mutually beneficial goals' (137). Yet Kaur also evades the conflict between the human population of the Sundarbans and man-eating tigers on the endangered species list. The hideous problem is not really engaged in his statement that, by seeing the tiger as a magnificent but amoral force of nature like a typhoon, the novel somehow 'goes beyond taking sides in the conservation debate over the Bengal tiger' (136).

Few environmental texts confront such issues as starkly as Holmes Rolston's 'Feeding People versus Saving Nature'. Stressing that the right of the poor is to a more equitable distribution of the wealth that already exists, Rolston expresses a frightening challenge, 'one ought not always to feed people first, but rather one ought sometimes to save nature'.[27]

The environmental crisis must multiply problems such as this, with no acceptable resolution (who on earth is 'one' in Rolston's sentence?). If the very 'eco-fascism' feared by western liberals is already a fact in some post-colonial states, how many ecocritics would yet feel comfortable working for increased human access to the world's national parks? If environmentalists now expect the poor in other parts of the world to forgo treating natural resources in the same way that the West has done, then 'it is difficult to see how anything other than a redistribution of assets could solve the problem' (Mark A. Michael).[28]

Eighth quandary: overpopulation

In the 1960s and 1970s the exponential growth in the human population became the often leading concern of environmental movements. The human population is still soaring today, moving from about 6 billion in 2000 towards a projected 9 billion by 2060, a trend ecologists would see in any other species as leading inevitably to a crash. Phrases like 'population explosion' were associated with the often apocalyptic arguments of Paul R. Ehrlich's *The Population Bomb* (1971)[29] or the Club of Rome report, *Limits to Growth* (1972).[30]

In literature the topic often took the form of science fiction scenarios in which various futures were depicted in terms of an intolerable lack of personal space and loss of identity among anonymous herds. In J. G. Ballard's short story 'Billennium' (1961), for instance, characters live in a city of 30 million people, each confined to a cubicle of four square metres.[31]

However, in later decades overpopulation became far less prominent in environmentalist contexts. Arguments tended to focus more on issues of distributive justice. The social and economic pressures that lead to overpopulation were understood to be the insecurities of poverty, to be addressed by programmes to increase basic welfare, and the oppression of women, to be addressed by reforms giving them genuine power over their own lives.

Such arguments, however, can sometimes have their own evasions. It would be just too convenient to assume that population pressures on the environment will ease simply if more people live like many inhabitants of Europe or North America. The sharper focus has been less on numbers of people so much as on the kinds of pressure different groups put on resources, an argument that puts the onus firmly on the squanderings of the so-called developed world.[32]

Overall, the issue of overpopulation highlights perhaps more glaringly than any other the inherent clash between a broadly liberal politics and environmental realities. Since measures to do with curbing population concern sexual behaviour and family life, they immediately breach perceived boundaries of what is private and what is public. Those ecologists who start to develop at a public meeting fairly obvious points about curbing human population growth are even liable to find themselves shouted down. A recent letter in *Wildlife* magazine claims: 'All this talk of reducing carbon emissions is just avoiding the real issue: the increasing human population' (David Walker, *Wildlife*, November 2009, 115).

In an interview Donna Haraway observes, as a biologist, 'in the face of a planet that's got well over 6 billion people now',

> the carrying capacity of this planet probably isn't that. And I don't care how many times you talk about the regressive nature of anti-natalist ideologies and population control ideologies. All true, but without serious population reduction we aren't going to make it as a species, and neither are thousands or millions of other species . . . So you can hate the Chinese for the one-child policy and also think they are right [*Laughing*].[33]

As an issue provoking even this sophisticated environmental thinker to acknowledged contradiction and awkward laughter, overpopulation still seems to present unavoidable but also unacceptable choices.

One issue may be this: if full environmental justice requires that a duty to future generations and to non-human life informs contemporary decision-making, then the conception of those 'rights' held by living people must shift accordingly, perhaps informed by consideration of how the predominantly western concept of 'human rights' itself evolved in the seventeenth and eighteenth centuries 'in low-level population-density and low-technology societies, with seemingly unlimited access to land and other resources', in a world, that is, that has now been consumed (Dale Jamieson).[34]

Chapter 13

Questions of scale

The local, the national and the global

There is one way in which environmental issues patently encompass and largely determine the politics and cultures of colonialism and post-colonialism. Over the past three centuries colonisation – and now global capitalism – has invariably expressed itself in the supplanting of local biota in favour of an imported portmanteau of profitable species: cattle, wheat, sheep, maize, sugar, coffee, palm oil, and so on. Thus it is that most of the world's wheat, a crop originally from the Middle East, now comes from other areas – Canada, the United States, Argentina, Australia – just as people of mainly European descent now dominate a large proportion of the earth's surface.[1]

This huge shift in human populations, including slaves as well as domesticated animals and plants, has largely determined the modern world. It is still widely reflected in kinds of racial and cultural prejudice linked to modes of food production. In Australia and North America the obliteration or displacement of indigenous ways of life by pastoralism and the growing of cereal crops justified itself in assertions that such farming was 'superior' to hunting and gathering. As a result of such processes the Caribbean, for instance, with its plantations of sugar cane, coffee and so on has become 'one of the most radically altered landscapes in the world'. 'The forced transplantation of peoples, plants and animals to the primarily island species of the region created a complex layering, a hybridization of diverse cultural and environmental forms,'[2] a condition that may soon become a global norm.

There is a close connection between destructive monocultures in food production, exploitative systems of international trade and exchange and the institution of the modern state. In this context, the social and political movement known as *bioregionalism* remains challengingly subversive of the institution of the modern nation state and the legal systems of international trade in which it is embedded. Bioregionalism proposes that human societies, their modes of production and cultures should reform themselves from the bottom up, decentralising to become communities with close and sustainable relations to their local bioregions.

Long centuries of environmental globalisation are to be put into a qualified reverse. The ideal is to reduce to a minimum the physical, cultural and psychological distance between the consumers and producers of food and other essentials. This would also be to let the geographical, climatic and biological nature of a region become once more a crucial agent in human identity and social organisation. Kirkpatrick Sale writes of a region as a 'life-territory, a place defined by its forms, its topography and its biota, rather than by human dictates'.[3]

Peter Berg and Raymond Dasmann's pioneering definition of bioregionalism in the 1970s referred 'both to geographical terrain and a terrain of consciousness – to a place and the ideas that have developed about how to live in that place'.[4] Unlike other political movements, bioregionalism accords the non-human a decisive place in conceptions of human polity: 'For a genuinely contextualist ethic to include the land, the land must *speak* to us; we must stand in *relation* to it; it must *define* us, and not we it.'[5]

The world-wide bioregional movement is also an instance of globalisation 'from below'. Mike Carr claims that it is the only environmental movement to combine 'many of the features and concerns of social ecology, deep ecology, and ecofeminism as well as a number of other radical movements'.[6] Bioregionalist campaigns and practice also offer a positive alternative to what has been criticized as the largely oppositional, repetitively negative emphasis of postcolonial readings, 'their panoply of rhetorical flourishes in which "unsettling", "disrupting", "decentering", "displacing", "resisting", become the only possible way of opposing "modes-of-production" narratives' (Priyamvada Gupal).[7] In former settler colonies like Australia or United States bioregionalism involves a rapprochement with the original cultures.

Methodological nationalism

'Methodological nationalism' is a term taken from A. D. Smith and used by Ulrich Beck.[8] It refers to modes of thought still dominant in the public sphere and intellectual life but which are arguably anachronistic in the contemporary globalised reality, including the planetary environmental crisis. 'While reality is becoming thoroughly cosmopolitan, our habits of thought and consciousness, like the well-worn paths of academic teaching and research, disguise the growing unreality of the world of nation-states.'[9] That is, we often still work and think as if the territorial bounds of the nation state act as a self-evident principle of overall coherence and intelligibility within which a history and culture can be understood, ignoring anything that does not fit such a narrative. One might also inflect Beck by observing that, ecologically, national borders have always been unreal. Even so innocent a title as 'regional novels in the United States' may instantiate methodological nationalism in proportion to the degree in which the national and its cultural agenda serve to enframe, contain and shape the analysis. For a long time, even a large body of environmental criticism remained pigeonholed as part of 'American studies', a situation now in the process of being reversed.

Beck writes:

> Globality means that from now on nothing which happens on our planet is only a limited local event; all inventions, victories and catastrophes affect the whole world, and we must reorient and reorganize our live and actions, our organizations and institutions, along a 'local–global' axis.[10]

Given the all-embracing power of international capitalism, it may not be surprising that, in practice, bioregional programmes almost always exist as isolated modes of resistance or as correctives to the previous misuse of a natural resource. A bioregional stance also remains stronger in outlining the dangers, shortcomings and destructiveness of existing arrangements than in modelling fully an alternative kind of society, bar a programme of the decentralisation of power and a limitation of destructive practices. The bioregionalist is also challenged by the question of how far reference to the authority of local 'nature' can be a sufficient guide for political decisions ('a region is governed by nature, not legislature' [Kirkpatrick Sale]).[11] For instance, would the bioregional ideal involve reintroducing dangerous predators long vanished, or the removal of invasive foreign species, something that may be prohibitively expensive and could, after all, also include such useful things as poultry and wheat? Daniel Berthold-Bond asks: 'But what if there is no "natural design" to be uncovered and followed? What if values are not "intrinsic" or "discoverable", there to be "found", in nature (or anywhere else, for that matter!)'[12] What a 'region' is can also remain rather vague: a look at work in the so-called 'new geography' of the past twenty years shows how a 'region' may be more determined by human actions and culture than might at first be thought.[13]

Literary 'reinhabitation'?

A writer, Derek Walcott affirms, is essentially provincial. 'If you took [Thomas] Hardy out of his countryside and [William] Faulkner out of his, you would have a different person.'[14] The bioregional idea seems very suited to such traditional conceptions of literature as a mode of communicating the particular, affirming the specific and otherwise untranslatable nature of life worlds as opposed to modes of language more complicit with generalisation and commodification. If 'reinhabiting' a land or region means 'learning to live-in-place in an area that has been disrupted and injured through past exploitation',[15] then a bioregional literacy may also provide a useful reorientation for assessing a whole range of regional writers, as well as offering students skills that feed into local activism.[16] Elsewhere, Walcott surmises that 'If the fusion had been possible between industry and, say, the American Indian idea of nature, then that would have been America.'[17]

Walcott's own Caribbean is particularly suited as a testing ground of the force and coherence of bioregional ideas, as well as their practicability in the current world. In an archipelago whose indigenous population has all but vanished, victims centuries ago of the genocide and diseases of European colonisation, appeals to the native and indigenous as standard can have little force. Just like the people, arriving either as colonisers, slaves or workers, the crops that formed the basis of the plantation systems in the Caribbean were transplants. Island economies were established on the eradication of native island flora in favour of large plantations of sugar cane, coffee, mangoes, bougainvillea and breadfruit. Divisions between human beings, in terms of gender, class and economic status, both reflected and helped perpetuate the work of the plantation economy. Ironically, it is nowadays as the image of a pristine 'paradise' – white beaches and palm trees – that the Caribbean is commodified and demeaned in so many tourist images. In either case, the given landscape of the islands is supplanted, literally or culturally, by the violent effects of global trade.

Bioregional thinkers are wary of their thinking lapsing into a merely atavistic idealisation of some lost organic community. Martinican writer and theorist Édouard Glissant sees such romantic notions of community as implicated in discredited forms of nationalism, the notion of a proper, exclusive territory, of *this* land for *this* people. He criticises those environmental thinkers who would sacralise the indigenous or the local as a basis of ideas of rootedness. Such thinking, he argues, is 'untenable in the Caribbean' – and undesirable, for such would-be sacred rootedness all too often means a territorial intolerance of others. Glissant endorses another 'ecology', which would be a politics of relation, questioning ethnic and cultural purism and stressing interdependence and interrelation across the earth.[18]

Caribbean thought and writing tend to be anti-essentialist. As a place in which several belief systems, languages and cultural traditions coexist, 'Caribbean everyday discourse is engaged in an extensive use of multiple logics, code-switching, and artistic and satiric solutions of possibly not resolvable contradictions and paradoxes.'[19] With history and ancestry of limited guidance for people of such mixed descent looking to affirm an identity, atavism is a less practicable and less acceptable option than Glissant's celebration of *créolité* or Walcott's affirmation of the Adamic possibilities of the archipelago, of new cultures that can name things again or as if for the first time ('the exultation of the landscape . . . no one has done justice to it').[20] This stance contrasts strongly with, for instance, Aimé Césaire's dated idealisation of negritude as closer to 'nature' than the artificial constructs of white colonialism.[21] Ecocritical essays from or concerning the Caribbean have been more open than others to modern developments in ecology, their stress on ecosystems as 'dynamic, unstable, and open . . . in which new species are incessantly settling, intermingling, and crossing with earlier species'.[22]

Glissant's novels in relation to Martinique form a strange and fascinating case study from a bioregional point of view. Incorporated in 1946 as simply an integral part of mainland France, Martinique is a peculiar case of what Glissant sardonically calls 'successful colonization'.[23] It has become a relatively prosperous but oddly purposeless place, with little sustainable work of its own, supported by money from Paris, importing almost all its food. In this strangely second-hand culture there is little real productive work, and, inverting bioregional aims, no 'creative link between nature and culture . . . vital to the formation of a community'.[24] Glissant describes Martinicans as forming perhaps the world's most alienated community, living the cultural dissolution of the 'happy zombi'.[25] The newly emerged middle class emulate the consumerism and lifestyle of modern French society, while the urban and rural poor live in deprived conditions, dependent on the welfare that 'perversely, renders them grateful to the very system that deprives their lives of real productiveness, and makes them at once passive and resentful, spiritually and psychologically destitute yet pathetically fearful of change'.[26] The island's remnant Creole culture drifts towards being a folksy vestige of the past, something for tourists and self-caricature.

Glissant's novels, especially after the 1960s, depict and enact the formal, cultural, aesthetic and psychic disruptions of this peculiar French colony. The disorientation of the novels may also be read in relation to the constraints that would currently suffocate any realisation of a bioregional ideal in the Caribbean. Glissant advocates Martinican independence from France as part of some Caribbean federation of islands. Nevertheless, with Martinique's current levels of population, Glissant can only envisage a realistic post-French future as one in which the island would survive by producing expensive food to export to the emerging niche market for organically grown produce.[27]

The experimental *Malemort* [*The Undead*] (1975) was the third of Glissant's novels, reconstructing a version 'from below' of Martinican history from colonisation to the present day. Martinique is seen as a place whose people lack the secure cultural resources to be able to affirm themselves. All the characters, as Celia Britton argues, show a peculiarly displaced, intentionally or unintentionally parodic or quasiparodic relation to the French they speak.[28] The mayor's secretary, Lesprit, for instance, speaks such an elegant and self-consciously 'good' French that it seems a vehicle of sarcasm, though it is in fact a kind of unknowing parody, for Lesprit talks in this way about matters of which he approves. In this novel speech is not connected to an expressed identity in the way most people assume, but is a kind of theatrical behaviour adopted with varying degrees of self-awareness and yet to which there is no secure or 'natural' alternative. In *Caribbean Discourse* Glissant mocks the weird habit of some Martinicans, living in the tropics, of referring to their environment in terms of the four seasons of the temperate zone: 'At the window in an administrative office, on 21st March 1978, a pleasant sixty-year-old greets me heartily: "So, M. Glissant, it is spring!"' (56). This is the language of a community 'lost in the unreal' (56).

In *Malemort* three unrelated agricultural workers, named Dlan, Médellus and Silacier, struggle to come to terms with unemployment after the collapse of the plantation system. Lack of a secure sense of any cultural past deprives people of ways to engage in meaningful or viable activities directed towards the future. At first the three figures are associated with each other so closely that they are referred to simply as 'Dlan Médellus Silacier'. Dlan takes psychic refuge in millenarian religion, Silacier in a stance of intellectual refusal, but Médellus tries to set up a utopian agricultural community. Its site is seemingly protected by the desolated land that surrounds it, though in fact the scheme is doomed in advance, for the commune is living on land already purchased for development by a construction company. Becoming mad, speaking a peculiarly private language, Médellus ends up only creating a kind of psychic refuge for himself from an intolerable space.

In this way, the weird, almost despairing disorientation of language and identity in Glissant's novels, with their strong attention to place and landscape, forms a kind of literary bioregional practice in extremis. They may be aligned here with the texts of the post-colonial theorist Franz Fanon (also from Martinique), who argued that in colonial contexts the distinction between sane and insane, normal and abnormal, ceases to work, for it is the overall context that is abnormal.[29] In the twenty-first century such a challenge to normality may now extend beyond the topic of overt colonialism, to the effects of environmental disruption on a continental or planetary scale. Médellus, watching a huge yellow and red tractor tear up his dream of agrarian reform with a din like thunder,[30] becomes brother to the narrator of Christa Wolf's *Accident*, tending her garden in rubber gloves as a protection against radiation from the Ukraine.

Questions of scale

The fragility of some bioregional ideas relates to the prior and crucial question: at what scale or scales should one think and work in environmental politics? For instance, 'Think globally, act locally', the famous slogan of the Sierra Club, involves work on at least two scales at the same time. It says, in effect: try to understand ecological systems on the largest possible scale and then take action locally in accordance with that understanding. Its inherent logic is also, paradoxically, that one cannot only act locally, that any action affects the whole world, however minutely.

The issue of climate change also undermines the very possibility of acting only locally. Environmental slogans urge us 'eat less meat and help save the planet', or they follow horrifying predictions of climate chaos with injunctions, no less solemn, not to leave electrical appliances on standby or overfill the kettle. Such language would have seemed surreal or absurd to an earlier generation and enacts a bizarre derangement of scales, collapsing the trivial and the catastrophic into each other. At the same time, to focus solely on individual behaviour and consumer choice risks projecting the crisis as the result merely of bad shopping or lifestyle decisions, evading deeper engagement with those national and global structures of economics and forms of government that are ultimately more responsible.

Disconcertingly, engaging climate change may also suggest that many eco-critical arguments are taking place on the wrong scale, or will now need to think on several scales at once. Essays affirming regional agrarianism and the wisdom of indigenous management are being published within a broader context that is already starting to erode their very conditions of possibility. Successes in reform environmentalism in one country may be negated by the lack of such measures in others or simply by increased prosperity elsewhere. In sum, just as '*we have no politics of climate change*' (Anthony Giddens),[31] so we still have little sense of how so overwhelmingly global an issue must affect methodologies of reading and interpretation.

Ursula K. Heise is one of the very few ecocritics to address climate change at length in relation to literary criticism. She challenges the cult of localism in environmental circles, including the bioregional ideal that one's life and sense of self should be as intimately formed by the local environment as possible. Is

Figure 10 Disorientation: luxury and pollution (the author)

not a new environmental cosmopolitanism more suitable to a world in which environmental effects so immediately disregard borders?

Rather than focussing on the recuperation of a sense of place, environmentalism needs to foster an understanding of how a wide variety of both natural and cultural places and processes are connected and shape each other around the world, and how human impact affects and changes this connectedness.[32]

Heise criticises almost all literary representations of climate change for falling short of its peculiar, counterintuitive demands, redeploying instead either trite clichés of apocalypse, as in the film *The Day after Tomorrow*, or inherited modes of narrative inadequate to the challenge of working on several scales at once, of linking individual lives with global transformations across multiple cultures, with counterintuitive jumps between the normal and the catastrophic. David Brin's *Earth* (1991) is accorded mixed success with its fantasy science fiction plot of global disaster (the earth being consumed by a black hole from within) conveyed through a multiplication of fragmented narrative viewpoints and through various generic modes – myth, epic and allegory – techniques, that is, previously associated with the urban modernist novel (James Joyce, John Dos Passos).[33]

Gary Snyder's late modernist poetry works, like the novels Heise cites, use multiple scales of space and time to form a critique of the destructive, one-dimensional and ultimately fragile sphere of the modern neoliberal state. Snyder is perhaps the best-known bioregional writer, turning it into an environmental cosmopolitanism informed by both Buddhism and modern science. For Snyder, the more powerful environmental reading is not to satirise the human city for being 'cut off' from the natural world, but to take a perspective whose spatial and temporal scale can encompass even Los Angeles as only a very peculiar and fragile part of nature. Spatially, Snyder's poem 'Night-Song of the Los Angeles Basin' depicts the city as a set of intersecting pathways, with the sweeping lights of the cars passing oblivious over the ancient tracks of the small creatures who preceded the city and who will survive it, as well as over the unobtrusive and abused watercourse on which all finally depend.[34] Like much of the sequence *Mountains and Rivers Without End* (1996), the poem projects a global context that embraces human beings of the Palaeolithic and those of the present and recorded history, with jumps to the points of view of animals and birds. Structures of human construction or order are seen in relation to huge ecological cycles of water, air and geology, those vast, long-term cycles of energy transfers in which humanity must live, even if they distort or deny them for a time. Such ecological literacy informs the poem's seemingly sudden or counterintuitive jumps in scale and perspective, that is, from the 'calligraphy of cars' in one line to the 'Vole paths. Mouse trails worn in / On meadow grass' in the next. There are corresponding jolts of connection between the meal thrown to ornamental carp in their 'frenzy of feeding' and those 'platters / of tidbit and wine, / snatch of fame' being presented to human celebrities in buildings high above. The 'Marmot lookout rocks' of line 21 are followed directly and in parallel by the 'Houses with green watered gardens' of line 22, and these precariously 'Slip under the ghost of the dry chaparral'. 'Slip' is in the present tense, under only the 'ghost' of the formerly dominant 'dry chaparral', but this is a ghost whose referent seems as much in the future as in the past. The time when the chaparral will return is already at work there. The poem ends with the calling owl with which it opened, as if once more in long-term, non-human cyclical time:

> The calligraphy of lights on the night
> freeways of Los Angeles
>
> *will long be remembered.*
>
>   Owl
> calls;
>   late-rising moon.
>   p. 64; emphasis added

The poem refuses to think on normal human scales of space or time. The song is 'of' the Los Angeles *basin* and seems to cover a time span beyond the likely duration of the ultimately self-destructive human city. The grass, viewed over a long enough time, becomes more significant than the geometry of roads and buildings. The unnamed animals, simply by being there, form in their very indifference a satire on notions of 'importance' and status connected with the celebrity culture. A cosmopolitan bioregionalism of this kind gestures towards a redefinition of human identity, a rejection of the individualism of the liberal property- and rights-holding tradition in favour of the need to recognise that 'our place is part of what we are', and that that place is both local and global at once.[35]

Ecopoetry

Snyder's *Mountains and Rivers Without End* is often described as an example of 'ecopoetry', but what kind of poetry is that, a whole new subgenre or just a name for any poetry with a vaguely green subject matter? At present, in a critical anthology such as J. Scott Bryson's *Ecopoetry: A Critical Introduction* (ed., 2002),[36] the term *ecopoetry* still has an opportunistic feel. It is hard to see this particular coinage becoming as useful as critical categories like 'postmodernism' or 'ecofeminism'. What is referred to in Bryson's collection of essays is a distinctive though largely American tradition of modernist poetry with often strong romantic elements. Poets who have been called ecopoets at some time include: Robinson Jeffers, Wendel L. Berry, Linda Hogan, Ted Hughes, W. S. Merwin, Denise Levertov, Seamus Heaney, Arthur Sze. The English poet Charles Tomlinson voices a characteristic challenge, in his 'Song':

> To enter the real,
> how far
> must we feel beyond
> the world in which we already are.
>
> It is all here
> but we are not.[37]

As with Heise's affirmation of the technique of the urban modernist novel as a way to engage the challenges of representing climate change, a loosely 'ecological' poetic emerges in the development and extension of modernist techniques that had been initially pioneered in the first four decades of the twentieth century. At issue is an aesthetic interested in formal experimentation and the conception of the poet or poem as forming a kind of intellectual or spiritual frontier, newly coupled with a sense of the vulnerability and otherness of the natural world, distrust of a society dominated by materialism and instrumental reason, and sometimes giving a counteraffirmation of non-western modes of perception, thought or rhetorical practice. The poem is often conceived as a space of subjective redefinition and rediscovery through encounters with the non-human. What was taken to be in the romantic lyric an aggrandisement of the personal ego, the appropriation of natural forms and encounters as a too easy source of personal meaning and endorsement (see Hess's reading of William Wordsworth in Chapter 10), gives way to a more chastening ethos of personal, bodily finitude and respect. Some texts move beyond the conception of the poem as the dramatisation of individual consciousness to create a space of multiple voices or stances, such as Snyder's *Mountains and Rivers Without End*. The stance is 'ecological' both in a loose sense of affirming interrelationship and possibilities of reading that work in several directions simultaneously (rather than in the straight line of an unfolding narrative), and, in Snyder's case, the modernist technique of juxtaposition and cutting ('parataxis' and 'ellipsis') also serves some strictly ecological points, as in the jumps between human and other animals, between Palaeolithic and modern realities, or between a human perspective and those of various mythical or religious agencies expressive of the deeper natural systems in which all life unfolds.

Sometimes, however, 'ecopoetry' does just mean work with a vaguely green message. In response, some critics, most notably John Elder (who introduces Bryson's anthology), push hard the notion of a poem itself as forming a kind of 'ecosystem', an interesting if forced analogy to name kinds of poetic presentation that invite readings in terms of a non-linear interrelation and illumination of image and theme, a process taking place both within the text and in relation to other texts, contexts and places.

There is also an online journal, Ecopoetics, which describes itself as 'a (more or less) annual journal dedicated to exploring creative-critical edges between making (with an emphasis on writing) and ecology (the theory and praxis of deliberate earthlings)'.[38]

Science and the struggle for intellectual authority

The relation of ecocriticism to the natural sciences is uniquely close, for unlike most political movements environmentalism claims a scientific basis. Green arguments often rest on the authority of scientific modelling and prediction. Science is also an ally in critiques of the illusory self-sufficiency of the cultural or of notions of 'nature' as mere cultural construction. The timeframes of geology or intimate studies of lives of other creatures undermine at a stroke any narrowly human-centred perspective on things.

At the same time ecocritics are often profoundly critical of the institutions of science. Science has become deeply implicated in techno-industrial society as both a practice and as an ideology. The growth of reform environmentalism has also seen the increasing co-opting of scientists into systems of global surveillance in not always comfortable ways.

Other critics challenge the basic assumptions that underlie the scientific claim to an exclusive understanding of reality through causal, material laws to be formalised mathematically. Scientific notions of 'objectivity' are accused of having unjustly discredited other modes of understanding and of having generally drained all ethical, spiritual and even aesthetic value from the world.

Sometimes, however, science appears in rather caricature forms. The multiplicitous work of scientists gets identified with a kind of totalitarian monolith whose aim is simply the domination of nature, for which all knowledge is a mode of power, and which threatens every remaining island of subjective freedom and individual responsibility with modes of administrative procedure. This view is sometimes pertinent but it does no justice to the plurality or the internal divisions of the sciences.

In sum, environmental criticism finds itself in the difficult position of needing, at the same time, both to draw on scientific knowledge and expertise and also to criticise the social power and intellectual authority of science. This situation reflects the way the environmental crisis is also one of culture, values, politics and ethics as well as the functioning of ecosystems. One manifestation of this is that issues engaging environmentalist thinkers no longer fit inside currently institutionalised divisions of knowledge, with the natural sciences on the one side and the social sciences and humanities on the other. Val Plumwood writes of the current, fragile demarcation of intellectual disciplines: 'The idea that we humans are completely immersed in a self-enclosed sphere of our own we can call "culture" while non-humans are part of a non-ethical sphere of "nature" is the leading assumption that corresponds to and structures these disciplinary exclusions.'[1]

Chapter 14

Science and the crisis of authority

The disenchantment thesis

Disenchantment: that the natural world has lost its magic, that rivers are reduced to an energy source for hydroelectric dams, the sea to a thoroughfare for oil tankers and a vast waste disposal site – these are now widespread perceptions. In intellectual life they often feed into the so-called disenchantment thesis: that is, that the more the world becomes thoroughly mapped and understood in formalised scientific laws, the less personally and immediately meaningful it seems to become. Jane Bennett traces the thesis that the domination of science has deprived the world of all human significance to the work of Max Weber and others. She offers the following summary:

> There was once a time when Nature was purposive, God was active in the details of human affairs, human and other creatures were defined by a pre-existing web of relations, social life was characterized by face-to-face relations, and political order took the form of organic community. Then, this pre-modern world gave way to forces of scientific and instrumental rationality, secularism, individualism, and the bureaucratic state – all of which, combined, disenchant the world.[1]

Bennett, however, argues that the disenchantment thesis is exaggerated. That modern science is not necessarily a mode of disenchantment is suggested, among other things, by the rise of the popular science book. The success of books such as Richard Fortey's *Trilobite! Eyewitness to Evolution* (2001) shows public fascination even for an unsensational family of extinct arthropods. Public demand for accessible overviews of whole fields of science has been met by works such as John McPhee's *Annals of the Former World* (1981); books about cosmology or the nature of life (Paul Davies, Carl Sagan, Stephen Jay Gould, Richard Dawkins); studies of individual discoveries or research projects, such as Richard Osborne's *The Floating Egg: Episodes in the Making of Geology* (1999) or Jonathan Weiner's *The Beak of the Finch: Evolution in Real Time* (1995); and books that blend nature writing with scientific work and natural history, such as Barry Lopez's *Arctic Dreams: Imagination and Desire in a Northern Landscape* (1986). Overall such texts and related television documentaries show the emergence of an influential 'third culture' (John Brockman), one lying between and overlapping old demarcations of the sciences and humanities.[2]

Popular science presents itself as making esoteric information available in a form that reaches a wide audience, a publicly responsible and important role. The sociologist Ron Curtis, however, is more sceptical, and argues that 'Popular science, written in a narrative mode, is a powerful tool for promoting a particular normative view of science while, at the same time, rendering that view immune to criticism.'[3] He stresses especially the way such writing is dominated by narratives of resolution with a strong sense of progression and closure. A standard pattern is for a book or documentary to begin by setting up some initial mystery crying out to be resolved, then offering a plethora of possible explanations, many mutually exclusive but also impossible to rank, till the story of sudden moment of insight or decisive discovery is followed by dramas of dispute in which an advance is nevertheless gradually confirmed. It is a kind of suspenseful detective story, a tale of persistence, of patience rewarded, leading to a full narrative closure. The reader tends to be cast in the role of satisfied spectator.[4] Popular science books can also exaggerate a view of science as solely the disinterested investigation of natural phenomena, downplaying deep disputes between scientists about the method, philosophy and social function of science, presenting these often as little more than clashes of personality (e.g., maverick newcomer pitched against a dismissive old guard, etc.). Such narratives also implicitly endorse the dominant conception of humanity's mission as the gradual but inevitable conquest of nature.

Such accounts of science have increasingly occupied a space of cultural legislation and that of philosophical and even religious overview that used to be the preserve of the humanities or the churches. Their success highlights the failure of traditional literary and cultural critics to engage public attention and discussion in the way that, say, Richard Dawkins, Richard P. Feynman or Stephen Hawking have done. Ecocriticism is one of the few branches of received literary scholarship to have engaged with this cultural shift.

Curtis argues that popular science needs to move away from offering only 'narratives of resolution' (451) and that 'This will change only if there is a systematic effort to represent science with a variety of forms' (452). What, for instance, if a scientific issue were presented not in the form of a progressive narrative but in the ancient form of the dialogue? This would counter the tendency to view true scientific understanding as the exclusive domain of specialists, with the public able only to glean 'popularised' versions. The dialogue form is not the presentation of a fait accompli: it foregrounds opposed methods of argument. The reader of a dialogue is positioned less as a spectator and more as a kind of judge between differing positions. Its dual nature also downplays the sense of closure inherent to the progressive narrative. Some nature writing and ecocriticism also differs from many popular science books in an explicit concern with the social and political issues that pervade the actual work of scientists.

Facts versus values? a reading, Annie Dillard's 'Galápagos'

Scientific work often presents itself as defined by its respect for 'objective fact'. A professional scientist looks to offer a dispassionate theory of how things are, one whose impersonality and rigour is supposedly guaranteed by the exclusion of all judgements of value. Such a model of strict objectivity highlights a crucial problem for any defence of the literary in a predominantly scientific culture – how to defend the claim that the literary arts are themselves a genuine and distinct mode of knowledge, not just a realm of subjective preferences and emotional escapism? If the scientific attitude would condemn a great deal of environmental writing as a sloppy mixture of fact and moralism, yet workers in the humanities often demonstrate the hidden values latent in the supposed objectivity of scientific practice. Ecocriticism, environmental writing and popular science have become the site of a general struggle between differing conceptions of cultural authority.

The 'naturalistic fallacy'

If any one issue may focus these struggles for cultural authority, it is the status of the so-called 'naturalistic fallacy' as it pervades and even defines crucial issues in the relationship of ecocriticism and science.[5] The supposed fallacy is simple enough to describe. It names the seemingly false assumption that any kind of judgement of value necessarily follows from any establishment of fact. Arguments about *what is* are of a totally different kind from arguments about what *ought to be*. As Stephen Jay Gould writes, 'My technical knowledge of the genetics of cloning gives me no right, or expertise, to dictate legal or moral decisions about the politics, sociology, or ethics of creating, say, a genetic Xerox copy of a grieving couple's dead child.'[6] Although the so-called 'naturalistic fallacy' is most explicitly an issue in philosophy and environmental ethics, the fact–value distinction is at play in almost every controversy about the environment and is sometimes explicitly criticised (see below). For instance, to cite scientific authority showing that a policy will destroy the habitat of a particular species is just not the same as arguing why that species should be valued in the first place.

The environmental writing of Annie Dillard is distinctive as a site in which these struggles of authority are unusually legible. In her essay 'Life on the Rocks: The Galápagos' (1982) the challenge is that of many environmental writers in the tradition after Thoreau.[7] How does one continue to write in a mode originally grounded in transcendentalist conceptions of nature, that is, producing analogies and sometimes even moral parallels between natural processes and human attitudes and behaviour, but to do so now within a modern scientific understanding of geology, evolution and cosmology? At times, a sense of clumsy anachronism remains, as in, for instance, Dillard's sentence, 'What if we the people had the sense or grace to live as cooled islands in an archipelago live, with dignity, passion, and no comment.'[8]

Dillard's piece instantiates another characteristic problem in the use of scientific research in modern nature writing. Whereas Thoreau was writing at a time when his own observations could still make original contributions to natural history, only a few modern writers (Carson, Leopold) can write about science as practitioners. A literary essay about evolution and the Galápagos must primarily occupy the stance of a mediator, presenting material gathered from others. This effects a substantial shift in the stance of authorship compared to other kinds of modern literature. In Dillard's case this restriction, as in her classic *Pilgrim at Tinker Creek* (1974), leads to a would-be virtuoso cultivation of the rhetorical and poetic skills of presentation, for any space for invention will lie more in the presentation of evolutionary theory than in its content.

Dillard's essay takes up this challenge by depicting events inferred by science but actually far outside the dimensions of human experience, doing so within a pseudo-religious stance that presents the Galápagos as an image of general processes of genesis. There are rhetorical jumps between accounts of events spanning millions of years and Dillard's own visit to the Galápagos, as in the sentence, 'The ice rolled up, the ice rolled back, and I knelt on a plain of lava boulders in the islands called Galápagos' (109). Dramatised accounts of geological change are interspersed with fragments of biblical quotation: 'And the rocks themselves shall be moved. The rocks are not pure necessity, given, like vast, complex molds around which the rest of us swirl. They heave to their own necessities, to stirrings and prickings from within and without' (127). There are also passages of more conventional reportage on Darwin's visit in the 1830s and on the later contributions of genetics to neo-Darwinism.

'Life on the Rocks: The Galápagos' reads as a site of conflict between Dillard's evident attachment to an inherited romantic ideal of the writer as the vehicle of individual creative vision and the very different ethos of scientific research. The reader suspects an underlying insecurity that the writer's role may dwindle to that of provider of info-tainment. In the Galápagos essay the occasional fragility of the rhetoric lies in the attempted forcing of the *facts* of evolution and geology into a would-be celebration of their *value*. As it proceeds, Dillard's essay becomes more and more a personal vision of life, conveyed in figurative language that spirals higher and higher above the empirical referents it started with. It becomes a kind of festive account of continents in motion like 'beautiful pea-green boats' (127) and of life as a great multiplicitous wave of adapted freedoms:

> Life is more than a live green scum on a dead pool, a shimmering scurf like slime mould on rock. Look at the planet. Everywhere freedom twines its way around necessity, inventing new strings of occasions, lassoing time and putting it through its varied and spiralled paces. Everywhere live things lash at the rocks.   127

The essay becomes an ambitious exercise in an imaginative perception informed by scientific understanding. However, Dillard's evaluation of evolutionary processes as a matter of joyful celebration can seem rather more arbitrary ('what shall we sing?' [128]). To image life over eons as if it could become the directly perceived object of personal experience, comparable to watching waves break against rock, may translate scientific knowledge into a vivid image, but one that also enacts the illusory fiction of transcending or surviving the implications of that knowledge. Life as a planetary phenomenon cannot convincingly be depicted as some kind of continuous super-subjectivity with which a reader can easily identify, for, as Dillard acknowledges elsewhere, 'Evolution loves death more than it loves you or me.'[9] Contemplating this, one could argue that a sense of horror and even despair would be as rational a response as Dillard's sense of rapture.

Overall, the vaguely religious stance of the essay may seem fragile. The clash of fact and value is arguably not overcome by depicting geological processes vastly accelerated and in a figurative way to inspire a sense of wonder. Dillard ends in this mode, with a quote from S. T. Coleridge's visionary poem 'Kubla

Khan'. This famous passage acts as a kind of coda, summary and epitome of the Galápagos 'paradise' itself:

> Weave a circle round him thrice,
> And close your eyes with holy dread,
> For he on honey-dew hath fed,
> And drunk the milk of Paradise. 129

This is also, finally, Dillard's implicit claim as author for the authority of the inspired poet, a stance incorporating but also transcending that of the scientist.

Against the facts–values split

Simon Critchley traces how the disenchantment thesis, figuring the everyday world as banal, has defined the understanding of much romantic and post-romantic literature. Again and again people have looked to writers to recreate that sense of wonder and significance in things that scientific rationalism is held to have destroyed, whether this be through fantasy literature like Tolkien's *The Lord of the Rings* (1954–5), environmental non-fiction or the defamiliarising strategies of modern poetry. Dillard's essay clearly enacts just such a conception of the writer, trying to cast a vaguely religious colouring over the accepted understanding of the evolution of life.[10]

Critchley also describes some intellectual traps for such a conception: 'The dilemma seems to be intractable: on the one hand the philosophical cost of scientific truth seems to be scientism', so that human life is reduced to amoral physical laws with no ethical content or meaning. On the other hand, 'the rejection of scientism through a new humanization of the cosmos seems to lead to obscurantism', so that we inhabit only our own fantasies.[11]

It is very rare to find an ecocritic who merely rejects the findings of the natural sciences. The issues are rather two. Firstly, there is a refusal to accept that scientific understanding is the *only* admissible form of knowledge, with exclusive authority against which one cannot appeal. Are not in fact some notions of objectivity already effectively a judgement of value?

Among ecocritics, especially ecofeminists, a refusal to accept the exclusive claim of science to the understanding of human life leads to a reaffirmation of the prereflective or of bodily experience. The world as actually lived is immediately full of human significance and meaning and it is, after all, from out of this primary, unreflective immediate knowledge of things that science, through certain procedures, comes to abstract and construct its particular account of reality. The relation to nature exemplified by the natural sciences is hardly culturally neutral: its very ideal of objectivity means that 'Nature, in this tradition, becomes truly accessible only when it is alienated from human feeling and desire' (George Levine).[12] For science, in other words, nature can only be objectively known if the observer is effectively dead or absent ('The human sciences are precisely the knowledge of self-alienation, the transformation of self into object').[13] Scientific writing purveys a would-be cultureless ideal of a terminology of pure denotation, a totally factual language without metaphor or cultural or aesthetic association. To posit such a complete divide of fact and value is also to enshrine in knowledge a total and uncrossable dualism between the natural world and the human observer, precisely the kind of alienation some environmentalist thinking tries to address.

This brings us to the second major point of contestation between ecocriticism and the institutions of science. This is the deep implication of science in politics, both as a support and resource for the techno-industrial project of dominating the natural world and also in relation to the way 'the scientific' so often functions as a kind of ideology, restricting important decisions to a culture of approved experts. Reference to science often serves to disguise issues of moral and political contestation under blunt assertions of supposed fact.[14] Science in the modern world patently acts often as an ideology: Bruno Latour defines 'Science' (with a capital S) as '*the politicization of the sciences through epistemology [the theory of what knowledge is] in order to render ordinary political life impotent through the threat of an incontestable nature*'.[15] Against this, environmental thinkers may open up such issues as the cultural imperialism of scientific classifications (e.g., how the Linnaean system of scientific names for species discredits the authority of local names) or the quirkier one of possible sexism in field guides to birds ('The Female is Somewhat Duller: The Construction of the Sexes in Ornithological Literature').[16]

The institutions of science are becoming newly contested and politicised as places in which environmental problems are defined, their risks predicted and often adjudicated, with huge implications in economics, politics and law. Some fear that such work, however vital, is also fostering the emergence of a culture of global managerialism: 'global constructs of environmental issues involve a universalizing discourse that steers us away from the difficult politics of enduring structural inequalities and differentiated interests and towards technomanagerialist remedies, preferred (and constituted) by élite, Northern-based scientists and bureaucrats' (Michael Goldman and Rachel A. Sherman).[17] In this respect the environmental crisis becomes a crisis in the social and political function of science. Scientists find themselves increasingly recruited to form advisory panels on all kinds of issues, from climate change to radiation levels or the

Figure 11 Global warming science (Pixelbrat)

design of fishing nets. Such pressure takes people well beyond any pretence that scientific work is merely factual or apolitical. The list of issues that patently transgress supposed borders of fact and value grows longer each year. Latour lists some of them:

> – Questions of medicine: for instance, how is it that the life-style of some Americans triggers diabetes?

> – Questions of ideology: Is aggression among males rooted in primate society in chimpanzees as much as in humans? This question is clearly mixed, pertaining as much to the ethnologists biases as to apes and monkeys.

> – Questions that are clearly technical and political imbroglios: What is a safe level of radiation from nuclear tests in the Nevada desert? What is the amount of carbon dioxide an industry may be allowed to release safely in the atmosphere?[18]

In these cases, to insist on a strict distinction of fact and value is to ask for the impossible.

This doubtful distinction also helps maintain arguably unhelpful boundaries between the various intellectual disciplines. Environmental issues may refuse to be encompassed by boundaries between the natural sciences on the one side and the social sciences and humanities on the other. Such intellectual and institutional divisions may already seem problematic for building a rigid nature–culture or human–non-human opposition into the very constitution of areas of inquiry. Such dubious distinctions even become reinforced by the way these disciplines try to keep themselves supposedly pure or 'rigorous'. For instance, the reaction of people in the humanities against such scientific initiatives as sociobiology shows how defensively many protect the stakes of studying 'the cultural *as* the cultural'. Sociobiology proposes to study and explain the social behaviour of animals – including human beings – in evolutionary terms, that is, as built-in adaptations to the conditions in which they evolved. For many in the humanities, however, any suggestion that something, xenophobia for instance, is 'natural' or ingrained as having been perhaps evolutionarily advantageous in the past becomes suspect immediately as disguised cultural prejudice.

In sum, ecocritical work both stresses and questions the way the authority of western scientific institutions is being changed by the environmental crisis itself, giving scientists new forms of power. For Latour the main force of radical environmentalism is that, in openly destabilising the fact–value distinction upon which so much modern thinking and practice is based, it also demystifies 'Science' as a political ideology, calling scientists to new forms of thought and responsibility.

Ecology, 'ecology' and literature

That environmental criticism should have a close connection to ecology is stating the obvious. As that science which studies living things in their complex interdependence, ecology is both a source of insight into the nature of life and, in some ways, a source of guidance for an emergent green ethics.[19] Ian Marshall, for example, makes the jump from natural science to politics when he writes, 'Perhaps the insights of ecology could do more to advance the cause of multiculturalism than any amount of politically correct preaching. To recognize the advantages of diversity and the verities of interrelationship and interdependency – that is the ecological way of knowing.'[20]

Other critics are more cautious. Nevertheless, in a world in which human activities are so evidently destructive, the science that focusses on the interrelations of all living things easily acquires the status of a kind of grim providence, as in Keith Tester's statement, 'So long as we *civilized men* imagine ourselves to be apart from the land, and from our fellow creatures, we shall attempt to exploit them for our private gain, and the attempt will kill us.'[21]

A closer look, however, suggests that things are not quite so simple. 'Ecology' actually names two usually separate intellectual fields, such that references in environmental writing to 'the ecological' or 'ecology' will often need further thought. Firstly, there is ecology as the science first named by the German Darwinian Ernst Haeckel in the 1860s, the study of organisms in relation to each other and to the surroundings in which they live. On the other hand, the term 'ecology' has long come to name a school of thought quite distinct from ecology as an empirical science. Its subject is really ethics and its issue the kind of relationship that human beings ought to have to the natural world. The gap between ecology as science and ecology as ethics becomes apparent if one turns to a modern university textbook, *Ecology: Principles and Applications*.[22] To open the bibliography of this work of scientific ecology, looking for such names as Murray Bookchin, Donald Worster or other political ecologists, is to draw a blank. Scientific ecology is itself the often heavily statistical analysis of energy flows, population dynamics and behavioural studies. In effect, 'ecology' names two quite different things, the one a natural science, the other, including 'deep ecology' and 'social ecology', a speculative part of the humanities and social sciences.

Because the two senses of ecology are often blurred, references to ecology in environmental writing have sometimes functioned in an underexamined ethical/political way. Josef Keulartz sees a great many modern appeals to ecology as continuing that long and dubious tradition in which what are essentially political arguments present themselves as grounded on the supposed facts of nature. He observes how radical environmentalism 'is in the habit of making an appeal to the cognitive authority of ecology – under the motto "Nature knows best" – on the understanding that ecology can provide social and personal rules of conduct'.[23] A dated and now frequently questioned model of scientific ecology still sometimes functions as a kind of moral norm in some environmentalist discourse. According to this model, a natural ecosystem supposedly exists in a state of harmony, diversity in unity, balance, and so on, already, that is, as an image of coexistence and mutual dependence ripe to be transmitted as an ideal of human politics – exactly what happens, in fact, in the influential 'social ecology' of Murray Bookchin. Keulartz writes:

> [radical ecology/environmentalism] is a discourse which calls
> incessantly for a humble holism and a submission of the individual to
> the greater whole while at the same time using 'the' ecology to silence
> dissenting voices and thus smother the debate on alternative future
> scenarios. Meanwhile, we are left completely in the dark as to the true
> essence of nature and confronted time and time again with the now

familiar litany of mantras about the whole being greater than the sum of its parts, about balance and harmony, stability and diversity, etc.[24]

Contrast the biologist Richard Lewontin: '*The*environment has never existed and there has never been balance or harmony.'[25] The assumption that a natural state of things, untouched by humanity, would be one of an harmonious or at least balanced interaction, a sustainable and continuous diversity, was often so entrenched that it acted more as a template through which people discussed such things as human interventions in ecosystems, rather than coming itself under examination. In fact, however, as Daniel Botkin showed in a series of case studies, actual ecosystems often show drastic transformations, sudden imbalances or irreversible shifts.[26]

Hubert Zapf, *Literature as Cultural Ecology*

One of the most sustained appropriations to date of ecological thinking to literary theory and criticism is Hubert Zapf's *Literatur als kulturelle Ökologie: Zur kulturellen Funktion imaginativer Texte an Beispielen des amerikanischen Romans* [*Literature as Cultural Ecology: On the Cultural Function of Imaginative Texts with Examples from the American Novel*] (Tübingen: Niemeyer, 2002).[27] This book has been influential among German critics and remains representative of the way in which some ecocritics use references to ecology. Zapf argues that literature represents what he calls 'an ecological principle or ecological force' within culture, working against tendencies towards rigidity in society. Literary texts offer a 'Sensorium and symbolical principle of compensation in relation to cultural deficits and imbalances' (3), a space in which socially repressed or marginalised people or issues may voice themselves. As a counterweight to social forces of homogeneity and conformity, literary works renew continually the cultural imaginary, language and perception.

In relation to scientific ecology itself, this function is presented cautiously as a matter of *analogy*. Nevertheless, Zapf still clearly implies that literature acts as a kind of 'natural' corrective of distortions and imbalances in the workings of human culture. His reading of Herman Melville's *Moby Dick* (1851) is a good example. Zapf reads Captain Ahab's quest to destroy the white whale as an extreme image of the anthropocentric drive to control and master all that is other and unknowable in the natural world, a drive that is itself also expressed in the whale industry's ghastly cutting up and exploitation of almost every body part or fluid in its prey. Demonising the white whale, Ahab himself becomes the white fiend he thinks he is pursuing. Against this, Zapf argues, such instances of the ultimately self-destructive drive to total authority and control are counterbalanced by other elements of the novel, by a 'cultural–ecological counter-discourse', for instance in the realm of dreams and fantasy in the narrator, Ishmael, and other characters, including crew members from non-western cultures, as well as in non-human nature itself. This 'cultural–ecological counter-discourse' dramatises the normally overlooked matrix or condition of Ahab's 'civilised' order in universal vital forces, common to all life. In this way *Moby Dick* stages how a drive to dominate the unknowable otherness of nature forms only an unbalanced denial of being part of the original interconnection of all life.

For Zapf, the analogy between the working of great literature and a certain understanding of 'ecology' renders texts such as *Moby Dick* agents of cultural self-stabilisation. Nevertheless, the analogy between 'ecology' and the social function of literature may seem rather forced on examination. Words such as 'distortion' and 'imbalance' are normative terms, and they are arguably appropriating references to scientific ecology to serve what is really a familiar contemporary politics of social inclusion. Zapf projects an implicit norm of culture as achieving the maximised 'vital' (7) working together of all its previously divided elements and, as such, his 'cultural ecology' could be said to blend a now common conception of the social function of literature with a recognisably romantic cultural ideal, of maximised social integration and interrelation. Is there much that is strictly 'ecological' in the social/political ideal of literature as an agent of cultural homeostasis in which marginalised subcultures find recognition?

Zapf's idealisation of the literary as a principle of natural counterbalance within the work of culture has been questioned by pointing to a counterexample, as Anne D. Peiter has done in relation to Ernst Jünger's unquestionably unbalanced *In Stahlgewittern* (1920).[28] In the genealogy of literary theories, moreover, Zapf's work recalls the kind of romantic modernism associated with mid-twentieth-century literary criticism, with for instance the New Critics' defence of the intellectual and moral complexities of literary language as against the one-sided terminologies of scientism.[29] The moral critic F. R. Leavis offers another analogue here: his vitalist language and references to 'life' as a norm of critical judgement often worked in a way that was very similar to references to ecology in Zapf and other modern ecocritics. Leavis defended creative writers for their 'more penetrating consciousness of that to which we belong', and their rendering of a language uniquely 'alive to [its] own time',[30] making the literary a sensitive conduit of cultural energies, uniquely alert to interrelationship and to the 'vital' or 'deadening' tendencies in its surrounding culture.

In effect, in both Leavis and Zapf, 'life' and 'ecology' are primarily moral and political concepts, not biological ones, backing up relatively traditional theories of the social function of literature as an anti-doctrinaire agent of social counterbalancing, inclusion and moderation.

Even in the sphere of environmental management, references to 'ecology' as a science may mask what are actually major political and social decisions. Adrian Franklin's study of controversies about introduced and invasive species in Australia may illustrate this. At issue are Australian efforts to restore indigenous ecosystems and eradicate or at least control such introductions as the red fox or the feral cat. Such programmes usually take 1788, the date of the first European settlement, as a kind of benchmark for restoration. Franklin writes:

the orthodoxy in Australia holds that native animals are those that were here at the time of *white settlement*. However, this traps environmental action in the enigma of an ecosystem they can never aspire to restore: the extensively burned pre-colonial landscape of Aboriginal Australia, or indeed the dominance of acacias on the continent before they were displaced by eucalypts. By this logic the dingo that came before the whites visited Australia is a native animal but the brumby [a local breed of horse gone feral] is not because it came just after.[31]

As Franklin's point shows, what 'natural' may finally mean is hard to gauge in this context. Ecological restoration projects may be a valuable response to the devastation wrought by settlement, as are calls for more suitable kinds of farming practice and water use. However, such projects may also feed an unacknowledged and problematic kind of eco-nationalism or even eco-cleansing (indigenous equals good, introduced equals bad), a policy dubious in itself for its dogmatism and with uncomfortable overtones in a country often torn by debates about human immigration. Franklin shows that the people who might be imagined most to support such eco-cleansing, the Aborigines, are in fact often against it. For instance, they value and exploit the introduced cats and have in some cases made them part of their culture. Tim Low argues that Australia's now hybrid fauna and flora need sometimes to be accepted and celebrated for what they are.[32]

In sum, environmental politics cannot be decided for us by the science of ecology. Ecology offers a vital and chastening understanding of how ecosystems function, their fragility, instability or endurance. It cannot, however, take on the role of a political authority. Recognising this, environmental politics is increasingly becoming more like politics elsewhere, the art of making the least bad decision in the face of often incompatible, singular claims.

Chapter 15

Science studies

Studying science as a kind of behaviour

What if the work of scientists is itself studied as just another kind of human behaviour, on a par with courtship rituals or competitive sport? Ullica Segerstråle's account of a scientific controversy of the 1970s and 1980s is just such an exercise in socio-anthropology.[1] Donna Haraway likewise describes 'science studies' as 'about the behavioral ecology and optimal foraging strategies of scientists and their subjects'.[2]

Scientists are usually baffled when their culture is studied in that way (Segerstråle, *Defenders*, 356). The issue, however, is not to discredit scientific work by supposedly explaining one scientist's theory in terms of personal prejudices or cultural background. That would be to make the untenable claim that sociology itself is somehow the true science that trumps the others (and then, would not the behaviour of sociologists in turn be studied by their own methods . . . ?). To use a sociological theory of human competitive behaviour to partly account for the claims of scientists does not itself discredit the scientific method, for the sociology itself rests on it.

Segerstråle's focus is the fierce and sometimes nasty arguments that arose about the status of sociobiology after the publication of E. O. Wilson's *Sociobiology* in 1975.[3] What caused the trouble was Wilson's one chapter about trying to understand human culture in evolutionary terms. Some of the stakes of this have already been outlined above. Segerstråle also found, surprisingly perhaps, that 'moral/political concerns, far from being an obstacle to be eliminated, were in fact *a driving force* both in generating and criticizing scientific claims in this field, and that the field was better off because of this'.[4]

The aim is to see scientific practice in terms broader than its own sometimes blinkered focus on strict disciplinary boundaries and 'objective facts'. In practice, questions of value are often deeply implicated, not necessarily for the worse. What Segerstråle also finds is that disputes about sociobiology often hinged on different presuppositions, not only about data but also about what science is or should be in the first place. 'A scientific controversy is always at the same time a second-order controversy: it is a conflict about the game rules of science as well, about *what counts as "good science"*.'[5]

The Selfish Gene[6]

Similar to the natural history essays of Stephen Jay Gould, the books of Richard Dawkins show how powerful scientific work can be done in a mode that need not respect the distinction between a popularising text and one engaged in debate with peers. His hugely influential study *The Selfish Gene* (1976) arose from work on the rising theory of 'kin selection' as a crucial feature of evolution ('kin selection' meaning crudely that a creature will behave altruistically for its close relatives, behaviour that makes no sense in terms of individual self-interest but which becomes intelligible – to use the pop-science language for which Dawkins is partly responsible – because it is acting on behalf of a creature that 'shares a large number of its own genes').

More than the comparable popular science essays of Gould, Dawkins's book employs often forceful and virtuoso modes of pedagogy. However, its vivid but figurative title also led to misconceptions that persist to this day. The 'selfish gene' has now become a phrase widely used to name any sort of genetic determinism, the implausible view, explicitly attacked by Dawkins, that all animal or human behaviour can be traced fatalistically to some inexorable genetic cause. In fact, however, Dawkins's 'gene' was a complex invention of explanatory modelling, not a unitary substantive entity, let alone one with any motives, naming what is essentially a logical function (for its referent would actually be the working of several microbiological processes).

Segerstråle writes:

> Dawkins brings in vivid examples and hypothetical scenarios, he entertains, he anthropomorphizes, he stretches the reader's imagination – all in the service of explaining evolutionary theory. Dawkins wants to present the *logic* of the gene's eye perspective – how we may look at evolution in a new way, considering the interest of a gene in producing replicas of itself rather than working for the survival of the individual organism.   70

What was in Dawkins essentially a matter of modelling, of finding the most logically simple algorithm for evolutionary processes by a focus on its minimal elements, that is, the principles of replication, soon came to circulate at second and third hands as a simplistic factual claim – that human behaviour, however objectionable, is just an inevitable consequence of evolution.

Dawkins's very success in rendering his explanatory logic concrete with an anthropomorphic term ('selfish') also made it liable to unjust claims that he had undermined the whole basis of human morality by promulgating the notion that all action is necessarily self-interested,[7] or that he was even lending support to reactionary arguments that tried to justify xenophobia or the oppression of women by reference to the supposed facts of human nature. Out of this context and other loosely sociobiological approaches also arose that contentious but now commonplace language that narrates animal life as a process of continuous cost–benefit analysis, for which every choice of food, mate, food source or habitat becomes part of what might be called its gene survival optimisation plan. As with Darwin's partially metaphoric phrase, 'the struggle for existence', Dawkins's misjudged term for an underlying model for the facts of evolution led to a reductive projection of late capitalist values into the whole biosphere.[8]

Donna Haraway

Donna Haraway's *Primate Visions* (1989)[9] is widely seen as having set a standard for subsequent work in science studies. This, and her concept of 'situated science' (see below), have also made her perhaps the most frequent reference in ecotheory.

Primate Visions is the book that launched Haraway's reputation. In it she contrasts differing ways in which cultures and scientists have regarded and studied non-human primates such as baboons, chimpanzees and gorillas. Given that humans are themselves primates, disputes in primatology are soon inevitably laden with questions or assumptions about human nature and origins, especially gender roles. Arguing that '[t]he detached eye of objective science is an ideological fiction' (13), Haraway shows in great detail how would-be 'scientific' accounts of primate behaviour too often draw upon modern human norms and assumptions. She studies the rhetoric and language of scientific studies with a view to foregrounding all kinds of decisive presuppositions and projections. What is really going on when a scientific observer interprets primate behaviour through the language of 'family', 'courtship', 'home' and so on, or modes of personhood based on competitive individualism? Haraway writes:

> Nonhuman primates' status both as surrogates and as rehabilitants rested on their semiotic residence on the borderland between western contestations of nature and culture. Many heading for laboratory

colonies, some for forests, simians were literally in a busy two-way traffic between these two domains because they lived in an epistemological buffer zone.   132

Let us turn now to a specific case study, Jeanne Altmann's work on baboons in the 1970s. As a result of her field studies Altmann, who is also a feminist, came to challenge the then dominant understanding of evolutionary adaptation in primate studies. This saw males as the primary source of genetic diversity in a species: that is, because one male can mate with many females, producing numerous offspring, it might seem initially that male competition for sex would be the crucial factor in genetic inheritance. Altmann, however, showed that female baboons were far more than mere prizes in rivalry between males, that they were agents and strategists in their own right, and in often decisive ways.

Altmann emphasised in interviews her view that a feminist would be discredited by directly putting 'politics', that is, her own gendered social identity, into 'science'.[10] To transgress in that way the fact–value distinction would be seen as contaminating the status of her work as 'scientific', even in the scientist's own eyes. To merely offer an explicitly feminist account against the male bias in studies of baboons would not help:

> because she is simultaneously annoyed as a woman and a scientist by the primate literature's overtly sexist accounts of categories called leadership and control, the one thing she specifically should not do is substitute the mirror-image reverse account or method, except perhaps as caricature to show the sad status as science of the original masculinist version.
>
> *Primate Visions*, 309–10

This is the kind of dilemma that recurs again and again in the material Haraway studies. How to show up the way in which supposedly objective studies of animal behaviour actually incorporate and project a human cultural politics, without at the same time reducing scientific work to nothing more than the play of competing human values, or to claims that 'all is relative', that there is no such thing as external reality and so on – to cite some familiar caricatures of science studies.

Haraway's method is to read primatology through a kind of multiple literacy – scientific, political, rhetorical, literary and philosophical. The aim is to become sensitive to the way in which something achieves the status of a scientific fact through, for instance, the complex mediations of technology and laboratory equipment, the publishing and review mechanisms that enable a paper to be published, and the whole history of the field of science at issue, its social make-up and sociopolitical standing:

> It is impossible to account for . . . developments without appealing to personal friendship and conflict, webs of people planning books and conferences, disciplinary developments in several fields (including practices of narration, theoretical modeling, and hypothesis testing with quantitative data), the history of economics and political theory, and recent feminism among particular national, racial, and class groups. The concept of *situatedness, not bias*, is crucial.   emphasis added[11]

The effect of considering all these dimensions together is not to 'relativise' a 'fact' out of existence, but to demonstrate the plurality of its conditions of being accepted as a 'fact', to blur the boundaries between what is literal and what may be social/symbolic in the scientific papers or narratives.

Haraway's multiple literacy is illustrated by her account of modern studies of chimpanzees. After the 1960s, as with studies of baboons, primatologists came to question the earlier focus on male competition as the crucial factor for genetic inheritance in chimpanzee groups. As with Altmann and baboons, new observations of female chimps in the field led to a sense of the subtle strategies they seemed to use to maximize their own reproductive success, thus, as they say, passing on more of their own genes to the next generation. However, Haraway would not be content to stay with this new result as a newly discovered scientific fact. While such a focus on female chimps contrasts strongly with earlier attention to male aggression and competition, it still remains, in Haraway's view, necessarily as 'situated' as the other approaches, that is, conditioned by a whole context of changing factors, some of which may induce more questions. For instance, the new observations on female chimps were in line with the new sociobiological focus on the strategies and ruses that individual animals use to maximize their reproductive success, and this focus, Haraway argues, involves its own projections and presuppositions. It tends, for instance, to project certain unexamined, liberal assumptions about personhood, seeing each chimp itself as a kind of separate calculating individualist, seeking always to maximize individual reproductive advantage: 'In socio-biological narrative, the female becomes the calculating, maximizing machine that males had long been.'[12] However, 'Such [assumptions are] unthinkable in naturalcultural worlds that do not *think* action in terms of bounded possessive individuals.' Illustrating this point, Haraway contrasts the different situatedness of Japanese primatologists, for whom *groups* were the seemingly self-evident issue of any study, not the individual.[13]

As this example shows, to read scientific work with a multiple and interdisciplinary literacy is to refuse the distorting effects of hard boundaries between intellectual disciplines:

> My mode of attention causes me to mix things up that sometimes others have high stakes in keeping separate, and I might often be wrong-headed. But my way of working will also, sometimes, usefully avoid reductive notions of what is 'inside' or 'outside' scientific primatology, what is popular and professional, and what is 'cultural' or 'political' and what is 'scientific' about our notions of primates.[14]

Haraway anticipates a new kind of provocative, open science, one that would be more scrupulous and rigorous than much modern practice in that its work would always be attentive to the multiple frames and contexts whereby something is accorded, perhaps only for a time, the status of a recognised fact or an accepted observation. Dogmatic divisions between science and cultural politics would be refused, in favour of thinking through multiple, intersecting grey areas, each yet defined as precisely as possible and made explicit in its stakes. For instance, the 'facts' about female chimps' reproductive strategies remain, but as part of an overall picture that must include a comprehensive account of the context that helped bestow them with the status of 'facts', the changing social scene (1970s feminism, for instance), the nature of the scientific institution at the time, the choice of study method in the field (e.g., the use of 'time and motion' and management efficiency studies originally taken from industry), and liberal assumptions about personhood. There are always more questions to ask, more contexts to unravel.

Haraway rarely uses the concept of *nature* unqualified. She prefers the compound term *natureculture*, highlighting the falsity of separating the one from the other. When the issue, however, is to affirm the natural world as an agent in its otherness from human conceptions, Haraway may use the name *coyote*, the wily actor or trickster spirit of some Native American cultures. Like her earlier coinage of *cyborg*, highlighting the way human beings in themselves transgress the natural–mechanical distinction, *coyote* is a kind of provisional 'fiction', situated in the space between the ideas we have of things and what things actually are or do. To call nature 'coyote' as opposed to, say, 'mother', is to project some expectations rather than others. 'Tropes matter, literally'.[15] 'Coyote', for example, is arguably preferable as a trope for a crucial agency in living processes to Dawkins's trope of the '*selfish* gene'. Dawkins defended his personification as a 'fruitful metaphor',[16] yet it led to widespread misunderstandings he has had to clarify ever since. To call nature 'coyote' helpfully affirms nature's agency as that of a wily trickster with which we are learning to interact, as opposed to 'nature' seen solely as an object of human constructions or representations.

To write, like Haraway, with a multiple literacy, is one way of engaging nature as a capricious and unstable agency in its own right. Extrapolating some implications and possibilities for literary ecocriticism, Christa Grewe-Volpp writes:

> Climate, wilderness conditions, technologically altered landscapes, topographies and many other environmental elements – never as pristine nature, never as mere text – function as a powerful force that human beings have to – and do – react to. Some writers represent this force by giving nature a 'voice' which, rightly understood, has nothing to do with anthropomorphising the non-human world. It does not mean projecting human feelings to a realm other than human, but is instead a paradoxical effort to realise and to appreciate nature's own laws, to at least come close to its fundamental difference.[17]

To acknowledge the agency of nature clearly accords already with all kinds of strategies of literary representation – mythic, magical realist, animist and fantastic. The problem for future ecocriticism may be not the plurality of ways of voicing the agencies of nature that already exist in the literatures of the world. It is in developing kinds of critical articulacy able to do justice to such agency and not, for instance, reading all figurations of the non-human and so on solely as a function, a 'construct' (see below), of human cultural contexts.

These issues also reflect themselves in the plurality of Haraway's own writing. Joseph Schneider observes of *Primate Visions*: 'Closure, totalization, self-certainty and self-righteousness, essentialism, and claimed or desired detachment or "objectivity", all are pointedly avoided.'[18] *Primate Visions* 'is replete with representations of representations, deliberately mixing genres and contexts to play with scientific and popular accounts'.[19] Haraway's coined terms express the complexity of the issues and their resistance to inherited kinds of language: 'natureculture' and 'subjectobject'. (The coinage 'factvalue' might in turn express both new freedoms and new difficulties.) The bizarre form of such expressions shows, once again, how quickly environmental and related issues collide with the demarcations between inherited concepts and disciplines.

Like science studies, environmental thought and writing places itself in the difficult, unstable but potentially radical space opened up by fissures in competing conceptions and justifications of science. Latour even argues that the importance of radical environmentalist arguments (what he calls 'political ecology') lies not in their own terms, those of the protection or reaffirmation of the natural, but in the way environmental issues destabilise in practice basic distinctions between science and politics, nature and culture, fact and value.[20] Environmentalist debate is about competing conceptions of natureculture. Thus the natural sciences may find themselves accused of complicity in technological imperialism, while an ecocritic may attempt a stance that would defend, say, the deeper rationality of phrases such as the 'language or message of rocks' or the wisdom of prescientific cultures.

Environmental issues are creating the need for new types of interdisciplinarity, greater interchange between the natural and social sciences and the humanities and even a questioning of the rationale of the division between them. Ecocriticism, however falteringly, is part of the difficult emergence of new kinds of literacy.

Ninth quandary: constructivism and doing justice to non-human agency

In 'Darwin's War-horse: Beetle-Collecting in 19th-Century England' the naturalist Peter Marren quotes A. A. Gill's speculations on why making collections of beetles was such a common pursuit among the Victorians:

> Beetles embody all the talents of the middle classes. They are not aristocratic, vain esoterics, like butterflies or moths, or communists, like ants and bees. They're not filthy, opportunistic carpetbaggers, like flies. They are professional, with a skill. They're built for a job, and get down to it without boastfulness or hysterics. And there is nowhere that doesn't, sooner or later, call in a beetle to set up shop and get things done.[21]

Thus, humorously, the interests of innumerable amateur naturalists become seen as a kind of cultural narcissism. It is as if Gill were lampooning that powerful paradigm in cultural and literary studies according to which whenever a writer or scientist considers the universe, through a telescope or microscope, some version of race, class or gender politics is always reflected back. A first generation of green literary critics argued that the environmental crisis was not just being ignored by mainstream literary criticism, but that its dominant assumptions were complicit with that crisis. Thus beetles are assumed to hold no interest in themselves: their fascination was only, to use the current terminology, a 'construct' of intra-human cultural politics.

To stress the extent to which something is a 'construct' or a 'social construct' has been a widespread gesture of demystification in the modern humanities. Its target is precisely a concept of 'nature'. It refuses the prejudice inherent, for instance, in notions of women as 'naturally' x or y or of any human group as 'naturally' inferior or superior in some sense. These conceptions are rather social 'constructs' whose artificiality can now be seen and dismantled. Hence the passionate controversies that can arise when some scientist claims to find natural differences between genders or ethnicities, as in the vehement disputes around sociobiology.

Although the rejection of cultural constructivism was an important gesture in earlier ecocriticism, the turn towards issues of ecojustice in the late 1990s led to a qualified use of constructivist arguments, not to assert that 'nature' is *only* a cultural construct, but to study the ways in which different cultural conceptions and notions of identity project different versions of nature. Such arguments have been productive of useful insights. They have opened again, for instance, those dominant masculinist conceptions of identity in the American pioneer tradition, of self-definition through the mastery and domestication of wilderness.

At the same time, the constructivist gesture is a two-edged weapon. It may slide in practice towards being a more dogmatic 'culturalism', to modes of thinking for which the cultural is taken as all there is, or at least all that is studied, instead of its making up, as it surely does, an evanescent and fragile bubble suspended vulnerably in a web of material conditions. Again, the choice of determining metaphors is crucial. Eileen Crist scrutinises some disconcerting assumptions at work in those usually 'productionist' or even 'industrial' terms that do so much work in some contemporary accounts of cultural processes:

> Metaphors of human labor regarding the creation of knowledge abound – familiar examples are building, constructing, assembling, manufacturing, inventing, or producing knowledge. Such vocabulary trades heavily on received distinctions between nature/natural and culture/artifactual, and through its semantics pushes the constructivist envelope – viz., that knowledge is primarily man-made, not imparted by nature.[22]

Scott Hess, for instance, contrasting three versions of nature projected in texts by William Wordsworth (see pp. 108–110 above), by Clare and by Dorothy Wordsworth relates various kinds of human self-conception to differing 'constructs' of nature. Dorothy, unlike William, is seen as '*constructing* a communal, relational and participatory version of the environment'.[23] Such language not only uncomfortably suggests a model of the psyche as a kind of mini-industrialist, but, whatever construct of 'nature' is at issue here, however participatory, reciprocal and so on, it is still being figured as passively built by a human agent. The natural world could never, within the terms of such an anthropocentric politics of 'identity', be acknowledged as an agent in its own right.[24] By contrast, Haraway defends the use of figurative and mythic language to express the agency of the non-human in its own right (nature as 'coyote') as well as offering a means for articulating issues that transgress given disciplinary boundaries.

Chapter 16

Evolutionary theories of literature

On the whole environmental criticism is defined more by its issues and challenges than by any particular method. There is, however, a small but striking body of work that attempts to offer an approach to literature from the viewpoint of Darwinian evolutionary science.[1] This means to confront directly the enormous, fraught meta-contextual issues that others sometimes evade: can literature be understood in terms of human evolution? What *is* human nature? Are there biological bases for morality, or even for aesthetic judgement? Such questions knowingly transgress deep boundaries between the humanities, social sciences and natural sciences, finding such boundaries often anachronistic and misleading.

It is not just a matter of particular arguments or issues in one discipline seeming dubious when viewed from the perspective of another, but of alleged falsities in the ways the disciplines are constituted. Glen Love sees thinkers in the humanities and social sciences as working 'for the most part, as if the monumental discoveries of Darwin and his followers had never taken place, as if we are "above nature"'.[2] For Love this aligns 'many humanists with creationists, backwoods school boards, and others whose efforts are devoted to not wanting to know what is true'.[3]

The Standard Social Science Model

Evolutionary critics would argue against almost all contemporary literary criticism, seeing it as an offshoot of the now suspect assumptions still used to differentiate the social sciences and humanities from the natural sciences. These assumptions form the so-called 'Standard Social Science Model'. According to this, human beings are uniquely and essentially social beings whose behaviour and thinking are overwhelmingly determined by their cultures. The human mind at birth is held to be a 'blank slate' or a general-purpose hardware awaiting the software of language and culture. This means that cultural factors, not evolutionary ones, are what are crucial for an understanding of human behaviour. In other words, the study of human cultures can form an autonomous discipline, independent of but not inferior to the natural sciences.

This argument seemed bolstered in the 1950s and 1960s by the success of the structural anthropology of Claude Lévi-Strauss, with its use of the model of linguistics to study human cultures as self-contained signifying systems, each with its rules of kinship, taboos, rituals and identity rites: 'anthropologists saw the developing theory of structural linguistics as providing a non-biological yet equally scientific basis for the study of culture' (Dylan Evans).[4] In effect, the SSSM meant that the social sciences and natural sciences could function separately and with seemingly equal authority. The blank slate model of the human mind – the original sense, in fact, of 'environmentalism' – was also motivated by the felt need to reject discredited social Darwinism, eugenics or bigoted theories of race. Jonathan Gottschall argues that the SSSM was 'sustained for a period of more than thirty years... as much for ideological expedience as for its success in bringing coherence to information'.[5]

The debt of literary criticism to the SSM is now usually forgotten and its basic premises or assumptions overlooked. To assume the autonomy of culture as an object of study has become a given for almost all cultural studies and literary criticism from the 1980s till the present day, whether mediated by work in the Marxist tradition, the influence of Michel Foucault on the nature of social power, or in various studies of the cultural politics of texts that map out competing claims to 'identity'. The assumptions of the SSSM also legitimate current disciplinary boundaries. This is also, perhaps, why it is so hard to shift – it is built into the very dividing walls of academic and research institutions. It remains far easier for a cultural critic to describe competing views of some natural entity as 'constructions' referable exclusively to cultural and social factors, than to engage issues outside his or her expertise, such as the evolution of the brain. Critics will happily refer to changing concepts of what they call 'the self' in relation to speculations in psychoanalysis or in 'new historicism' but show no knowledge of or interest in empirical research in developmental psychology. Dylan Evans even writes that, by erecting a huge wall between the social and the natural sciences, the SSSM creates 'the last refuge for the shaky creationist notion of a radical gap between humans and other animals'.[6]

Literature and human nature

It seems incontrovertible that the SSSM often works in literary criticism as a fragile and discredited strategy of intellectual containment, and that its doctrine of human exceptionalism may have environmentally destructive consequences. It is still very unclear, however, how to break it down. Nevertheless, rejecting the SSSM underlies one controversial feature of such Darwinian literary criticism. This is, its need to offer, in a context in which culturalist arguments are widespread, some defensible account of what a universal human nature might actually be. Joseph Carroll offers: 'all cultures have marriage, rites of passage, social roles defined by age and sex, religious beliefs, public ceremonies, kin relations, sex taboos, medical practices, criminal codes, storytelling, jokes, and so on'.[7] Marcus Nordlund represents the kind of broad points Darwinian critics make of the dominant assumptions of cultural and literary criticism:

> The otherwise eminent Shakespearean critic Richard Levin gives voice to a broad consensus among literary critics with his assertion that 'what is called romantic love cannot be universal, natural, or essential because it is socially constructed, and we know this because it is constructed differently in different societies'. To someone who is versed in modern evolutionary theory, this position is bound to appear misguided since it revives an obsolete dichotomy between nature and culture and assumes that cultural variation in a trait or behavior is sufficient evidence that it is 'cultural' rather than 'natural'.[8]

Evolutionary thinking has repeatedly had to rebut misreadings that its arguments involve the claim that people are totally determined by their genetic inheritance.[9] The consensus now is rather that what distinguishes human beings among the animals is 'the emergence of a flexible general intelligence', an ability 'to adapt to variations within an environment that is itself complex and unstable' (Joseph Carroll).[10] To recognise variability and adaptability as the distinctive human trait is already to refute the possibility of a crude genetic determinism. As Alison Jolley observes, 'It no longer seems obvious that proposing biological bases for understanding human behavior leads straight to justifying the gas chambers.'[11]

How have such evolutionary overviews been deployed? Joseph Carroll challenges the idea that Darwinian criticism need mean only to identify in texts seeming universal or archetypal forms of human behaviour, thus using literature to verify the claims of evolutionary psychology. Nevertheless, such a description does fit a lot of the work in this area. Tony Jackson, for instance, considers Robert Storey's 'evolutionary' reading of the force of Sophocles' drama *Antigone* and the tragic conflict at work in the heroine Antigone's decision to bury her brothers in defiance of King Creon, against whom they had rebelled. He concludes:

> What Storey says seems true enough, but except for the fact that it is now backed up by evolutionary psychology, it hardly needs to be argued for. Who would deny that Antigone's dilemma involves 'a conflict between immediate family obligations and obligations to civil authority'?[12]

Perhaps Jackson's scepticism is inevitable. If evolutionary critics see their Darwinian constants of human nature as features of ourselves that should be immediately recognisable and (mostly) uncontentious, then any literary reading based on observing them may be in danger of seeming to state the obvious.

In another 'evolutionary' reading Marcus Nordlund writes of the sexual tension between Troilus and Cressida in Shakespeare's play:

> From the perspective of parental investment theory, it is only to be expected that the average man will be slightly more prone to 'idealize' a prospective sexual partner, at least in the sexual short term, while the average woman will have a greater incentive to prolong the courtship (which means more time for assessment and choice).[13]

A difficulty many critics have with this kind of approach is legible here. If such work tests finally inadmissible barriers between the humanities and sciences, it also suggests possible dangers in doing so too dogmatically. It is a small step from saying that male idealisation and haste in courtship are 'only to be expected' in a neutral sense to morally condoning it. How far should an understanding of biological differences inform the making of moral and critical judgements? Alternatively, are references to 'evolution' really functioning often as a covert moral code?

A difficulty latent here is that by setting up evolutionary science as an umpire of ultimate truth to which the readings should ultimately refer, critics also risk denying the extent to which the science itself is split by even fundamental debates. For instance, the presumption that all human behaviour, including art, serves some kind of evolutionary adaptive function is challenged by arguments that some aspects of an animal's anatomy or behaviour may actually serve no purpose at all in evolutionary terms. Steven Pinker, for instance, argues that such is the case with human art and literature themselves.[14]

Because the science is already in itself so contentious, evolutionary criticism can become vulnerable to claims that its use of Darwinism as a source of intellectual authority could with more justice be called an appropriation of selected scientific arguments for cultural/political ends. For instance, when evolutionary critics attack 'post-structuralists' and other alleged relativists the views they offer in response can read as effectively restatements, in superficially scientific vocabulary, of traditional and conservative liberal humanist defences of literature as broadening the mind by exposing it to universal values shared across the centuries, as supposedly uniting us in a sense of shared humanity. Thus Carroll writes that 'the elemental dispositions of human nature provide a common basis for understanding what is intelligible in these novels and . . . also what is confusing and unsatisfactory'.[15]

The fragility of this critical method is also suggested by the fact that Darwinism is just as easily appropriated by critics in the left-liberal progressive tradition, often the alleged deniers of human nature whom Carroll and others claim to refute. Considered on the broadest scale, the theory of evolution by natural selection can also be affirmed as proving the provisional, makeshift nature of all identities and species. The fluidity of all boundaries in biology can seem to refute at a stroke all assertions of essence. Timothy Morton stresses the deconstructive implications of Darwinism in proposing a 'queer ecology' that mocks the domination of masculinist, heterosexual norms in modern culture. He writes:

> In a sense, molecular biology confronts issues of authenticity similar to those in textual studies. Just as deconstruction showed that, at a certain level at any rate, no text is totally authentic; biology shows us that there is no authentic life form . . . All life forms, along with the environments they compose and inhabit, defy boundaries between 'inside' and 'outside' at every level . . . evolution theory is anti-essentialist in that it abolishes rigid boundaries between and within species . . . Life forms are liquid: positing them as separate is like putting a stick in a river and saying 'This is river stage x' (Quine).[16]

Morton draws on Darwin's anti-essentialism to attack dogmatic claims that human nature is essentially x or y, meaning in this case especially attitudes that inform homophobia as well as the masculinist sexual politics of some conceptions of 'the outdoors', or prejudices against people with disabilities. At the same time, the intellectual jumps made in Morton's work here, from molecular biology to a familiar social ethic, are huge ones, most defensible perhaps as answering the cultural politics of conservative Darwinists by copying their own method of deducing ethical stances from evolutionary arguments, but to different effect.

In sum, the interest of evolutionary literary theories still lies mainly in the very perplexity of the issues they raise, underlining the difficulty of the space between the disciplinary lines that they attempt to cross. Overall, things seems currently to be at an impasse, a variant of the antinomy described at the end of Chapter 10 ('the antinomy of environmentalist criticism'). On the one hand, the destructive narrowness of the SSSM now seems unanswerable and its dismantling an urgent task for environmental thought. On the other hand, ecocritics who draw on Darwinism to transcend the SSSM, whether this is Carroll's use of it to endorse a familiar cultural conservatism or Morton's to endorse an equally familiar ethos of social inclusion, are still making themselves vulnerable to the criticism that they are using a selective interpretation of evolutionary science to bolster ethical or political positions already held for other reasons.

Chapter 17

Interdisciplinarity and science

Two essays on human evolution

Tenth quandary: the challenge of scientific illiteracy   *176*

Ian Marshall observes that 'If there is a methodology that sets ecocriticism apart from other modes of literary scholarship, it is its inherent interdisciplinary nature.'[1] This chapter examines the mode, stakes and success of two interdisciplinary essays that engage the difficult space between the natural sciences and the humanities. How do differing kinds of intellectual method, generic expectation and convention negotiate this space?

One text is an autobiographical and speculative essay in ecocriticism, Marshall's own 'Tales of the Wonderful Hunt' (2003),[2] concerning evolution, literature of the hunt and the author's own peculiar experiment with hunting. The other is Stephen Jay Gould's 'Posture Maketh the Man' of 1977, on how cultural assumptions about human brain size led to misreadings of human evolution.[3] Both the relaxed essay form of Marshall and the popular science essay of Gould knowingly refuse to stay within the recognised boundaries of single academic disciplines. Both, in different ways, exemplify Julie Thompson Klein's argument that '[all] interdisciplinary work is critical in that it exposes the inadequacies of the existing organization of knowledge to accomplish given tasks'.[4]

Let us take the seemingly more straightforward piece of writing first. Gould, who died in 2002, remains famous as a populariser of natural history. His very success as a writer made him controversial as a scientist, for his essays were widely seen as giving his own idiosyncratic theory of evolution ('punctuated equilibrium') a public authority it did not really warrant.[5] 'Posture Maketh the Man' is not an exercise in ecocriticism as such: it precedes accepted use of that term and is not devoted to interpreting a primary text. Nevertheless, it enriches environmental criticism in a broader sense. Gould's essays over thirty years repeatedly demonstrate how deeply cultural prejudice and political motives have distorted science in the past, especially in studies of human beings. 'Posture Maketh the Man' concerns the difficult terrain of human self-definition in the face of the findings of palaeontology. It comes to conclusions that necessarily reflect on the relation of theory and practice and its own cultural context.

At issue is the question of the decisive element in human evolution. Is it a relatively large brain size or is it standing upright, bipedalism? For decades workers in human evolution assumed, like the great nineteenth-century embryologist Karl Ernst von Baer, that 'Upright posture is only the consequence of the higher development of the brain . . . all differences between men and other animals depend upon construction of the brain'.[6] It seemed self-evident that growth in brain size over the millennia was the decisive element in the emergence of humanity among the great apes. Sigmund Freud, however, was one voice of dissent, arguing that it was walking upright that first reoriented the human sensorium around vision rather than scent and that ultimately led to changes in sexual behaviour from which something like the family group emerged as the basis of human reproduction. In fact, the current consensus, with strong fossil evidence, is that bipedalism evolved first, in the form of apes which stood upright but with the brain size of chimpanzees. Standing upright in turn led to new possibilities. It freed the hands to manipulate and exploit objects, enabling new observations and deductions and thus stimulating development of the brain.

Gould was a Marxist. Although he always denied a direct connection between his politics and his scientific research,[7] his basic arguments about evolution are fully compatible with Marxist dialectical materialism. 'Posture Maketh the Man' endorses Friedrich Engels for his 'trenchant political analysis of why Western science was so hung up on the a priori assertion of cerebral primacy' (211). The overvaluation of brain size as the determining factor in human evolution may well reflect social structures that denigrate and degrade manual work and exalt the directing intelligence of the ruling classes: 'Labor, the source of all wealth and the primary impetus for human evolution, assumed the same low status of those who labored for the rulers' (211).

Gould's essays take on and illuminate scientific controversies on racial difference, IQ and sociobiology, determined to expose science based on false presuppositions. Ultimately, he argues, distortions in scientific practice, such as the overvaluation of conscious thought and brain size, reflect social imbalances. Gould's seems the classic enlightenment correlation of good science and social progress. He concludes a review from 1988 with Karl Marx's famous remark: 'Philosophers thus far have only interpreted the world in various ways: the point, however, is to change it'.[8]

'Posture Maketh the Man' ends by relating ingrained prejudice about brain size to scientists' idealisation of 'pure' as opposed to applied research. One issue here is the opprobrium that scientists who are also popularisers often receive from their colleagues. Gould's own work as an essayist is itself a more impure kind of labour, uncovering unrecognised kinds of cultural politics in the institutions and workings of science. If, he writes, 'we recognized our belief in the inherent superiority of pure research for what it is' then scientists might force a salutary union 'between theory and practice' (213).

Marshall's 'Tales of the Wonderful Hunt' is a more ambitious but ultimately far less successful essay. Marshall sets up an interesting experiment, based on the contrast between two theories about the prehistoric hominid species, *Australopithecus africanus*. For the palaeontologist Raymond Dart, working in the 1920s and after, the fact that fossilised bones of this hominid were found with many other animal bones indicated that this creature was a fierce hunter, even a cannibal. The image of 'man the hunter' was to become popular and dominant for some decades in the middle of the twentieth century. For C. K. Brain, however, writing in 1981, the evidence suggested that these australopithecines were not hunters but the hunted. Their bones were being found stashed with other victims of the large cats, hyenas and so forth that had eaten them.

Which might be correct? Marshall proposes to test various hypotheses about whether an original human nature is predisposed to hunting or not. Taking himself to be 'a certain representative human subject' (189) he takes himself to the woods to see if, while backpacking, he can find it in himself to kill something by his own hands and eat it. This anecdotal travelogue forms one strand of his essay.

'Tales of the Wonderful Hunt' is essentially structured as a kind of quest narrative in the familiar way of the romantic wilderness tradition, namely the affirmation of 'nature' as a space for the recovery of a supposedly more authentic identity. What seems essential in human 'nature' is to be retrieved through engagement with 'nature' in the sense of non-man-made environments.

> I lay plans to test the Brain and Dart hypotheses. Perhaps I am inspired by the familiar notion, reduced to the status of cliché, that backpacking is a way for us to get 'back to nature'. What is usually meant by that is a combination of getting reacquainted with the world around us and rediscovering something of our essential self, our own nature, once the foofaraw of contemporary civilization is left behind.   189

Marshall's knowingly comic account of his killing and eating a snake, along with his musings on human evolution, follows the familiar romantic plot of 'nature' as a scene of escape and self-discovery.

'Tales of the Wonderful Hunt' instantiates one of the more experimental strands of literary ecocriticism. The essay is a form of 'narrative scholarship' in the mode of Marshall's own *Story Line* (1998), a work of mixed travelogue and critical work about the Appalachian Trail and writers associated with it. 'Narrative scholarship' is a term coined by Scott Slovic to name a field-based and interdisciplinary literary criticism.[9] Other examples are John Elder's *Reading the Mountains of Home* and Terry Gifford's *Connecting with John Muir*.[10] Slovic urges ecocritics to 'encounter the world and literature together, then report about the conjunctions'.[11] *Story Line* hovers between being a travelogue, a guidebook, cultural history, natural history, academic study and personal memoir. Thus an authority on Cherokee myths is quoted as Marshall narrates walking through a related part of the Appalachian Trail, not in the mode of academic analysis but more in the relaxed form of a kind of conversation on the way.

The invented genre of 'narrative scholarship' is one response to the challenges of interdisciplinarity. In effect, it relaxes the constraints of professional academic rigour and enables Marshall to bring in all sorts of material – on palaeontology, folklore and so on – that normally falls outside the expertise of a literary critic. 'Tales of the Wonderful Hunt' is an entertaining mix of personal travelogue, natural history and a survey of American hunting literature. At the same time, it demonstrates some limits of the personal non-fiction essay as a mode of dealing with environmental issues. For even if some of the subject matter of palaeontology can be carried over into a literary essay, its hard-won standards of argument and demonstration cannot.

Marshall's quest to discover something about human nature through a mix of personal experience and speculations on palaeontology is engaging but arguably on thin ground scientifically. He writes that because *Australopithecus Africanus* was, if not a direct human ancestor, closely related to one, then the issue of whether it was a savage hunter or not 'has profound implications for our conceptions of what human nature is – and what role hunting has in that nature' (189). He also turns to Abenaki folklore, following Jung's claim that folklore gives access to an original, collective human nature.

The scientific literacy of Marshall's essay seems limited. *Australopithecus africanus* is in fact such a distant figure in hominid evolution that the issue of whether it hunted or not would have little relevance to humans: in fact, some of its descendants or relatives hunted and some did not. Marshall does not mention another australopithecine species also found by Dart, *Australopithecus robustus*, which is both of more recent date and believed to have been vegetarian,[12] nor more direct human ancestors like *Homo erectus* or *Homo habilis*. In fact, whether a hominid species hunted or not is generally taken to be a variable, relating to opportunity and skill in tool use, not the expression of some underlying original 'nature'.

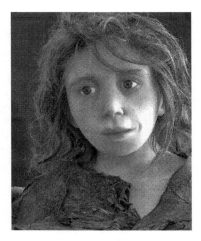

Figure 12 Neanderthal child (Christoph P. E. Zollikofer)

Marshall's understanding of prehistory as the site of an original human nature seems also questioned by both the large number and the sheer variety of prehuman hominid species. This alone destabilises any claims of some 'original' human nature. It also unsettles the lines of difference between human animals and others.[13] If any image might undermine at a stroke all assertions of human exceptionalism, it might be that of the face of a Neanderthal child, reconstructed from fossil remains. 'Its' gaze encounters ours with the unspeakable poignancy of an extinct species.

Other basic problems of method surface late in Marshall's essay, when he draws on an argument that would effectively undermine the premises of his experiment. He observes that both Dart and Brain's theories about *Australopithecus africanus* can be seen as cultural products of their times, that is, with Dart and the promulgators of a 'man the hunter' stance writing at a time of global violence and its aftermath, but with Brain much influenced by 1960s pacifism (200). However, such a constructivist argument, if taken seriously, would cause the bases of the whole essay to collapse. For if the supposed original human 'nature', hinted at through study of one australopithecine species, is really just a projection of topical concerns that change over a few decades, then it can make no sense to search for that nature by going hunting oneself or to assume it exists in pristine form in folklore. To then claim that 'the findings of science turn out to be as ambiguous and indeterminate and open to interpretation as any story' (201) also undercuts the reasons for turning to palaeontology as any kind of authority in the first place.

In sum, 'narrative scholarship' of this kind serves perhaps as a reminder of just how difficult a rigorous interdisciplinarity would be, one, that is, attentive to strict modes of argument, to scientific method, as well as subject matter.

'Tales of the Wonderful Hunt' is interdisciplinary only through a dubious relaxing of intellectual standards. Gould, however, used interdisciplinary work responsibly to challenge the self-enclosure of the scientific institution, as well as using the essay form to make its work more widely accessible. Charles Bazerman writes of another essay of Gould's, co-authored with Richard Lewontin (a famous attack on sociobiology and the paradigm, in models of evolution, that everything in animal life is intelligible as an environmental adaptation of some sort):

> Gould and Lewontin implicitly . . . question the enclosure of biology itself by setting biological explanation side by side with aesthetic and cultural explanation. They do this because their cause ultimately reaches beyond biology. They must remove the protection of biology from the sociobiology they believe is wrapping itself in untenable biological reductions. To wean us, the readers, from sociobiology, they must first wean us from 'our biological prejudices'.[14]

In practice, as Gould's very last book made explicit, his ideal of science involves a perpetual vigilance, suspicious of the culture of modern science as a kind of obscure priesthood defended by the 'myth' of a 'special status' freed 'of constraining social bias' and seeing 'nature directly'.[15] Such vigilance would mean being critical of the premature claims of E. O. Wilson and other committed reductionists, that the bases for human moral judgements can be understood from studies of their evolutionary contexts, while, equally, having little sympathy with the scientific illiteracy that frequently mars work in the humanities. A genuine interdisciplinarity would not entail a relaxing of the standards of any one discipline, but instead the intense strain but also excitement of bringing each strictly to bear upon the other.

Tenth quandary: the challenge of scientific illiteracy

Gretel Ehlich's *The Future of Ice* has already been described as an adventurous ecofeminist exercise in creative non-fiction. With its depiction of various parts of the earth newly perceived under the destabilising knowledge of climate change, Ehlrich's prose is steeped in perspectives gained from reading popular science, a kind of interdisciplinarity seemingly 'felt on the pulses'.

At the same time, what Ehrlich asserts as given scientific fact is sometimes very inaccurate – that the sun will 'be gone in 5 million years' (93), that snow is technically a '"black body" that absorbs 100 percent of the energy incident upon it' (81), and that (contradictorily) without snow and ice to reflect UV radiation back into space then 'earth will become a heat sponge and only smoke from a volcano could shield us' (46).

What effect does such scientific illiteracy have on a text of this kind and what critical issues does this raise? This seems to be a new kind of critical problem, one specific to the ethical commitment of this kind of environmentalist writing and quite distinct from, say, Thomas Hardy getting his astronomy wrong in *Two on a Tower* (1882). Environmentalist non-fiction, as we saw, often subjects itself to an ethic of truthfulness, accuracy and coherence of a kind more normally associated with scientific or professional academic work. Ehrlich's revisionist project is not refuted by her errors in basic science, but it is surely undermined. Her alternative sensuous dialogue with the natural world owes much of its authority to the scientific findings she garbles, whereas Hardy's errors, as they are now known to be, do not undermine the whole plot and rationale of *Two on a Tower*, with its study of love, ambition and ageing.

The animal mirror

In the question of the animal, or rather of other animals, ecocriticism finds perhaps its most striking ethical challenge. James Rachels writes:

> We kill animals for food; we use them as experimental subjects in laboratories; we exploit them as sources of raw materials such as leather and wool; we keep them as work animals. These practices are to our advantage, and we intend to continue them. Thus, when we think about what animals are like we are motivated to conceive them in ways that are compatible with treating them in these ways. If animals are conceived as intelligent, sensitive beings, these ways of treating them might seem monstrous. So humans have reasons to resist thinking of them as intelligent or sensitive.[1]

A first issue is that of animal ethics: how should animals be regarded and treated? What questions are raised by the way humans differentiate themselves from other creatures? What happens if 'person' is no longer understood so as to exclude the non-human?

Writing about animals poses a challenge distinct from writing about places, ecosystems, landscapes or pollution. Whereas ecology in the strict sense will consider animals only as a group or species, in relation to threats to population size, habitat and so on, and may happily talk of the need of a cull of some species to 'protect the environment', an animal ethics will often concern the animal as an individual existence, more in the way in which a person is considered.

This will bring us to the challenge of *anthropomorphism*. How to represent animal lives in human language and culture without illusion or injustice?

Figure 13 Animal trails (Pavel Konovalov)

Eleventh quandary: animal suffering versus ecological managerialism

After Peter Singer's *Animal Liberation* (1975) on the extent and cruelty of human exploitation of animals, Tom Regan published his *The Case for Animal Rights* (1983), followed by such studies as Carol Adams's *The Sexual Politics of Meat* (1990) and Mary Midgley's *Animals and Why They Matter* (1984).[2] Regan argued that animals' evident capacity for sentience and suffering made them worthy of moral consideration as individuals with inherent value.

   This is a strikingly different defence of a creature's value from that of ecologists. These tend to esteem a species in terms of its place in an ecosystem: value lies in the ecosystem as a whole, not in the individual. Hence the controversies that flare up about animal cruelty when a scheme of ecological restoration involves the wholesale slaughter of an invasive species, with images like those of flocks of feral goats on the Galápagos being shot one by one from a helicopter.

There is a real, intractable dispute here. J. Baird Callicott, defending Leopold's 'land ethic', condemns the animal liberation movement for too exclusive a focus on the welfare of individual creatures, missing the arguably more fundamental issue of the health of ecosystems as a whole.[3] Regan, on the other hand, sees the land ethic as leading to ecological fascism.[4] His point here can be focussed simply by turning such ecological thinking on humanity itself as an invasive pest: 'A large scale cull is urgently needed to save the environment. Humans are in no danger of extinction, and their population would remain healthy and sustainable.'

Chapter 18

Ethics and the non-human animal

In David Garnett's novella *A Man in the Zoo* (1924) a young man, as an extreme gesture in a row with his fiancée, has himself placed for weeks in a cage in the Ape House at London Zoo. Spectators find him on display as a species between the orang-utan and the chimpanzee. In many scenes of this novella the mere presence of the cage wires marking a strict line between the human-as-spectator and the animal-as-exhibit produces defamilarising and disturbing effects. Take the scene in which the fiancée, Josephine, arrives among the crowd of spectators:

> At that moment he was engaged in walking up and down (which occupation, by the way, took up far more of his time than he ever suspected). But she could not speak to him; indeed she dreaded that he should see her.
>   Back and forth he walked by the wire division, with his hands behind his back and his head bent slightly, until he reached the corner, when up went his head and he turned on his heel. His face was expressionless.[1]

The scene is both comic and disturbing. Normal conventions of significa-tion are transgressed in a view of the human as animal and of caged animal behaviour (walking up and down) as human boredom.

Such a scene may highlight the way in which most human societies depend on assumptions of a basic distinction between 'human' and 'animal'. Of his-torical English society Keith Thomas writes, 'consciously or unconsciously, the fundamental distinction between man and animals underlay everyone's behaviour'.[2] This remains as much a matter of daily practices of eating and language as one of theories reserving to people some characteristic no other

Figure 14 Cage wire, woman and lynx (the author)

animal could supposedly share, whether that be reason, a soul, language, imagination or humour.

As Garnett's passage exemplifies, non-humans are not just objects of thought, they have always been used to map out constitutive features of human culture. Some of these are obvious, for instance the use of animal names as insults ('motorists are pigs!'). As Kate Soper writes: 'It is as if through the semiotic use of animals we are spared the embarrassment of a more direct confrontation with our own follies and aggression.'[3] Soper also argues that derogatory references to animals help human beings sustain an image of themselves as both part of but also above nature, as an unstable amalgam of the 'civilised' and the 'merely animal'.

Animal terms seem implicated in all systemic human oppression. An association of women with the bodily has historically aligned them with the animal, even as meat-eating has often been associated with virility. Racism's first move is usually to dissociate its object from the respect normally accorded other people, with the use of animal names as insults ('pig', 'rat', 'dog'). However, a response that objects 'these people are not rats' and so on, does not undo the force of hatred at work in the animal terms themselves. It does not confront what Cary Wolfe, following Peter Singer and others, terms 'the *institution* of speciesism' lying behind such language, manifest in 'the ethical acceptability of the systematic, institutionalized killing of nonhuman others'.[4] The work of dissociating rats from 'rats', pigs from 'pigs', snakes from 'snakes', and so on (at least as understood in most western cultures) has become one of the tasks of writers and broadcasters in natural history.

In the 'developed' world animals have become less and less visible in reality but more and more prominent as images. Wildlife television documentaries have done much to awaken a general sense of the threat facing the natural world, but has this been at the cost of transforming it into a kind of consumerist spectacle? Do they sometimes misrepresent the actual elusiveness and inaccessibility of many creatures, giving a disproportionate amount of attention to violence and predation, becoming in fact sometimes a modern kind of bear-baiting or cock-fighting at one remove?[5] In sum, the non-human, whether sentimentalised as Bambi, bred and slaughtered for a civic or religious feast, sterilised and then cosseted as a pet, watched on television or revered in its 'rarity' on some eco-tourist holiday, is caught up claustrophobically in various kinds of human practice and self-image, and yet for all that still extraordinarily remote.

Literary texts have often drawn their power from the way distinctions of human and non-human can be unstable. The animal, like the ghost or the good or evil spirit with which it is often associated, has been a manifestation of the uncanny, token of either an attractive disruption of species boundaries, as in many children's stories, or a disconcerting one, as in the horror stories of writers like H. P. Lovecraft, M. R. James or in Algernon Blackwood's tales of actively malevolent wild places.[6] The mere presence of a non-human animal can raise questions that engage the very definition of the human and human culture: 'it is impossible to disentangle what the people of the past thought about plants and animals from what they thought about themselves'.[7]

'Kiss goodbye to the idea that humans are qualitatively different from other animals'[8]

Most recent thinking on the distinction of the human and (other) animals now finds the very terms of the debate misleading. To pose the issue in ways that place 'the animal' on one side and 'the human' on the other, then to attempt to trace the line of demarcation between them, already conveys the assumption of a major divide between the two, the seeming issue being only to locate just where it lies.[9] Cary Wolfe writes: 'the humanities are . . . now struggling to catch up with a radical revaluation of the status of nonhuman animals that has taken place in society at large'.[10]

This brings us to a point made most forcefully by Derrida, that the term '*the animal*' in the singular is already preposterous for lumping together such a diversity of living creatures. The phrase itself bears all the weight of the crudity of the human–animal distinction. Derrida writes:

> it is rather a matter of taking into account a multiplicity of heterogeneous structures and limits. Among nonhumans and separate from nonhumans there is an immense multiplicity of other living things that cannot in any way be homogenized, except by means of violence and wilful ignorance, within the category of what is called the animal or animality in general.[11]

Human beings could not exist but as part of a community of animals. For Haraway, '*Human nature is an interspecies relationship*'.[12]

Human–animal

Critical thought on the human–animal border line immediately raises fundamental, multidisciplinary issues. However, the challenge is frequently unmanageable and seems often to be resisted, either consciously or unconsciously. For instance, if there were as straightforward an analogy as some claim between human rights and putative animal rights, then one would expect there to be numerous literary readings equivalent to schools of interpretation elsewhere, namely, we would have readings of classical texts highlighting in them elements of prejudice or of the systematic misrepresentation of animal life. A demystification of the civilised sphere would take the form of demonstrating its basis in modes of food production requiring mass servitude, imprisonment and slaughter. There would be widespread arguments that 'the canon' itself needs to be overhauled in view of its systematic endorsement of pastoral, hunting and religious practices implicated in animal suffering. There would be a broad questioning of the general association of animals with 'mere' children's books, leading perhaps to new evaluations of books such as Williamson's *Tarka the Otter* (1927) or Jack London's *The Call of the Wild* (1903). Might not even Norman Maclean's *A River Runs Through It* find itself recategorised as an instance of 'speciesism', together with subgenres of writing on hunting and fishing?

However, apart from a few essays in scattered places, no literary movement with such modes of reading exists.[13] Even the landmark *Ecocriticism Reader* of 1996 contained not one essay devoted to the issue of an animal or animals. Why is engaging with non-human creatures so difficult?

In most canonical literary texts, the place of non-human life is both pervasive but unseen. It is simply so uncontroversial as to make alternative readings centred on animals seem almost like a change of discipline. Any study of a text on the non-human always becomes a study of humanity in some sense. A survey of texts in which animals appear in some symbolic guise or other leads John Simons to conclude: 'the human experience bulks too large and is so important to us that it tends to blot out all other concerns whenever we encounter them'.[14] At the same time, once the issue of animal exploitation is raised about a text, it immediately becomes obvious in ways that may leave little more to say.

Surprisingly perhaps, the most fruitful readings of these issues appearing this century have not taken their crucial moves from the arguments of thinkers in the animal rights movement such as Tom Regan, Mary Midgley or Stephen Clark, arguments that move outwards from a given understanding of the human as having certain attributes (moral worth, capacity for suffering, sentience, etc.) to argue the implications of the fact that other creatures have them too.[15] Instead, the more fruitful critical practice has derived from work that makes our very concepts of the human problematic in the first place, as with arguments loosely associated with post-humanism. Critiques of essentialist, dogmatic and exclusive notions of the human lead necessarily to new attitudes of respect towards those animals from which people can no longer be so confidently distinguished. More than that, it can be shown that it is precisely in making the gesture of saying that 'animals don't have x' or 'animals can't y' that a dogmatic humanism is sustained.

Cary Wolfe's *Animal Rites* (2003) is an example of such questioning. Wolfe puts 'speciesism' and the issue of the animal at the crux of numerous literary, philosophical and cultural debates. His detailed readings show, skillfully and yet with an almost surprising lack of resistance, how the issue of animals disrupts even basic methodological assumptions: 'much of what we call cultural studies situates itself squarely, if only implicitly, on what looks to me more and more like a fundamental repression that underlies most ethical and political discourse: repressing the question of nonhuman subjectivity'.[16] The very presence of an animal can show up the fragility of speciesism and the violence of the practices that sustain it.

A simple initial point is this: images of non-human animals in literary texts are rarely taken seriously as such. In Ernest Hemingway's novels, for example, there are numerous images of animals. Wolfe yet observes:

> the discourse of species, and with it the ethical problematics of our
> relations to nonhuman others, continues to be treated largely as if species

is always already a counter or cover for some other discourse: usually gender (Spilka, Comley and Scholes, Burwell), sometimes race (Toni Morrison) or ethnicity (Walter Benn Michaels), still more rarely, class.[17]

Wolfe takes up critical readings of texts or films and examples of given critical methods to show how they fail to engage deeper assumptions about the animal–human and nature–culture divide, and thus perpetuate the cultural bases of speciesism. Thus a psychoanalytic reading of Hemingway's *The Sun Also Rises* (1926) is placed within the wider context of the human–animal distinction, something it merely takes for granted. Picking up on the way references to animals structure accounts of human sexuality, Wolfe strives to prise open space for writing of non-human species as something

> *other* than a figure for the relation of the symbolic order to the Real, or if you like, the Oedipal subject with its drives to the body, instinct and the biological . . . the psychoanalytical 'outside' of the subject is subtended by another, even more remote outside against which psychoanalysis persists in an essentially humanist effort to secure the human . . . by relegating the nonhuman other to the realm of senseless matter, inert organicity, brute instinct, or at best mindless repetition and mimicry.[18]

Wolfe also offers a reading of a well-known attack on the environmentalist movement, Luc Ferry's *The New Ecological Order* (1995). Ferry had been alarmed by some of the political implications of deep ecology and by dubious appeals to 'nature' as a source of values. Seeing environmentalism as an implicitly totalitarian and regressive discourse of the comfortable and privileged, Ferry reaffirmed the stock ideals of liberal humanism. He argued that a certain freedom from natural causes, a kind of self-making and perfectibility, is definitive for the human being alone: 'nature is not an *agent*, a being able to act with the *reciprocity* one would expect of an *alter ego*. Law is always for men, and it is for men that trees or whales can become *objects* of a form of respect tied to legislation – not the reverse'.[19] The emphasis here is Wolfe's. It highlights how Ferry's argument hinges on the preconception of the sovereignty of the human over the non-human. This is also implicit in Ferry's understanding of ethics, which is 'contractarian', that is, it acknowledges rights to others only within a reciprocal framework (an implicit contract) in which they acknowledge our rights in turn, something other animals probably cannot do. Correspondingly, within such circular conceptions, any question of the moral standing of the non-human can only be a matter of how it relates to the human. Wolfe continues, '"Animals", Ferry argues, "have no rights . . . but . . . we do have certain indirect duties towards them"', if only because the respect with which we treat animals reflects on the way we view ourselves and treat each other: '"the most

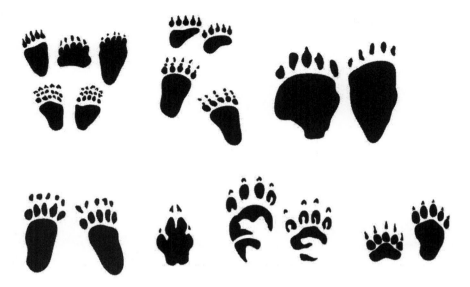

Figure 15 Animal trails (Pavel Konovalov)

serious consequence of the cruelty and bad treatment inflicted on [animals] *is that man degrades himself and loses his humanity*".[20] In other words the non-human has moral worth only as a kind of sounding board and mirror for human self-conceptions. In sum, Ferry's arguments against environmental-ism rest on a dogmatic and unexamined understanding of the human–animal opposition, one allowing subjectivity and ethical consideration to the human alone.

Wolfe's readings are extremely sophisticated, but their sophistication lies mainly in their engagement with the 'humanist' assumptions at work in the depth structure of even the most progressive critical methodology. If the issue becomes instead one of simply tracing the work of the human–animal divide in a primary text, the critical work involved seems less demanding. For instance, one can take a canonical text in which animal concerns seem at first to play no part at all, say Dickens's *David Copperfield*, and then trace in it the fault lines of the animal–human distinction. In this case we would move from, say, consideration of the lap dog 'Jip' who serves as a kind of double to David's spoilt and decoratively genteel first wife, Dora (dog and mistress even dying at the same time), to his aunt Betsey's phobia of donkeys (and men), and the ubiquity of horses and animal imagery and metaphors. Once removed from its customary blind spot, the place of animals in the work of human self-imaging becomes peculiarly and even disturbingly obvious. '[O]nce we have seen through our self-serving, anthropocentric thinking about other animals, we are and should be left disarmed, ill-equipped to calculate our proper response.'[21] However, a basic 'speciesism' is so fundamental and all-pervasive that it is still hard to imagine what society would be like without it. A critic can ask 'What would *War and Peace* be without horses?', but then what?

Twelfth quandary: reading the animal as 'construct'

Do some methods of argument dominant in the modern humanities make a crude speciesism inevitable? Take the familiar method of analysing a text by mapping out representations – of flowers, of animals, of the landscape – in terms of how they project and negotiate the perceptions, values and interests of specific human groups. Thus Hindu conceptions of the cow may be compared to those of Maasai in East Africa, or US hunting culture examined through changing conceptions of the wolf. Clearly, however, animals cannot be thought of solely in this way: cows and wolves have interests of their own that transcend their image and status within any human culture.

A specific reading may illustrate the difficulty created by animal ethics for the dominant critical method of analysing how the cultural politics of differing human groups leads them to 'construct' the non-human realm in different ways. Lisa J. Kiser's 'Chaucer and the Politics of Nature' appears in the critical anthology *Beyond Nature Writing* (41–56). Geoffrey Chaucer's *Parliament of Fowls* (c. 1380), Kiser's concern, is a dream-vision poem in which the humanised and aristocratic figure 'Lady Nature' is pictured presiding over the mating rituals of a host of birds of various rank. She is especially and most favourably concerned with an aristocratic female eagle, faced by three eligible eagle suitors. Thus both the figure of Lady Nature and the birds, Kiser observes, are necessarily 'constructed' according to then available codes of human aristocratic privilege. Other birds, ranked according to their eating habits, appear in various 'lower-class' guises, their descriptions evidently modelled on human castes and stereotypes of Chaucer's time. As in other Chaucer texts, the subordinate voices are critical of the roles in which others put them. The courtly speeches of the eagle's three wooers are interrupted in various comic ways by the 'lesser' birds. This brings us to the crucial point of Kiser's argument. Chaucer, she argues, is unusually aware, in using these socially derived constructions of birds, that they are just that:

> What is remarkable about Chaucer's poem, however, is that its author seems to know all about his complicity in the practice of social construction and to want to signal this knowledge to his wisest readers . . . Chaucer reminds us forcefully that there is indeed a nonhuman world, one that lies unrepresented in his poem, for readers to contemplate.   47–9

Kiser is proposing that Chaucer's caricatures of birds invite an ironic reading, as a self-mocking rhetorical strategy:

> By aggressively appropriating the nonhuman world in his representation of it, and ensuring that his readers notice this act of appropriation, Chaucer suggests that there is a natural world outside the parameters of his artistic colonization, one that has been silenced and suppressed and about which he has no authority to write.   50

This leads towards the conclusion that Chaucer anticipates 'an issue that has preoccupied modern ecological critics', namely, 'of the extent to which it is philosophically sound (and politically justifiable) to insist on extreme social constructivism as the basis on which to ground one's views of the environment' (50).

Without going on to offer an actual alternative to cultural constructivism, Kiser's essay effectively highlights the inherent anthropocentricism of currently dominant modes of reading, the now standard assumption that all human representations are instrumental modes of cultural 'construction'. In fact, the only recourse for any critical essay aspiring to a non-human viewpoint but following such assumptions would be the kind of irony Kiser claims to find in Chaucer, that is, representations that stage their own artificiality but can say nothing about the non-human as such.[22]

Once again, environmental criticism seems poised on the difficult intellectual question of how to conceptualise non-human agency. As the inhabitant of undeniably real worlds, alien to us and not fully comprehensible, the animal's gaze into the human realm may seem profoundly to shake it, refusing it the illusion of totality or of self-evidence in its modes of coherence.[23]

Anthropomorphism

Anthropomorphism, the concept seems easy, even self-evident. Anthropomorphism is 'the attribution [usually falsely] of a human form or personality to a god, animal, or thing' (*Illustrated Oxford Dictionary*). The issue has recurred at key points in this book. It related to what may be the inherently anthropocentric nature of human language, projecting as it does a world usually understood according to our own scale, dimensions, interests and desires (see Third Quandary in Chapter 4). Alternatively, language that may seem problematically figurative or 'merely anthropomorphic' can also acquire provocative value as a way of doing justice to the agency of the non-human, as in Haraway's naming nature 'coyote' or even Cheney's talk of the 'watchfulness' of rocks. Finally, in this last chapter the category of 'anthropomorphism' is considered in relation to ethical questions of the just representation of the non-human. The issue of 'anthropomorphism', positioned on the hazy borderlines between human and non-human, can become a powerful tool for questioning the complacency of dominant human self-conceptions.

As a simple example of anthropomorphism, in parts of Jack London's *The Call of the Wild* it remains all too obvious that the hero, the dog 'Buck', is essentially a compound of still human traits, for all London's efforts. When he is new as a sledge dog and unfamiliar with snow, Buck is puzzled that the other dogs seem suddenly to disappear when it is time to sleep – in fact they have dug themselves for shelter under the snow. Incongruously, like the surrogate human being he really is, Buck cannot scent the other dogs, but he must wander about using his eyes to locate them: 'To his astonishment [his team-mates] had disappeared. Again he wandered about through the great camp, looking for them, and again he returned. Were they in the tent? No, that could not be, else he would not have been driven out. Then where could they possibly be?'[1] The question raised by such anthropomorphism is this:

how on earth can one represent an animal in ways that do justice to its own perceptions and interests? At one extreme, there are those who maintain that any anthropomorphism is simply a category mistake, that is, to attribute pride to a dog is like attributing colour to a mathematical equation. This view, however, only assumes in advance what ought to be at issue, an absolute and impermeable difference between the human and the rest. So extreme a position would also delegitimise almost all references to animal life in human speech. More reasonably, anthropomorphism could mean the undue ascription of human qualities to a non-human animal, for example, accusing a garden snail of religious heresy. Nevertheless, this would still leave a whole range of creatures and situations for which 'anthropomorphism' would need to float as a term of uncertain and perhaps undecidable status, as in the claim that a sparrow 'enjoys' its dust bath.

Given that all human representations project a human measure of some sort, it soon becomes debatable where 'anthropomorphism' stops (as was demonstrated by controversies about the so-called 'selfish' gene). All human knowledge must needs be anthropomorphic in some way. Beyond that, is a question like 'Why does the universe exist?' anthropomorphic, or not? It would be nice to know.

In Chapter 3 Eileen Crist's work was used to show how even seemingly trivial choices of language project totally different conceptions of an animal's nature. Is there a simple opposite to anthropomorphism? To return to *The Call of the Wild*, to say that Buck 'scented out' his colleagues would be an improvement but would also demand a more difficult act of imagination for the human reader, conveyed into a canine world without colour, without human language but where scents form strong and complex messages. Then the writing would need to confront the issue of how to render a canine thought process (how plausible is London's 'Then where could they possibly be?'?). Sustained writing of this kind would require subtle shifts in reference in some words ('high' for a dog is not 'high' for a horse) and a total redefinition of others ('delicious' for a dog is rarely 'delicious' for a human being), as well as somehow addressing the question of anthropomorphism in the nature of syntax, with its built-in models of coherence, sequencing and causation.

Crist nevertheless defends anthropomorphism as a genuine source of understanding: 'in the hands of impeccable observers of animals the anthropomorphic perspective deserves serious attention, for it discloses the nature of animal life with the power and internal cohesion that real worlds possess' (*Images of Animals*, 7). She believes that scientific evidence for the commonality of humans and other animals gives credit to anthropomorphism as a

Figure 16 Animal trails (Pavel Konovalov)

pragmatic shortcut for understanding animal life. Darwin himself saw emotion and mind in both animals and humans not as secret interior states but as legibly enacted in features and behaviour: we just recognise when bees are 'angry' or when a dog is 'happy'.[2] Stephen Mithen argues that with the evolution of more fluid cognitive abilities, anthropomorphic thinking in the first modern humans led to far greater success in hunting, that projecting intentions, fears and so on on to prey helped people to anticipate it with a success that would have seemed magical to other hominid species.[3] However, to ascribe to anthropomorphic accounts 'the power and internal cohesion that real worlds possess' (Crist) may itself rest on an appeal to norms of self-evident narrative coherence and continuity of sense that might not always apply. Crist's own study included the deceptive case of the *Sphex* wasp, an insect whose seemingly planned actions become on analysis more akin to a set of built-in responses to stimuli.

Another issue with anthropomorphism is this. To describe a specific representation as 'anthropomorphic' necessarily makes certain assumptions about what human nature itself *is* in the first place: for example, that certain qualities are definitively human ones, whether also then attributed to other creatures or not. For instance, the legal tradition crucial for some advocates of animal rights is based on a set of specific presuppositions about supposedly incontestable human properties, a norm of the rights-holding person as both rational, self-interested and individual. This norm, however, is vulnerable to claims that it not only 'anthropomorphises' the non-human but also misconstrues the human by taking a specific western, individualist image of what a person is and then identifying it with human beings in general. For Heidegger[4] or for post-humanist thinkers, anthropomorphism becomes turned back on itself as the question of what a human being is.

In sum, questions of anthropomorphism in representations of the non-human open a decisive space in which several difficult issues – about the nature of other animals, of language, of the human – intersect in fascinating, provocative and perhaps ultimately irresolvable ways.

An art of animal interpretation

Cary Wolfe's approach is primarily to deconstruct unexamined assumptions about the human as these surreptitiously govern readings of animals in literature and film. However, a great many primary texts about animals fall outside such a remit. These are texts in which the animal in itself is already the explicit subject. Literary studies of animal species are not uncommon and often are very popular. Examples are Barry Lopez's *Of Wolves and Men*, John A. Baker's *The Peregrine* (1967), Diane Ackerman's essays in *The Moon by Whale Light* (1991) or Richard Mabey's *Book of Nightingales* (1997).[5] Such books typically blend details of natural history, anecdotes about behaviour, travelogue (the writer's own quest for the animal), interviews with naturalists, the history of various human attitudes to the creature, its cultural and religious associations. These works of hybrid genre admit of various kinds of reading, but one element in them remains distinctive and specific. This is the practice of a novel mode of interpretative art (an 'animal hermeneutics'?) that attempts to shape human language to express the specific life world of another species.

Writing that attempts an imaginary identification across the species barrier forms a beguiling and under-recognised practice. It is as if writers were taking up the supposedly impossible challenge of Thomas Nagel's famous article, 'What Is It Like To Be A Bat?'[6] Against the increasing appropriation of animals as images in the human environment, such literature strives to do justice to the non-human as an agent in its own right, pushing against the inherent anthropocentrism of inherited language towards a partial if always problematic overlapping of life worlds. Few projects in the arts of language are perhaps more difficult to judge, nor is there yet much discussion of why many people find such writing compelling, despite its seeming lack of 'human interest'.

The challenge is that of an art of language that conveys a creature's 'environment' in a phenomenological or hermeneutic sense, that is, as a field of significance or network of meaning within which a creature experiences and orients itself. Lopez, influenced by the controversial thinking of Jakob von Uexküll,[7] writes of the 'self-world' of an animal. Human attempts to understand an animal's world might also draw on Kalevi Kull and Peeter Torop's work on '*biotranslation*', describing the correspondence achieved between the signs in the world of one organism with those in another, as different species of bird understand others' alarm calls.[8]

One of the best considerations of the 'what is it like to be . . . ?' question is by Stephen W. Laycock ('The Animal *as* Animal: A Plea for Open Conceptuality').[9] The cognitive and ethical challenge here is that the quality of animal subjectivity and hence the question of anthropomorphism are fundamentally undecidable. 'I cannot know whether the "terror" and "suffering" exhibited by a wounded deer are authentic expressions of an inaccessible subjectivity or my own projection' (275). However, this undecidability is not, for Laycock, a problem to be wished away in favour of some objective answer. The most authentic way to approach a mystery is not to seek, vainly, to dispel it, but to become more open to its resistance and challenge:

> 'What is it like . . . ?', the openness to alterity in its own terms, not in ours, even if this openness can only suspend itself before a voiceless enigma, is at least innocent of the substitution of metaphysics for mystery . . . Mystery surrounds us. It is an index to the conceptual inviolability of the animate Other.   281

Laycock's argument offers a way of conceptualising and perhaps evaluating writings on animals like those of Lopez and others, this strange and largely unstudied element of literature. To take an example from Victorian 'nature writing', Richard Jefferies's essay 'Swallow-Time' (1889) offers a peculiar blend of personal observation, hackneyed association ('Now the swallows are, of all others, the summer birds')[10] and, yet, also passages of sustained prose poetry on the flight of the swallow. Jefferies offers several pages simply celebrating the flight of a bird, with apparently no further attempt to give it significance or make some more general point relevant to human life. The very fact that the essay ends lamely, with a sentence precisely trying to make such a connection (124), shows how far the writing was from needing such a flat gesture of closure:

> It is when they fly low, but just missing the grass, that their wonderful powers of flight appear . . . Imagine shooting an arrow from the strongest bow in such a way that it might travel about seven inches above the ground – how far would it go before it stuck a tall buttercup, a wiry bennet, or stick into a slight rise of the turf? You must imagine it given the power to rise over hedges, to make short angles about buildings, slip between the trunks of trees, to avoid moving objects, as men and animals, not to come in contact with other animated arrows, and by some mysterious instinct to know what is or what is not out of sight on the other side of the wall. I was sitting on a log in the narrowest

> of lanes, a hedge at the back, in front thick fir trees, whose boughs
> touched the ground, almost within reach, the lane being nothing more
> than a broader footpath . . . Suddenly a swallow slid by me as it seemed
> underneath my very hands, so close to the ground that he almost
> travelled in the rut, the least movement on my part would have stopped
> him. Almost before I could lift my head he had reached the end of the
> lane and rose over the gate into the road – not a moment's pause before
> he made that leap over the gate to see if there was a waggon or not in the
> way . . .   119–20

The passage enacts an 'openness to alterity in its own terms, not in ours', in
describing something that a human being cannot do or comprehend doing.
It is also the celebration of the virtuosity of bird flight. Analogies with post-
Victorian technologies are striking. The swallow is 'the perfection of a machine
for falling' (120). 'He does not fall perpendicularly, the angle of his fall is
prolonged and very low, and the swifter he goes the more nearly it approximates
to the horizontal' (122). Jefferies's passage, written a couple of decades before
cinema, also shows how animal writing anticipated what the philosopher Gilles
Deleuze saw as the philosophical challenge of film, a fascination with modes
of seeing other than those of an embodied human eye and which may explore
unknown modes of experiencing time and space.[11] When purists attack the
use of time-lapse photography or slow motion in films of animal behaviour,
they are perhaps missing a deeper point: that the speed with which the world
happens for a human being need not be a norm.

John Simons writes of texts in which the narrative focalisation shifts to the
point of view of a non-human:

> It is not only characters that are transformed but also the very world
> of the text. As we shift from a fictive world entirely organized around
> human perspectives to one in which non-human perspectives also have
> their place, we also shift in our ability to account for literary language
> and the strategies through which it structures our perceptions by
> offering a representational matrix which is, potentially at least, complete
> in itself.[12]

The animal not only disrupts an anthropocentric point of view but breaks
the illusion of a seemingly closed human horizon, the familiarity of given significances, dimensions. It 'offers a transgressive route not only across species
boundaries, but also between the closed formal universe of the linguistic arte-
fact and into the material world in which it exists'.[13]

Another way of thinking about such writing would be through the work
of Deleuze and Felix Guattari, important as instigators of post-humanist

thinking and a common reference in what criticism there is in relation to non-human animals.[14] In *A Thousand Plateaus* (1980) they offer a concept of a 'becoming animal'.[15] Linguistic experiment or virtuosity of the kind found in Jefferies or Woolf's *The Waves* can be seen as a letting go of the illusory fixity of the conventionally human standpoint and a becoming open to otherwise unimagined modes of perception and sense. One might even want to develop this perspective further to risk the objection that the swallow in Jefferies's essay is still being thought too anthropomorphically, that is, as a unified self-relating subjective agent to which events happen in narrative sequence or which is depicted as the consistent central wielder of certain abilities and skills. Might it be a matter of writing not 'he...reached the end of the lane and rose over the gate into the road – not a moment's pause before he had made the leap over the gate to see if there was a wagon or not in the way' but somehow of a multiple happening of relations in which definitive concepts of 'lane' and 'gate' do not exist, but instead a transitory and changing constellation of percepts, hunger and muscular flexing, metamorphosing itself as a variously focussed assemblage of co-ordinations and impulses? In sum, animal writing of this kind raises questions of anthropomorphism and its contestation that render the text a space of identification between human and non-human while also pushing its reader into a questioning of the even the most basic and assumed categories of sense-making and self-conception.

Deleuze and Guattari's post-humanism helps answer Dana Phillips's attack on environmentalist writing as working within an essentially romantic tradition in which identification with other creatures is just material for a cult of heightened personal experience, of escape into forms of psychic epiphany.[16] Nevertheless, Deleuze and Guattari also seem vulnerable to Haraway's critique that their notion of 'becoming animal' is a concept primarily designed to undo humanist conceptions of human sovereignty and superiority – there is little real interest in animals as such. That their interest remains fixated on questions of the human is clear in assertions that show little actual knowledge of non-humans, the showy and inaccurate claim, for instance, that all 'animals are packs'.[17]

A reading: *The Wind in the Pylons*

The issue of anthropomorphism poses the question of animal experience in all its power and ambivalence. It can be at once a mode of understanding non-human animals, a profound barrier to such understanding, a mode of

Figure 17 *The Wind in the Pylons* (Brill Books)

appropriating of animal otherness or a term that rebounds into the open question of what the human actually is. Finally, in the tension between these views, anthropomorphism in literary texts may enact an ethical and cognitive challenge to re-evaluate the bases of modern society. The non-human effects both a defamiliarisation of human perception, an undermining of 'speciesism' and a potentially revolutionary ethical appeal against the brutal human tyranny over the animal kingdom.

A look at Gareth Lovett Jones's *The Wind in the Pylons* (vol. I, 2003) can further open up some of these points. *The Wind in the Pylons* is a sequel to the Edwardian children's classic, Kenneth Grahame's *The Wind in the Willows* (1908). In it the figure of Grahame's Edwardian mole suddenly pops up one spring into a 1990s English landscape next to a six-lane motorway. Bewildered, he later finds himself caught up in a raid on a chicken prison camp led by 'the badger' and the Animal Restoration Front. A slogan is painted, 'These are also Animals / Remember / ARF'. The following exchange then takes place concerning the mole's acquaintance with some powerful corporate executives in the City:

Figure 18 Animal trails (Pavel Konovalov)

[Badger] 'With just a bit of persuasion you could become a mole for us. I mean – you understand – at Toad Transoceanic' . . .
[Mole] 'But I am . . . I am a mole.'
[Badger] 'Yes but I mean, a *mole*. An *underground animal*.'
'Ah. O.' The mole hesitated, thinking very hard. 'Surely, surely, the Badger could not be mad too.'[18]

Most of *The Wind in the Pylons* is what Simons terms 'trivial anthropomorphism': that is, the characters are essentially all types of human being, as in Jones's description of modern industrial society as a world dominated by 'weasels'. As in *The Wind in the Willows*, the very name 'weasel' draws on its use as an insult for a certain type of person and then projects these characteristics back upon the original mustelids. No fox is a major character in the original, but it is easy to imagine what kind of personality it would have if there were. Where Jones's version differs from Grahame's is, of course, in its satirical and even loathing account of modern Britain, depicted through the mole's inexhaustible horror at so brutally instrumentalised a landscape. The perspective is primarily environmental rather than an exercise in nostalgia for Grahame's earlier idealisation of the Edwardian society of the river.

Jones's weak anthropomorphism produces a curious paradox: that to make his fictional world coherent the book has to reinvent or reintroduce a human–animal distinction into it.[19] A distinction becomes necessary between those animals which, like all the main characters, have clothing and speak, and those that do not (see 208–9), like the wild fox the mole encounters being chased by a hunt (Jones underplays there what ought to be the bizarre image of a toad and a weasel hunting on horseback). This is in some ways a necessity of the narrative – no fully coherent parallel world can be invented without some 'animals' in it.

However, the redefinition of the human–animal distinction in terms of two kinds of animal also makes for some provocative conceptual transgressions, as in the slogan of the Animal Restoration Front ('These are also Animals / Remember / ARF').[20] At such times, though primarily a satire on modern capitalism, Jones's book achieves a genuinely non-human perspective, more like what Simons terms 'strong anthropomorphism': 'a category of representation which deals with animals as if they were humans but does it in such a way as either to show how the non-human experience differs from the human or to create profound questions in the reader's mind as to the extent to which humans and non-humans are really different' (120). Jones's satire redeploys the way the animal world has always offered a source of tropes for human cultures. Nevertheless, apart from the scene in which the ARF liberate the egg factory of chickens, Jones does not take much interest in one crucial feature of modern speciesism, the industrial mass production of sentient creatures for slaughter. The rescued chickens are given the voices of bewildered and institutionalised creatures who have taken their dark shed to be the whole universe, but Jones does not take up the challenge of actually depicting an abattoir. Such a scene would needs have shown scores of talking animals being shunted and forced through a conveyor belt to be killed by other talking animals.

Chapter 20

The future of ecocriticism

Since it emerged as a self-conscious movement in the 1990s, ecocriticism has transformed itself from a relatively minor body of work characterised mainly by a close relationship to environmental non-fiction, into a plural school with practitioners across the world, both vastly extending its scope and reconsidering its basic concepts.

Looking over the body of environmental literary criticism as a whole, it is still hard to see any specific 'ecocritical' method emerging. Instead, the issues are taking the more challenging form of a general uncertainty and revision of intellectual boundaries. The limitations as well as the excitement of ecocritical work to date may reflect the fact that environmental questions are not just a matter of aesthetics, politics, poetics or ethics, but can affect certain ground rules as to what these things mean. Who would have thought, even recently, that flicking off a light switch could become part of a new virtue ethic?

Above all, the crucial term *nature* is being questioned in some senses and reaffirmed in others. *Nature* and the *natural* cannot now convincingly function as self-validating norms underwriting a romantic, anti-modern politics or as the self-evidently desirable other of the artificial or the cultural. Instead, environmental criticism is increasingly coming to affirm a more explicitly amoral 'nature', in the sense of the wild, *physis*, coyote, that which is not a matter of human control or calculation. Far from being the sacral spectacle of some wilderness preserve or the object of various human 'constructions', this is nature acknowledged as an agent in own right, capricious, awesome and easily capable of wiping humanity off the face of the earth.

Final brief quandary: what place environmental criticism in the modern 'University of Excellence'?

David Orr sets out the challenge:

> The plain fact is that the planet does not need more successful people.[1]

Anyone who has worked through this book to this point will realise that one issue is to understand anew and differently what is meant by 'success'.

The main future challenge for ecocriticism may lie in the way environmental questions will continue to resist inherited structures of thought and are uncontainable within the competence of any one intellectual discipline. Donna Haraway's example of a genuinely plural interdisciplinary competence is an exciting but also forbidding model. Environmental issues can question the supposed cultural neutrality of scientific institutions like no other, but without yet being able to set up widely accepted alternative norms of intellectual authority. Bruno Latour writes: 'We are not witnessing the emergence of questions about nature in political debates, but the progressive transformation of all matters of fact into disputed states of affair' (*Politics of Nature*, 24–5).

Another thing stands out, the almost bewildering diversity of issues and problems that can be labelled *environmental*, a term perpetually in danger of dissolving. A sceptic might ask: what real relationship is there between a campaign to reduce the toxicity of a pesticide, efforts to 'green' an urban ghetto, advocacy of wind farms instead of nuclear power, and work to preserve threatened species of frog in Costa Rica? Is 'environmentalism' just an unhelpfully singular term for a host of diverse and even incompatible arguments and issues? The 'environment', after all, is, ultimately, 'everything'. On the other hand, the unprecedented challenge of things like climate change or overpopulation – issues at the same time of morality, ethics, biology, 'animal rights', statistics, geography and politics – may be the need, literally, to think everything, even to think everything at once. Anticipating the daunting but exciting kinds of literacy essential in the centuries to come, ecocriticism offers its emerging and still faltering voice.

Notes

Introduction

1 Ulrich Beck, *World Risk Society* (Cambridge, MA: Polity, 1998), 119.
2 Robert J. Brulle, *Agency, Democracy, and Nature: The US Environmental Movement from a Critical Theory Perspective* (Cambridge, MA: MIT Press, 2000), 48.
3 Lynn White Jr, 'The Historical Roots of our Ecologic Crisis', in Cheryll Glotfelty and Harold Fromm (eds.), *The Ecocriticism Reader: Landmarks in Literary Ecology* (Athens: University of Georgia Press, 1996), 3–14.
4 Brulle, *Agency, Democracy*, 48.
5 Murray Bookchin, *The Ecology of Freedom: The Emergence and Dissolution of Hierarchy* (1982; Edinburgh: AK Press, 2005), 34.
6 Raymond Williams, *The Country and the City* (1973; London: Hogarth, 1993).
7 See www.asle.org/
8 Sylvia Bowerbank, *Speaking for Nature: Women and Ecologies of Early Modern England* (Baltimore, MD: Johns Hopkins University Press, 2004); Alice Jenkins, 'Alexander von Humboldt's *Kosmos* and the Beginnings of Ecocriticism', *ISLE* 14.2 (summer 2007): 89–105; Angela Wilde, 'Challenging the Confines: Haiku from the Prison Camps', in Annie Merril Ingram et al. (eds.), *Coming into Contact: Explorations in Ecocritical Theory and Practice* (Athens: University of Georgia Press, 2007), 39–57.
9 Henry D. Thoreau, *Walden and Resistance to Civil Government*, ed. William Rossi, Norton Critical Edition, 2nd edn (New York: Norton, 1992), 216.
10 Peter Brand with Michael J. Thomas, *Urban Environmentalism: Global Change and the Mediation of Local Conflict* (London: Routledge, 2005), 104.
11 Timothy W. Luke, *Ecocritique: Contesting the Politics of Nature, Economy, and Culture* (Minneapolis: University of Minnesota Press, 1997), 195.
12 Raymond Williams, *Keywords* (London: Flamingo, 1993), 176.
13 David W. Orr, *Earth in Mind: On Education, Environment, and the Human Prospect* (1994; Washington, DC: Island Press, 2004), 56.
14 Bruno Latour, *Politics of Nature: How to Bring the Sciences into Democracy*, trans. Catherine Porter (Cambridge, MA: Harvard University Press, 2004), 28.
15 Michael P. Cohen, 'Blues in the Green: Ecocriticism under Critique', *Environmental History* 9.1 (January 2004), www.historycooperative.org/journals/eh/9.1/cohen.html

16 Henry Williamson, *The Lone Swallows* (1933; Gloucester: Alan Sutton, 1984), 51.

17 Ibid., 165.

18 Roger Deakin, *Wildwood: A Journey Through Trees* (London: Hamish Hamilton, 2007), xiii.

19 Kofi Annan, 'Climate Cost Made Clear', *New Scientist*, 6 June 2009, 6.

20 For a sober overview of likely scenarios see Mark Lynas, *Six Degrees: Our Future on a Hotter Planet* (London: Harper Perennial, 2008).

21 James Lovelock, 'We're doomed but it's not all bad', interview with James Lovelock, *New Scientist*, 24 January 2009, 30–1.

22 Ken Hiltner, 'Renaissance Literature and our Contemporary Attitude toward Global Warming', *ISLE* 16 (2009): 429–41, 436.

Romantic and anti-romantic

1 Jonathan Bate, *Romantic Ecology: Wordsworth and the Environmental Tradition* (London: Routledge, 1991), 9.

2 Robert Kirkham, 'The Problem of Knowledge in Environmental Thought: A Counterchallenge', in Roger S. Gottlieb (ed.), *The Ecological Community: Environmental Challenges for Philosophy, Politics and Morality* (London: Routledge, 1997), 193–207, 194.

3 Timothy Morton, 'Environmentalism', in Nicholas Roe (ed.), *Romanticism: An Oxford Guide* (Oxford University Press, 2004), 696–707.

1 Old world romanticism

1 See also Karl Kroeber, *Ecological Literary Criticism: Romantic Imagining and the Biology of Mind* (New York: Columbia University Press, 1994); Jonathan Bate (ed.), *Green Romanticism*, special issue of *Studies in Romanticism* 35.3 (1996).

2 Bate's Wordsworthianism is, however, only one major strand of ecocritical readings of the Romantics. See Further Reading for this chapter. Greg Garrard argues that it is an attention to the very instability of the nature–culture distinction that marked romanticism as proto-ecological, 'Radical Pastoral', *Studies in Romanticism* 35.3 (1996): 33–58.

3 From Appendix, Jonathan Wordsworth, *William Wordsworth: The Borders of Vision* (Oxford: Clarendon, 1982), 390–415, 401.

4 Bate, *Romantic Ecology*, 51.

5 John Ruskin, *On Art and Life* (1853; Harmondsworth: Penguin, 2004), 32.

6 Lewis Mumford, 'Let Man Take Command', *Saturday Review of Literature*, 2 October 1948, 35.

7 William Morris, 'The Society of the Future' (1887), quoted in Fiona McCarthy, *William Morris: A Life for Our Time* (London: Faber & Faber, 2003), 546. 'Nature', wrote Georg Lukacs, means 'the true essence of man liberated from the false,

mechanizing forms of society: man as perfected whole' (*History and Class Consciousness* [Cambridge, MA: MIT Press, 1971], 136). The Frankfurt School Marxist Herbert Marcuse also appeals to an implicit norm of human 'wholeness', drawing upon psychoanalysis in his call for non-repressive forms of work and the transformation of society that would ensue from a non-instrumental and even erotic relation to the natural world. Such a change would be a 'synthesis, reassembling the bits and fragments of a distorted humanity and distorted nature', *Counterrevolution and Revolt* (Boston, MA: Beacon, 1972), 70.

8 Morris, 'Society of the Future', quoted McCarthy, *William Morris*, 546.

9 Derek Ratcliffe, *Lakeland* (London: HarperCollins, 2002), 31.

10 See John Simons, *Animal Rights and the Politics of Literary Representation* (Basingstoke: Palgrave, 2002), 87–96; Chen Hong, 'To Set the Wild Free: Changing Images of Animals in English Poetry of the Pre-Romantic and Romantic Periods', *ISLE* 13.2 (summer 2006): 129–49.

11 Jim Cheney, 'Universal Consideration: An Epistemological Map of the Terrain', *Environmental Ethics* 20 (1998): 265–77.

12 David Kidner, 'Culture and the Unconscious in Environmental Theory', *Environmental Ethics* 20 (1998): 61–80, 79.

13 Jonathan Bate, *The Song of the Earth* (London: Picador, 2000), 64.

14 See J. Scott Bryson (ed.), *Ecopoetry: A Critical Introduction* (Salt Lake City: University of Utah Press, 2002), 77–87.

15 Geoffrey Summerfield (ed.), *Selected Poems* (Harmondsworth: Penguin, 1990), 172–8, 173, 175.

16 Timothy Morton, 'John Clare's Dark Ecology', *Studies in Romanticism* 47 (2008): 179–93, 191.

17 Crucial essays by Naess and others are collected in George Sessions (ed.), *Deep Ecology for the 21st Century: Readings on the Philosophy and Practice of the New Environmentalism* (Boston and London: Shambhala, 1995), 64–84, 80.

18 See Knut A. Jacobsen, 'Bhagavadgita, Ecosophy T, and Deep Ecology', and Deane Curtin, 'A State of Mind like Water: Ecosophy T and the Buddhist Traditions', in Eric Katz, Andrew Light and David Rothenberg (eds.), *Beneath the Surface: Critical Essays in the Philosophy of Deep Ecology* (Cambridge, MA: MIT Press, 2000), 231–52, 253–68.

19 Sessions (ed.), *Deep Ecology for the 21st Century*, 49–53.

20 *The Complete Works of P. B. Shelley*, ed. Roger Ingpen and Walter Edwin Peck, 10 vols. (London: Ernest Benn, 1926–60), VI, 299–306, 303.

21 Luke, *Ecocritique*, 24.

2 New world romanticism

1 Gretel Ehrlich, *The Solace of Open Spaces* (Harmondsworth: Penguin, 1986), 2.

2 Eric Kaufmann, '"Naturalizing the nation": The Rise of Naturalistic Nationalism in the United States and Canada', *Comparative Studies in Society and History* 40 (1998): 666–95, 668.

3 Adrian Franklin, *Animal Nation: The True Story of Animals and Australia* (Sydney: University of New South Wales Press, 2006), 131.

4 Michael L. Johnson, *Hunger for the Wild: America's Obsession with the Untamed West* (Lawrence: University Press of Kansas, 2007), 144.

5 See Daniel J. Philippon, *Conserving Words: How American Nature Writers Shaped the Environmental Movement* (Athens: University of Georgia Press, 2004).

6 Edward Abbey, *Down the River* (1982; New York: Penguin, 1991), 88.

7 Randall Roorda, *Dramas of Solitude: Narratives of Retreat in American Nature Writing* (Albany: SUNY Press, 1998), xiii.

8 Lawrence Buell, *The Environmental Imagination: Thoreau, Nature Writing, and the Formation of American Culture* (Cambridge, MA: Harvard University Press, 1995).

9 Vincent Serventy, *Dryandra: The Story of an Australian Forest* (Sydney: A. H. and A. W. Reed, 1970).

10 Cited in Martin Mulligan and Stuart Hill, *Ecological Pioneers: A Social History of Australian Ecological Thought and Action* (Cambridge University Press, 2001), 129. See also Nick Drayson, 'Early Perceptions of the Natural History of Australia in Popular Literature', in Patrick D. Murphy (ed.), *Literature of Nature: An International Sourcebook* (Chicago: Fitzroy Dearborn, 1998), 264–9.

11 See Harold Alderman, 'Abbey as Anarchist', in Peter Quigley (ed.), *Coyote in the Maze: Tracking Edward Abbey in a World of Words* (Salt Lake City: University of Utah Press, 1998), 137–49.

12 Edward Abbey, *Desert Solitaire: A Season in the Wilderness* (New York: Simon & Schuster, 1968), 191.

13 *The Journey Home* (New York: Dutton, 1977), 88.

14 Mulligan and Hill, *Ecological Pioneers*, 72–111.

15 Kathryn Morse, 'Putting History at the Core: History and Literature in Environmental Studies', *History Teacher* 37 (2003): 67–72, 69. An anti-romantic gesture informs Morse's alternative recommended reading list. Some titles she cites (69) may speak for themselves: Alfred Crosby, *Environmental Imperialism*, Elinor Melville, *A Plague of Sheep*, Charles Rosenberg, *The Cholera Years*, Donald Worster, *Dust Bowl*. For a recent critique of the romanticism of some American nature writing, and its denigration of the value of work in the land, such as farming, see William Major, 'The Agrarian Vision and Ecocriticism', *ISLE* 14.2 (summer 2007): 51–70.

16 Jane Bennett, *Thoreau's Nature: Ethics, Politics, and the Wild* (Lanham, MD: Rowman & Littlefield, 2002), 81.

17 Ibid., 83.

18 Philip Abbot, 'Henry David Thoreau, "The State of Nature, and the Redemption of Liberalism"', *Journal of Politics* 47.1 (1985): 182–208, 184.

19 Jane Bennett observes: 'Thoreau's vision of an inward life denies, at least rhetorically, that the conceptual content of "conscience" and "genius" is itself a social or cultural production' ('On Being a Native: Thoreau's Hermeneutics of Self', *Polity* 22.4 [summer 1990]: 559–80, 561).

20 Robert Sattelmeyer, 'The Remaking of *Walden*', in Rossi (ed.), *Walden*, Norton Critical Edition, 428–44, 436.

21 Bennett, *Thoreau's Nature*, xxviii.
22 Henry D. Thoreau, 'Walking', in *Collected Essays and Poems* (New York: Literary Classics of the United States, 2001), 225–55, 239.
23 Linck C. Johnson, '*A Week on the Concord and Merrimack Rivers*', in Joel Myron (ed.), *The Cambridge Companion to Henry David Thoreau* (Cambridge University Press, 1995), 40–56, 47.
24 Lawrence Buell, 'Thoreau and the Natural Environment', ibid., 171–93, 192.
25 Sharon Cameron, *Writing Nature: Henry Thoreau's Journal* (University of Chicago Press, 1985), 78.
26 Henry D. Thoreau, *Journal*, vol. III, 1848–51, ed. Robert Sattelmeyer, Mark R. Patterson and William Rossi (Princeton University Press, 1990), 151.
27 Leonard N. Neufeldt, 'Thoreau in his Journal', in Myron (ed.), *Cambridge Companion to Thoreau*, 107–23, 120.
28 Cameron, *Writing Nature*, 23.
29 David Rothenberg (ed.), *Wild Ideas* (Minneapolis: University of Minnesota Press, 1995); Gary Snyder, *The Practice of the Wild* (Washington, DC: Shoemaker Hoard, 1990); Richard Mabey, *Landlocked: In Pursuit of the Wild* (London: Sinclair-Stevenson, 1994).
30 Richard Mabey, *Nature Cure* (London: Chatto & Windus, 2005), 219.
31 Thoreau, 'Walking', 244.
32 Henry D. Thoreau, *A Week on the Concord and Merrimack Rivers*, ed. Carl F. Howe et al. (Princeton University Press, 1980), 304.

3 Genre and the question of non-fiction

1 Robert Root, 'Naming Nonfiction: A Polyptych', *College English* 65 (2003): 242–56, 245. For Root's own definition of non-fiction, see 255.
2 Barry Lopez, *Of Wolves and Men* (1978; New York: Scribner, 2004).
3 Terry Tempest Williams, *Desert Quartet: An Erotic Landscape* (New York: Pantheon, 1995).
4 Philip Garard, quoted in Lynn Z. Bloom, 'Living to Tell the Tale: The Complicated Ethics of Creative Nonfiction', *College English* 65.3 (2003): 276–89, 278.
5 For an overview of what writers have said about the essay as a form, see Carl H. Claus, 'Essayists on the Essay', in Chris Anderson (ed.), *Literary Nonfiction: Theory, Criticism, Pedagogy* (Carbondale: Southern Illinois University Press, 1989), 155–75.
6 Quoted ibid., 163. See Adorno's 'The Essay as Form' in vol. I of his *Notes to Literature*, trans. Sherry Weber Nicholson (New York: Columbia University Press, 1991).
7 Heather Dubrow, *Genre*, Critical Idiom Series (London: Methuen, 1982), 2.
8 See the clumsy historical overview that 'The Middle Ages were years of very deep frustration for human beings, caught in the twilight between the Dark Ages and the Renaissance. It was the time of the wolf. And anger that men felt over their circumstances, they heaped on wolves' (*Of Wolves and Men*, 228).

9 Ishimure Michiko, *Paradise in the Sea of Sorrow: Our Minamata Disaster*, trans. Livia Monnet (Tokyo: Yamaguchi, 1990).

10 Bloom, 'Living to Tell the Tale', 278.

11 For Dillard's inaccuracies and derivativeness see Donald Mitchell, 'Dancing with Nature', in Robert Pack and Jay Parini (eds.), *The Bread Loaf Anthology of Contemporary American Essays* (Hanover and London: University Press of New England, 1989).

12 Quoted in Roorda, *Dramas of Solitude*, 197.

13 Patrick D. Murphy, *Further Afield in the Study of Nature-Oriented Literature* (Charlottesville: University of Virginia Press, 2000), 10.

14 Timothy Morton, *Ecology without Nature: Rethinking Environmental Aesthetics* (Cambridge, MA: Harvard University Press, 2008), 111.

15 Dana Phillips, *The Truth of Ecology: Nature, Culture, and Literature in America* (Oxford University Press, 2003), 185ff.

16 John Burroughs, quoted in Frank Stewart, *A Natural History of Nature Writing* (Washington, DC: Island Press, 1995), 87.

17 From Lopez, 'Annotated Book List', in Daniel Halpern (ed.), *Antaeus: On Nature* (London: Collins Harvill, 1989), 295–7, 297.

18 Eileen Crist, *Images of Animals: Anthropomorphism and Animal Mind* (Philadelphia: Temple University Press, 1999).

19 E. M. Forster, *Aspects of the Novel* (1927; New York: Harcourt Brace World, 1955), 86.

20 Crist has chosen the very kind of wasp that had already led Douglas R. Hofstadter to coin the adjective 'sphexish' to describe apparently purposive behaviour that is revealed on investigation to be actually rigid and mechanical – for to deliberately interrupt the wasp's routine, no matter how many times, always makes it revert to an earlier stage and start again, however unnecessarily. See Hofstadter, *Metamagical Themas: Questing for the Essence of Mind and Pattern* (Harmondsworth: Penguin, Viking, 1985), 529.

21 Roorda, *Dramas of Solitude*, 14–15.

22 Mark Cocker, *A Tiger in the Sand: Selected Writings on Nature* (London: Jonathan Cape, 2006), 117.

4 Language beyond the human?

1 As an instance of such caricaturing see Leonard M. Scigaj, 'Contemporary Ecological and Environmental Poetry: *Différance* or *Référance*?', *ISLE* 3.2 (1996): 1–25. In fact, Derrida anticipated a crucial challenge in environmental criticism: 'Every week I receive critical commentaries and studies on deconstruction which operate on the assumption that what they call "poststructuralism" amounts to saying that there is nothing beyond language, that we are submerged in words – and other stupidities of that sort' ('Deconstruction and the Other', in Richard Kearney [ed.], *Dialogues*

with Contemporary Continental Thinkers [Manchester University Press, 1984], 123).
It is rather a matter of the challenge to language of 'The other, which is beyond
language and which summons language' (ibid.).

2 Michael E. Soulé and Gary Lease, *Reinventing Nature: Responses to Postmodern
Deconstruction* (Washington, DC: Island Press, 1995), xiii, xv.

3 See Claire Lawrence, '"Getting the desert into a book": Nature Writing and the
Problem of Representation in a Postmodern World', in Quigley (ed.), *Coyote in the
Maze*, 150–67.

4 Kate Soper, *What is Nature?* (Oxford: Blackwell, 1995), 151.

5 Buell, *Environmental Imagination*, 107.

6 Edouard Glissant, *Caribbean Discourse: Selected Essays*, trans. J. Michael Dash
(Charlottesville: University of Virginia Press, 1992), 145, see also 74, 105, 242.

7 Leslie Marmon Silko, 'Landscape, History and the Pueblo Imagination', in Halpern
(ed.), *Antaeus: On Nature*, 83–94, 85.

8 Phillips, *Truth of Ecology*, 18. Serpil Opperman criticizes those ecocritics whose
stress on realist conceptions of language leads them to caricature so-called 'post-
modernists' as reducing all issues to questions of textuality, supposedly asserting
that 'nature' is only a cultural signifier. He argues that environmental criticism can
be enriched by such critics' anti-dogmatic sensitivity to the multiple ways in which
nature is culturally framed and plural possibilities of interpretation ('Theorizing
Ecocriticism: Toward a Postmodern Ecocritical Practice', *ISLE* 13.2 [summer 2006]:
103–28).

9 Rebecca Raglon and Marian Sholtmejer, '"Animals are not believers in ecology":
Mapping Critical Differences Between Environmental and Animal Advocacy Literatures', *ISLE* 14.2 (2007): 121–40, 135.

10 David Abram, *The Spell of the Sensuous: Perception and Language in a more-than-
human World* (New York: Vintage, 1997), 40.

11 Carol H. Cantrell uses Merleau-Ponty to similar effect in '"The locus of compos-
sibility": Virginia Woolf, Modernism and Place', *ISLE* 5.2 (1998): 25–40. Arguably,
Abram romanticises the proto-language of bodily perception shared by all creatures, projecting a mainly benign and even celebratory life spirit, and not, as it
must be for so many, a realm including anger, puzzlement, trickery, deception and
terror.

12 '[W]riters who wrote in service to the more-than-human earth – from Rilke to
Rachel Carson, from John Muir to Jean Giono, from Wendell Berry to Barbara
Kingsover and Rick Bass', David Abram, 'Between the Body and the Breathing
Earth: A Reply to Ted Toadvine', *Environmental Ethics* 27 (2005): 171–90, 179.

13 David Brin, *Earth: A Novel* (London: Futura, 1990), 1.

14 See Snyder, *Practice of the Wild*.

15 Jacques Derrida, 'Eating Well: An Interview', in Eduardo Cadava et al. (eds.), *Who
Comes After the Subject?* (London: Routledge, 1991), 96–119, 116.

16 Cary Wolfe, 'In the Shadow of Wittgenstein's Lion', in Cary Wolfe (ed.), *Zoontologies*
(Minneapolis: University of Minnesota Press, 2003), 1–57, 35.

17 Snyder, *Practice of the Wild*, 121.
18 See also Val Plumwood's different defence of the rationality of ascribing purpose and intention even to non-sentient things, *Feminism and the Mastery of Nature* (London: Routledge, 1993), 131–40.
19 Snyder, *Practice of the Wild*, 100.

5 The inherent violence of western thought?

1 William McNeill (ed.), *Pathmarks* (1967; Cambridge University Press, 1998), 147.
2 Michael Zimmerman, *Heidegger's Confrontation with Modernity: Technology, Politics, Art* (Bloomington: Indiana University Press, 1990), 157.
3 McNeill (ed.), *Pathmarks*, 240.
4 Martin Heidegger, *Being and Time*, trans. John Macquarrie and Edward Robinson (Oxford: Basil Blackwell, 1980), 89.
5 Martin Heidegger, *Gesammtausgabe* 75 (Frankfurt-on-Main: Vittorio Klostermann, 2000), 260–1.
6 See especially 'On the Essence and Concept of *Physis* in Aristotle's Physics B, I', in McNeill (ed.), *Pathmarks*, 183–230.
7 'A subject... understands the presencing of a thing from itself with regard to the representedness [*Vorgestelltheit*]. Presence is understood as representedness. Thereby, presence is no longer taken as what is given by itself but only as how it is an object for me as the thinking subject, that is, how it is made an object over and against me' (Martin Heidegger, *Zollikon Seminars: Protocols, Conversations, Letters*, ed. Medard Boss, trans. Franz Mayr and Richard Askay [Evanston, IL: Northwestern University Press, 2001], 99).
8 Martin Heidegger, *Off the Beaten Track*, ed. and trans. Julian Young and Kenneth Haynes (Cambridge University Press, 2002), 1–56, 24–5.
9 Martin Heidegger, *Gesammtausgabe* 13 (Frankfurt-on-Main: Vittorio Klostermann, 1983), 75–86; translated as 'The Thinker as Poet' in Martin Heidegger, *Poetry, Language, Thought*, trans. Albert Hofstadter (New York: Harper & Row, 1971), 3–14. For a reading see my 'Can a Place Think?: On Adam Sharr's *Heidegger's Hut*', *Cultural Politics* 4.1 (March 2008): 100–21.
10 Martin Heidegger, *Hölderlin's Hymn 'The Ister'*, trans. William McNeill and Julia Davis (Indianapolis: Indiana University Press, 1993), 28.
11 Martin Heidegger, *Elucidations of Hölderlin's Poetry*, trans. Keith Hoeller (New York: Humanity Books, 2000).
12 Bate, *Song of the Earth*, 262.
13 Ibid., 206.
14 Martin Heidegger, *Vorträge und Aufsätze*, 3rd edn (Pfullingen: Neske, 1967), 99.
15 Quoted in Heidegger, *Elucidations*, 167.
16 Robert Pogue Harrison, *Forests: The Shadow of Civilization* (University of Chicago Press, 1992).

17 Harrison seems especially indebted to Heidegger's 'On the Essence and Concept of *Physis* in Aristotle's *Physics*'.

18 For both Harrison and Heidegger there would remain pressing questions as to whether the kind of access to the world they see as unique to human consciousness and language is not, in fact, experienced by other creatures in their ways. For a critique of Heidegger's exclusive privileging of the human, see Matthew Calarco, *Zoographies: The Question of the Animal from Heidegger to Derrida* (New York: Columbia University Press, 2008).

6 Post-humanism and the 'end of nature'?

1 Jacques Derrida, 'The Aforementioned so-called Human Genome', in *Negotiations: Interventions and Interviews 1971–2001*, trans. Elizabeth Rottenberg (Stanford University Press, 2002), 199–214, 204.

2 Ibid., 208. While defending a liberal humanist conception of human identity that many would certainly challenge, Francis Fukuyama expresses a similar anxiety. His concern is the possibility of a world in which notions of rights based on a shared and universally recognized human nature will have been lost: 'the posthuman world could be one that is far more hierarchical and competitive than the one that currently exists, and full of social conflict as a result. It could be one in which any notion of "shared humanity" is lost, because we have mixed human genes with those of so many other species that we no longer have a clear idea of what a human being is' (*Our Posthuman Future: Consequences of the Biotechnology Revolution* [New York: Farrar, Straus & Giroux, 2002], 218).

3 Slavoj Žižek, *In Defense of Lost Causes* (London: Verso, 2008), 435.

4 Catherine Waldby, *The Visible Human Project: Informatic Bodies and Posthuman Medicine* (London: Routledge, 2000), 43.

5 Teresa Heffernan, 'Bovine Anxieties, Virgin Births, and the Secret of Life', *Cultural Critique* 53 (winter 2003): 116–33, 128.

6 G. Bateson, *Steps to an Ecology of Mind: Collected Essays in Anthropology, Psychiatry, Evolution and Epistemology* (St Albans: Granada, 1973), 453.

7 Bernard Stiegler, *Technics and Time I: The Fault of Epimetheus*, trans. Richard Beardsworth (Stanford University Press, 1998).

8 John Lechte, 'The *Who* and the *What* of Writing in the Electronic Age', *Oxford Literary Review* 21 (1999): 135–60, 35.

9 Donna Haraway, 'A Manifesto for Cyborgs: Science, Technology, and Socialist Feminism in the 1980s', in *The Haraway Reader* (New York: Routledge, 2004), 7–45.

10 See Jon Turney, *Frankenstein's Footsteps: Science, Genetics and Popular Culture* (New Haven, CN: Yale University Press, 1998).

11 Morton, *Ecology without Nature*, 194.

12 Mary Shelley, *Frankenstein: or, The Modern Prometheus*, the 1818 text, ed. Marilyn Butler (Oxford University Press, 1994), 36.

13 Heffernan, 'Bovine Anxieties, Virgin Births', 131.

14 Cynthia Deitering, 'Toxic Consciousness in Fiction of the 1980s', in Glotfelty and Fromm (eds.), *Ecocriticism Reader*, 196–203, 197.

15 See Ursula K. Heise, *Sense of Place and Sense of Planet* (Oxford University Press, 2008), 178–203. Frederick Buell argues that the crisis of nature has become itself our habituated contemporary environment. In dystopian fiction and 'cyberpunk' such as William Gibson's *Neuromancer* (1984) or Bruce Sterling's *Schismatic* (1985) environmental apocalypse appears 'not as the end of everything but as a milieu people dwelt in as they moved out beyond the limits of nature' (*From Apocalypse to Way of Life: Environmental Crisis in the American Century* [New York: Routledge, 2004], 248).

16 Bill McKibben, *The End of Nature: Humanity, Climate Change and the Natural World* (1989; London: Bloomsbury, 2003).

17 Žižek, *In Defense of Lost Causes*, 442.

18 Franklin, *Animal Nation*, 236.

The boundaries of the political

1 Bob Pepperman Taylor, 'Environmental Ethics and Political Theory', *Polity* 23 (1991): 567–83, 567–70.

7 Thinking like a mountain?

1 J. Baird Callicott, 'The Land Aesthetic', in J. Baird Callicott (ed.), *A Companion to A Sand County Almanac: Interpretive and Critical Essays* (Madison: University of Wisconsin Press, 1987), 157–71, 157.

2 While Leopold's stance is generally read as straightforwardly biocentric, the issues are in fact more complicated. See Ben A. Minteer, *The Landscape of Reform: Civic Pragmatism and Environmental Thought in America* (Boston, MA: MIT Press, 2006), 115–52.

3 See McKay Jenkins, '"Thinking like a mountain": Death and Deep Ecology in the Work of Peter Matthiessen', in John Tallmadge and Henry Harrington (eds.), *Reading Under the Sign of Nature: New Essays in Ecocriticism* (Salt Lake City: University of Utah Press, 2000), 265–79.

4 See Dennis Ribben, 'The Making of *A Sand County Almanac*', in Callicott (ed.), *Companion*, 91–109, 104.

5 Buell, *Environmental Imagination*, 172.

6 Letter to Robert Marshall, 1 February 1935, quoted in Daniel J. Philippon, *Conserving Words: How American Nature Writers Shaped the Environmental Movement* (Athens: University of Georgia Press, 2005), 192.

7 Letter of 1936 to the editor of the *Journal of Forestry*, quoted in Philippon, *Conserving Words*, 198.

8 Callicott, 'Land Aesthetic', 160.
9 Walter J. Ong, 'Romantic Difference and the Poetics of Technology', in *Rhetoric, Romance and Technology: Studies in the Interaction of Expression and Culture* (Ithaca, NY: Cornell University Press, 1971), 255–83, 264.
10 Gernot Böhme, *Für eine ökologische Naturästhetik* (Frankfurt-on-Main: Suhrkamp, 1989); *Atmosphäre* (Frankfurt-on-Main: Suhrkamp, 1995).
11 See Edwin P. Pister, 'A Pilgrim's Progress from Group A to Group B', in Callicott (ed.), *Companion*, 221–32, 229.
12 Wallace Stegner, 'The Legacy of Aldo Leopold', in Callicott (ed.), *Companion*, 233–45, 237.
13 Ibid., 233–4.
14 Yaakov Garb, 'Change and Continuity in Environmental World-View: The Politics of Nature in Rachel Carson's *Silent Spring*', in David McCauley (ed.), *Minding Nature: The Philosophers of Ecology* (New York: Guildford Press, 1996), 229–56, 241. The page numbers from Carson are from the original edition (New York: Ballantine, 1962).
15 In Leopold's case, the gap between the radical nature of the land ethic and the fragility of the actual politics is covered by some arguably dubious speculations on the ethic as a possible future development of 'social evolution' (225), that a greater sense of duty to the non-human is bound to merge as society changes. Leopold lets the term *evolution* slide into phrases like 'social evolution' (225) to imply, falsely, a kind of simple continuity between evolution in the strict sense of slight physiological and behavioural alterations arising over time through natural selection and the way in which societies change. This is a striking piece of conceptual sleight of hand, especially considering that Leopold was a professional naturalist and would have known that Darwinian evolution could not be applied to cultural change in any simple way. See Kirkham, 'The Problem of Knowledge in Environmental Thought: A Counterchallenge'.
16 Andrew Dobson, *Green Political Thought*, 4th edn (London: Routledge, 2007), 16–17.
17 See Yang Ming-tu, 'Ecological Consciousness in the Contemporary Literature of Taiwan', in Murphy (ed.), *Literature of Nature*, 304–14.
18 Quoted from Brulle, *Agency, Democracy, and Nature*, 198.

8 Environmental justice and the move 'beyond nature writing'

1 See www.ienearth.org/index.html
2 Beck, *World Risk Society*, 39.
3 Cinder Hypki, 'Sustaining the "Urban Forest" and Creating Landscapes of Hope: An Interview with Cinder Hypki and Bryant "Spoon" Smith', in Joni Adamson, Mei Mei Evans and Rachel Stein (eds.), *The Environmental Justice Reader: Politics, Poetics and Pedagogy* (Tucson: University of Arizona Press, 2002), 284–307, 292.

4 Karla Armbruster and Kathleen R. Wallace, editors' introduction to *Beyond Nature Writing*, 3.

5 Adamson et al. (eds.), *Environmental Justice Reader*, 4.

6 Armbruster and Wallace (eds.), *Beyond Nature Writing*, 8.

7 Garrard, *Ecocriticism*, 128. Yet to open the index of *The Environmental Justice Reader* is to discover no entry for 'social ecology' or for the work of Murray Bookchin.

8 Murray Bookchin, *The Ecology of Freedom: The Emergence and Dissolution of Hierarchy*, 2nd edn (Oakland: AK Press, 2005); *Post Scarcity Anarchism*, 2nd edn (Oakland: AK Press, 2004). See also his 'What is Social Ecology?', http://dwardmac.pitzer.edu/Anarchist_Archives/bookchin/socecol.html

9 See Jozef Keulatz, *The Struggle for Nature: A Critique of Radical Ecology*, trans. Rob Kuitenbrouwer (London: Routledge, 1998), 91–8. See also Alan Rudy and Andrew Light, 'Social Ecology and Social Labor: A Consideration and Critique of Murray Bookchin', in McCanley, *Minding Nature*, 318–42.

10 Michael Bennett, 'Anti-Pastoralism, Frederick Douglass, and the Nature of Slavery', in Armbruster and Wallace (eds.), *Beyond Nature Writing*, 195–210, 200.

11 Norman Maclean, *A River Runs Through it and Other Stories* (University of Chicago Press, 1976), 104.

12 See Johnson, *Hunger for the Wild*, 250–1.

13 Also, 'I and the three Scottish women publicly declared our love for each other, given the restrictions Scots put on such public declarations' (78).

14 Maclean writes of the high rapids of Big Blackfoot River: 'It is a tough place for a trout to live – the river roars and the water is too fast to let algae grow on the rocks for feed, so there is no fat on the fish, which must hold most trout records for high jumping' (13). In fact, trout are exclusively carnivorous, feeding on various species of invertebrates.

15 *Animal Field Guide*, Montana Fish *Salmo trutta* (Salmonidae), http://fwp.mt.gov/fieldguide/detail_AFCHA04070.aspx

16 Franklin, *Animal Nation*, 106.

17 See ibid., 21; Daniel Simerbloff, 'Impacts of Introduced Species in the United States', *Consequences* 2.2 (1996), www.gcrio.org/CONSEQUENCES/vol2no2/article2.html

18 Terry Gifford, *Pastoral* (London: Routledge, 1999), 170.

9 Two readings: European ecojustice

1 Berbeli Wanning, 'Wenn Hechte ans Stubenfenster klopfen – Beschädigte Idylle in Wilhelm Raabes *Pfisters Mühle*' ['When Witches Knock at the Tavern Window: Damaged Idylls in Wilhelm Raabe's *Pfister's Mill*'], in Catrin Gersdorf and Sylvia Mayer (eds.), *Natur-Kultur-Text: Beiträge zu Ökologie und Literaturwissenschaft* (Heidelberg: Universitätsverlag, 2005),193–205, 196.

2 Ibid., 197.

3 Ibid., 193.

4 See Adamson et al. (eds.), *Environmental Justice Reader*, 22. Hindu pilgrims who seek to purify themselves through bathing in the Ganges are now risking their health (see Frank Kürschner-Pelkmann, *Das Wasser-buch: Kultur, Religion, Gesellschaft, Wirtschaft* [Frankfurt-on-Main: Lembeck, 2005], 154–8).

5 Wanning, 'Wenn Hechte', 203.

6 Wilhelm Raabe, *Pfisters Mühle: Ein Sommerferienheft* (Stuttgart: Reclam, 1980), 159.

7 Wanning, 'Wenn Hechte', 204.

8 Bate, *Song of the Earth*, 64.

9 Thomas Hardy, *The Woodlanders* (1887; London: Macmillan, 1975), 340–1.

10 See Fiona J. Stafford, *The Sublime Savage: A Study of James Macpherson and The Poems of Ossian* (Edinburgh University Press, 1988); Howard Gaskill, *The Reception of Ossian in Europe* (London: Athlone, 2002).

11 See, however, Timothy Oakes on Raymond Williams's view that the literary tradition of regional pastoralism in Wales is part of such a syndrome, 'Place and the Paradox of Modernity', *Annals of the Association of American Geographers* 87 (1997): 509–31, 517–19, 528.

12 Thomas Hardy, *The Return of the Native* (1878; London: Macmillan, 1975), 262.

13 See, for instance, Holly Davis, 'Hardy's Romanticism in *The Woodlanders*', *Deep South* 3.3 (spring 1997), www.otago.ac.nz/DeepSouth/vol3no3/holly1.html

14 Linda M. Shires, 'The Radical Aesthetic of *Tess of the d'Urbervilles*', in Dale Kramer (ed.), *The Cambridge Companion to Thomas Hardy* (Cambridge University Press, 1999), 145–63, 147.

15 Madeleine Bunting, 'Home is where the Heart is', *Countryside Voice* (Campaign to Protect Rural England, autumn 2007): 39.

16 Morton, *Ecology without Nature*, 109–23.

10 Liberalism and green moralism

1 Richard Kerridge and Neil Sammells, 'Introduction', in *Writing the Environment: Ecocriticism and Literature* (London: Zed Books, 1998), 6.

2 B. P. Taylor, 'Environmental Ethics and Political Theory', *Polity* 23 (1991): 567–83, 581.

3 Roderick Nash, *The Rights of Nature* (Madison: University of Wisconsin Press, 1989), 160.

4 Taylor, 'Environmental Ethics', 574.

5 Wilson C. McWilliams, *The Idea of Fraternity in America* (Berkeley: University of California Press, 1973).

6 John Locke, *Second Treatise of Civil Government* and *A Letter Concerning Toleration*, ed. J. W. Gough (Oxford: Basil Blackwell, 1946), [paragraph 26] 15. See also Val Plumwood, *Environmental Culture: The Ecological Crisis of Reason* (London: Routledge, 2002), 82, 153.

7 Michael E. Zimmerman, *Contesting Earth's Future: Radical Ecology and Postmodernity* (Berkeley: University of California Press, 1994), 241.

8 Catherine Albanese, 'Having Nature all Ways: Liberal and Transcendental Perspectives on American Environmentalism', *Journal of Religion* 77.1 (1997): 20–43, 24.

9 Robyn Eckersley, *The Green State: Rethinking Democracy and Sovereignty* (Cambridge, MA: MIT Press, 2004), 112.

10 Andrew Vincent, 'Liberalism and the Environment', *Environmental Values* 7 (1998): 443–59, 453.

11 Robert Frodeman, 'Radical Environmentalism and the Political Roots of Difference', *Environmental Ethics* 14 (1992): 262.

12 Wendy Brown, *States of Injury: Power and Freedom in Late Modernity* (Princeton University Press, 1995), 59.

13 See E. O. Wilson, *The Future of Life* (London: Little Brown, 2002), 23.

14 Beck, *World Risk Society*, 65–6.

15 Richard Kerridge, 'Ecothrillers: Environmental Cliffhangers', in L. Coupe (ed.), *The Green Studies Reader: From Romanticism to Ecocriticism* (London: Routledge, 2000), 242–9.

16 McKibben, *End of Nature*, 41.

17 Scott Hess, *Romanticism, Ecology, and Pedagogy*, www.rc.umd.edu/pedagogies/commons/ecology/hess/hess.html

18 Turning to issues of aesthetic form, the comparison again seems to work in Dorothy's favour. Her prose 'moves fluidly between various images, emotions, and metaphors, while William's verse uses punctuation, syntax and stanza breaks to frame the scene and separate observer and landscape' (8–9).

19 For instance, it is hard not find a moralistic personalising element in Hess's contrast of an egocentric 'male' William and a sensitive ecofeminist Dorothy. Also, as Hess acknowledges, the differences between these texts are also a matter of genre, of first-person lyric as opposed to prose journal: what if William had written a journal and Dorothy a poem?

20 See also Robert Harrison's reading of a non-liberal notion of freedom in Clare and Thoreau, *Forests*, 219–35.

21 Anthony Giddens, *The Politics of Climate Change* (Cambridge, MA: Polity, 2009), 117.

22 Kristian Ekeli, 'Green Constitutionalism: The Constitutional Protection of Future Generations', *Ratio Juris* 20 (2007): 378–401, 391.

23 Alan Carter, 'In Defence of Radical Disobedience', *Journal of the Society of Applied Philosophy* 15.1 (1998): 29–47, 43.

24 I have made some tentative steps in this direction in 'Towards a Deconstructive Environmental Criticism', *Oxford Literary Review* 30.1 (July 2008): 45–68.

11 Ecofeminism

1 Quoted in Noël Sturgeon, 'The Nature of Race: Discourses of Racial Difference in Ecofeminism', in Karen J. Warren (ed.), *Ecofeminism: Women, Culture, Nature* (Bloomington: Indiana University Press, 1997), 260–78, 260.

2 For an ecofeminist critique of deep ecology see Ariel Salleh, 'Class, Race, and Gender Discourse in the Ecofeminism/Deep Ecology Debate', in Max Oelschalager (ed.), *Postmodern Environmental Ethics* (Albany: SUNY Press, 1995).

3 Glynis Carr, 'Introduction', in *New Essays in Ecofeminist Literary Criticism* (Lewisburg, PA: Bucknell University Press, 2000), 15–25, 18.

4 Donna Haraway, 'A Manifesto for Cyborgs', *Haraway Reader*, 35.

5 Rachel Stein, '"To make the visible world your conscience": Adrienne Rich as Revolutionary Nature Writer', in Tallmadge and Harrington, *Reading Under the Sign of Nature*, 198–207, 203.

6 Quoted ibid., 206.

7 Ibid., 205.

8 Ehrlich, *Future of Ice*, 23. Ehrlich's work has been celebrated as a kind of 'postmodern pastoral' (Gretchen Legler, 'Towards a Postmodern Pastoral: The Erotic Landscape in the Work of Gretel Ehrlich', in Michael P. Branch and Scott Slovic [eds.], *The ISLE Reader: Ecocriticism, 1993–2003* [Athens: University of Georgia Press, 2003], 22–32).

9 Gretel Ehrlich, *Islands, the Universe, Home* (New York: Viking, 1991), 60.

10 Neil Everden, 'Beyond Ecology: Self, Place and the Pathetic Fallacy', in Glotfelty and Fromm (eds.), *Ecocriticism Reader*, 92–104, 95.

11 In Carr (ed.), *New Essays in Ecofeminist Literary Criticism*, 137–56.

12 Quoted in Waller, 'Woolf and an Ecology', 147.

13 Ibid., 149.

14 Waller refers to Patrick D. Murphy's extension beyond an exclusively human reference of Mikhail Bakhtin's notion of the polyvocal and dialogical nature of language. See Murphy, *Further Afield*, 96–8.

15 L. Elizabeth Waller, 'Ecofeminism and Nonhumans: Continuity, Difference, Dualism, and Domination', *Hypatia* 13.1 (1998): 158–97, 173–4.

16 Zimmerman, *Contesting Earth's Future*, 270.

17 Catriona Sandilands, *The Good-Natured Feminist: Ecofeminism and the Quest for Democracy* (Minneapolis: University of Minnesota Press, 1999), 68. See Haraway on such 'feminist paganism' as making sense only as an oppositional part of late capitalism, *Haraway Reader*, 32.

18 Louise Westling, 'Literature, the Environment, and the Question of the Post Human', in Gersdorf (ed.), *Nature in Literary and Cultural Studies*, 25–47, 43, 44.

19 Dominic Head, 'Ecocriticism and the Novel', in Coupe (ed.), *Green Studies Reader*, 235–41.

20 Lealle Ruhl, 'Natural Governance and the Governance of Nature: The Hazards of Natural Law Feminism', *Feminist Review* 66 (autumn 2000): 4–24, 21.

21 Sandilands, *Good-Natured Feminist*, xiii.

22 Ariel Kay Salleh, quoted in Zimmerman, *Contesting Earth's Future*, 239.

23 Janet Biehl, quoted in Dobson, *Green Political Thought*, 201.

24 Ruhl, 'Natural Governance', 5.

25 Ibid., 8.

26 Barbara Charlesworth Gelpi and Albert Gelpi (eds.), *Adrienne Rich's Poetry and Prose* (New York: Norton, 1975), 114.
27 Ibid.
28 Ibid.

12 'Post-colonial' ecojustice

1 William Slaymaker, 'Echoing the Other(s): The Call of Global Green and Black African Responses', *PMLA* 116.1 (2001): 129–44, 132.
2 Mark Dowie, 'Conservation Refugees', in Brian Greene (ed.), *The Best American Science and Nature Writing 2006* (Boston: Houghton Mifflin, 2006), 67–81, 68. In parts of Mesoamerica advocates and defenders of national parks have become known derogatively as *parquistas* (Thomas T. Ankersen, 'Addressing the Conservation Conundrum in Mesoamerica: A Bioregional Case Study', in Michael Vincent McGinnis (ed.), *Bioregionalism* [London: Routledge, 1999], 171–87, 173).
3 Dowie, 'Conservation Refugees', 70.
4 Quoted in Beth A. Conklin and Laura R. Graham, 'The Shifting Middle Ground: Amazonian Indians and Eco-Politics', *American Anthropologist* n.s. 97.4 (1995): 695–710, 699.
5 Richard White, *The Middle Ground: Indians, Empires, and Republics in the Great Lakes Region, 1650–1815* (Cambridge University Press, 1991), x. I am indebted to Conklin and Graham for this reference.
6 See Shepard Krech III, *The Ecological Indian: Myth and History* (New York: Norton, 1999).
7 J. Scott Bryson, 'Finding the Way Back: Place and Space in the Ecological Poetry of Joy Harjo', *MELUS* 27.3 (autumn 2002): 169–96.
8 Graham Huggan, '"Greening" Postcolonialism: Ecocritical Perspectives', *Modern Fiction Studies* 50 (2004): 701–33, 720.
9 Murphy, *Further Afield*, 146–89.
10 Quoted in Graham Huggan and Helen Tiffin, editorial 'Green Postcolonialism', *Interventions* 9.1 (2007): 4.
11 John McLeod, *Beginning Postcolonialism* (Manchester University Press, 2000), 59.
12 This point even applies to so sophisticated a reading as Lisa Perfetti's 'The Postcolonial Land that Needs to be Loved: Caribbean Nature and the Garden in Simone Schwartz-Bart's *Pluie et Vent sur Télumée Miracle*', and its argument about how 'looking closely at how nature and the land are represented in fictional works can help us understand how peoples resist colonial and neo-colonial ideologies' (*ISLE* 14.1 [summer 2007]: 89–105, 89).
13 Eric Katz, 'Imperialism and Environmentalism', in Roger S. Gottlieb (ed.), *The Ecological Community: Environmental Challenges for Philosophy, Politics and Morality* (London: Routledge, 1996), 163–74, 171.
14 Kiana Davenport, *Shark Dialogues* (New York: Penguin, 1995), 317.

15 Mayumi Toyosato, 'Land and Hawaiian Identity, Literary Activism in Kiana Davenport's *Shark Dialogues*', in Carr (ed.), *New Essays in Ecofeminist Literary Criticism*, 71–81, 75.

16 Ibid., 77.

17 Such an identification of interests is often vaguely asserted rather than defended in detail. In Paul Lindoldt, 'Literary Activism and the Bioregional', for instance, the conflicting interests of human inhabitants and wildlife are addressed by only a conveniently catch-all 'social ecological' statement: 'The bioregional agenda does not insist that environmental activism is more worthy in itself than activism for human rights, say, but it does insist that the subjugation of nature always involves domination of people, and the subjugation of peoples involves the domination of nature' (Branch and Slovic [eds.], *ISLE Reader*, 243–57, 252).

18 See Juliana Makuchi Nfah-Abbenyi, 'Ecological Postcolonialism in African Women's Literature', in Murphy (ed.), *Literature of Nature*, 344–9.

19 Some recent criticisms of Silko's novel argue that its depiction of Navaho culture is not as far removed from dominant romantic plots of 'the West' as might be supposed, with a familiar idealisation of native culture as a general 'antidote to modern or postmodern problems'. See Krista Corner, 'Sidestepping Environmental Justice: "Natural" Landscapes and the Wilderness Plot', *Frontiers: A Journal of Women Studies* 18.2 (1997): 73–101, 83.

20 See Murphy, *Further Afield*, 33.

21 The secular ethic of multiculturalism may also have some of the evasiveness of a pre-mature 'middle ground', with its language of according 'respect' to cultural difference also functioning to evade facing deep differences of belief. Hence, in Australia, for instance, Aboriginal traditions are accorded a certain legal respect under the liberal aegis of 'multiculturalism' while yet being embedded in governmental frameworks whose concepts of personhood, work, subjectivity, property and land all effectively negate those traditions. See Elizabeth A. Povinelli, 'Do Rocks Listen? The Cultural Politics of Apprehending Australian Aboriginal Labor', *American Anthropologist* n.s. 97 (1995), 505–18.

22 Huggan and Tiffin, editorial 'Green Postcolonialism', 9.

23 Rajender Kaur, '"Home is where the Oracella are": Toward a New Paradigm of Transcultural Ecocritical Engagement in Amitav Ghosh's *The Hungry Tide*', *ISLE* 14.1 (winter 2007): 125–41.

24 Amitav Ghosh, *The Hungry Tide* (London: HarperCollins, 2004), 397.

25 Huggan and Tiffin, editorial 'Green Postcolonialism', 5.

26 Kaur, '"Home is where the Oracella are"', 139.

27 In Gottlieb (ed.), *Ecological Community*, 208–25, 224.

28 Mark A. Michael, 'International Justice and Wilderness Preservation', in Gottlieb (ed.), *Ecological Community*, 311–32, 322.

29 Paul R. Ehrlich, *The Population Bomb* (Cutchogue, NY: Buccaneer, 1971).

30 D. Meadows, J. Randers and W. Behrens III, *Limits to Growth* (New York: Universe Books, 1972).

31 J. G. Ballard, *The Complete Short Stories* (London: Flamingo, 2001), 267–78.
32 Penti Linkola, a deep ecologist of unrepresentative extremism, advocates drastic authoritarian measures to reduce the human population. 'It is obvious to me that human morality during the population explosion is wholly unlike that adopted when in the beginning man was a sparse and noble species' (*Can Life Prevail?: A Radical Approach to the Environmental Crisis*, trans. Eeuto Rautio [London: Integral Tradition Publishing, 2009], 139).
33 Joseph Schneider, *Donna Haraway: Live Theory* (New York: Continuum, 2005), 153.
34 Dale Jamieson, 'Public Policy and Global Warming', *Science, Technology, and human Values* 17 (1992): 139–53, 148.

13 Questions of scale: the local, the national and the global

1 For studies of colonialism as an environmental history see Richard H. Grove's *Green Imperialism: Colonial Expansion, Tropical Island Edens, and the Origins of Environmentalism, 1600–1860* (Cambridge University Press, 1995) and Alfred W. Crosby's *Ecological Imperialism: The Biological Expansion of Europe, 900–1900* (Cambridge University Press, 1986).
2 Elizabeth DeLoughrey, 'Quantum Landscapes', in 'Green Postcolonialism', *Interventions* 9.1 (2007): 62–83, 64.
3 Kirkpatrick Sale, *Dwellers in the Land: The Bioregional Vision* (Philadelphia: New Vision, 1991), 43.
4 Peter Berg, *Reinhabiting a Separate Country: A Bioregional Anthology of Northern California* (San Francisco: Planet Drum Foundation, 1978), 218.
5 Jim Cheney, 'Nature/Theory/Difference', in Karen J. Warren (ed.), *Ecological Feminism* (London: Routledge, 1994), 158–78, 174–5.
6 Mike Carr, *Bioregionalism and Civil Society: Democratic Challenges to Corporate Culture* (Vancouver: University of British Columbia Press, 2004), 49.
7 Priyamvada Gupal, 'Reading Subaltern History', in Neil Lazarus (ed.), *The Cambridge Companion to Postcolonial Studies* (Cambridge University Press, 2004), 139–61, 160.
8 Ulrich Beck, *What is Globalization?* (Cambridge, MA: Polity, 2000), 21.
9 Ulrich Beck, *The Cosmopolitan Vision* (Cambridge, MA: Polity Press, 2006), 21.
10 Beck, *What is Globalization?*, 11.
11 Sale, *Dwellers in the Land*, 43. For further points on the political limitations of bioregionalism see Plumwood, *Environmental Culture*, 74–80.
12 Daniel Berthold-Bond, 'The Ethics of "Place": Reflections on Bioregionalism', *Environmental Ethics* 22 (2000): 5–24, 13.
13 See Sara Blair, 'Geography and the Place of the Literary', *American Literary History* 10 (1998): 544–67. Roberto Maria Dainotto has criticised some celebrations of the regional in literary criticism as idealising it in terms of 'the utopian possibility of a community considered as an undivided whole' ('All the Regions do Smilingly

Revolt', *Critical Inquiry* 22 [1996]: 486–505). At a time when nations can no longer present themselves in terms of some supposedly desirable cultural and ethnic wholeness, such ideals are nevertheless still projected upon the regional. Dainotto criticises elements of Jonathan Bate's reading of Wordsworth as a poet of place (discussed in Chapter 1) for enacting such a would-be 'purification of literature from history and politics, and, at the same time, the recuperation of an organic identity for literature – what Bate calls the "roots"' (504).

14 Derek Walcott, '"The argument of the outboard motor": An Interview with Derek Walcott', in Elizabeth M. DeLoughrey, Renée K. Gosson and George B. Handley (eds.), *Caribbean Literature and the Environment: Between Nature and Culture* (Charlottesville: University of Virginia Press, 2005), 127–39, 139.

15 P. Berg and R. F. Dasmann, 'Reinhabiting California', *Ecologist* 7.10 (1977): 399–401, 399.

16 Lindoldt, 'Literary Activism and the Bioregional', 243–57.

17 Walcott, '"The argument of the outboard motor"', 131.

18 Edouard Glissant, *Poetics of Relation*, trans. Betsy Wing (Ann Arbor: University of Minnesota Press, 1997), 146–7.

19 Holger Henke, 'Ariel's Ethos: On the Moral Economy of Caribbean Experience', *Cultural Critique* 56 (winter 2004): 33–63, 37.

20 Walcott, '"The argument of the outboard motor"', 138.

21 See Eric Prieto, 'The Use of Landscape: Ecocriticism and Martinican Cultural Theory', in DeLoughrey et al. (eds.), *Caribbean Literature and the Environment*, 236–46, 244–5.

22 Isabel Hoving, 'Moving the Caribbean Landscape: *Cereus Blooms at Night* as a Reimagination of the Caribbean Environment', in DeLoughrey et al. (eds.), *Caribbean Literature and the Environment*, 154–68, 160.

23 Edouard Glissant, *Caribbean Discourse: Selected Essays*, trans J. Michael Dash (1981; Charlottesville: University of Virginia Press, 1992), 89.

24 Ibid., 63.

25 Ibid., 59.

26 Richard D. E. Burton, 'Comment Peut-on être martiniquais?: The Recent Work of Édouard Glissant', *MLR* 79 (1984): 301–12, 307.

27 See Prieto, 'Use of Landscape', 244–5.

28 See Celia M. Britton, *Édouard Glissant and Postcolonial Theory: Strategies of Language and Resistance* (Charlottesville: University Press of Virginia, 1999), 83–118.

29 Ibid., 84–9.

30 Édouard Glissant, *Malemort* (Paris: Éditions du Seuil, 1975), 213–14.

31 Giddens, *Politics of Climate Change*, 4. See also David Shearman and Joseph Wayne Smith, *The Climate Change Challenge and the Failure of Democracy* (Westport, CT: Praeger, 2007). For an attempt to confront the imponderable questions of scale and scale effects in engaging climate change, see my 'Derangements of Scale' in Tom Cohen (ed.) *Telemorphosis: Essays in 'Critical' Climate Change* (Open Humanities Press, 2011), and open access book at openhumanities.org

32 Heise, *Sense of Place and Sense of Planet*, 21.

33 Ibid., 205–10.

34 In Gary Snyder, *Mountains and Rivers Without End* (New York: Counterpoint, 1996), 62–4.

35 Snyder, *Practice of the Wild*, 29.

36 J. Scott Bryson, *Ecopoetry: A Critical Introduction* (Salt Lake City: University of Utah Press, 2002).

37 Charles Tomlinson, *The Door in the Wall* (Oxford University Press, 1992), 47.

38 Ecopoetics can be found at http://ecopoetics.wordpress.com/
See also James Englehardt, 'The Language Habit: An Ecopoetry Manifesto', www.octopusmagazine.com/issue09/engelhardt.htm

Science and the struggle for intellectual authority

1 Plumwood, *Environmental Culture*, 51.

14 Science and the crisis of authority

1 Jane Bennett, *The Enchantment of Modern Life* (Princeton University Press, 2001), 7.

2 John Brockman, *The Third Culture* (New York: Simon & Schuster, 1996).

3 Ron Curtis, 'Narrative Form and Normative Force: Baconian Story-Telling in Popular Science', *Social Studies of Science* 24.3 (1994): 419–61, 434.

4 Ibid., 421.

5 The term 'naturalistic fallacy' was actually coined by G. E. Moore though in practice it is usually applied to an issue associated with the work of the eighteenth-century philosopher David Hume.

6 Stephen Jay Gould, *The Hedgehog, the Fox, and the Magister's Pox: Mending the Gap between Science and the Humanities* (London: Jonathan Cape, 2003), 53.

7 Annie Dillard, *Teaching a Stone to Talk* (New York: Harper Perennial, 1982), 108–29.

8 Ibid., 110.

9 Annie Dillard, *Pilgrim at Tinker Creek* (New York: Harper & Row, 1974), 179.

10 See Gary McIlroy, 'Pilgrim at Tinker Creek and the Burden of Science', *American Literature* 59 (1987): 71–84.

11 Simon Critchley, *Continental Philosophy: A Very Short Introduction* (Oxford University Press, 2001), 9. Holmes Rolston argues that the very root of the ecological crisis may be something awry with the fact/value distinction ('Are Values in Nature Subjective or Objective?', *Environmental Ethics* 4 [1982]: 125–51).

12 George Levine, 'By Knowledge Possessed: Darwin, Nature, and Victorian Narrative', *New Literary History* 24 (1993): 363–91, 363.

13 Ibid., 371.

14 Stephen Yearley, reaffirming the close dependence of environmentalism on science, also reminds us that 'the green movement is dependent on extra-scientific, moral considerations' ('The Green Ambivalence about Science: Legal-Rational Authority and the Scientific Legitimation of a Social Movement', *British Journal of Sociology* [1992]: 511–32, 529). In fact, precisely this same point applies to science itself as an institution. As soon as scientists start to defend what science is ultimately *for*, they are no longer talking as pure scientists but appealing to generally shared values and goals, such as the virtues of knowledge, of ameliorating suffering, improving the quality of life.

15 Latour, *Politics of Nature*, 10.

16 Margaret Van de Pitte, in *Environmental Ethics* 20 (spring 1998): 23–39; Jennifer C. Wheat, 'Mindless Fools and Leaves that Run: Subjectivity, Politics, and Myth in Scientific Nomenclature', in Ingram, *Coming into Contact*, 209–20.

17 Michael Goldman and Rachael A. Sherman, 'Closing the "Great Divide": New Social Theory on Society and Nature', *Annual Review of Sociology* 26 (2000): 563–84, 75. David Demeritt considers how climate change alters and challenges the social role of scientists in 'The Construction of Global Warming and the Politics of Science', *Annals of the Association of American Geographers* 91 (2001): 307–37.

18 Bruno Latour, 'The Impact of Science Studies on Political Philosophy', *Science, Technology, and Human Values* 16.1 (winter 1991): 3–19, 4.

19 See Robert Kirkham, 'Why Ecology Cannot be all Things to all People: The "Adaptive Radiation" of Scientific Concepts', *Environmental Ethics* 18 (1997): 375–90.

20 Ian Marshall, *Story Line: Exploring the Literature of the Appalachian Trail* (Charlottesville: University Press of Virginia, 1998), 45.

21 Keith Tester, *Animals and Society* (London: Routledge, 1991), 8.

22 J. L. Chapman and M. J. Reiss, *Ecology: Principles and Applications*, 2nd edn (Cambridge University Press, 1999).

23 Keulartz, *Struggle for Nature*, 18.

24 Ibid., 13.

25 Quoted in Phillips, *Truth of Ecology*, 72.

26 Daniel B. Botkin, *Discordant Harmonies: A New Ecology for the Twenty-First Century* (Oxford University Press, 1990).

27 See also Zapf's 'The State of Ecocriticism and the Function of Literature as Social Ecology', in Gersdorf and Mayer (eds.), *Nature in Literary and Cultural Studies*, 49–70.

28 Anne D. Peiter, 'Kriegslandschaften: Umwelt und Sprache in Karl Kraus' *Die letzten Tage des Menschheit* und in Ernst Jüngers *In Stahlgewittern*', in Gersdorf and Mayer (eds.), *Natur-Kultur-Text*, 229–56, 236–7.

29 See Art Berman, *From the New Critics to Deconstruction* (Urbana: University of Illinois Press, 1988), 7–82.

30 F. R. Leavis, quoted in Michael Bell, *F. R. Leavis* (London: Routledge, 1988), 31.

31 Franklin, *Animal Nation*, 147.

32 Tim Low, *The New Nature* (Ringwood, Victoria: Penguin Australia, 2002).

15 Science studies

1 Ullica Segerstråle, *Defenders of the Truth: The Sociobiology Debate* (Oxford University Press, 2000).

2 Donna Haraway, 'Morphing in the Order: Flexible Strategies, Feminist Science Studies, and Primate Revisions', *Haraway Reader*, 200.

3 Edward Wilson, *Sociobiology: The New Synthesis* (Cambridge, MA: Harvard University Press, 1975).

4 Segerstråle, *Defenders of the Truth*, 408. Olivia Frey's 'Beyond Literary Darwinism: Women's Voices and Critical Discourse' studied all the articles in *PMLA* from 1975 to 1988 and found that almost all employ adversarial and even aggressive modes of argument in relation to other critics in a kind of Darwinian struggle for authority (*College English* 52.5: 507–26).

5 Segerstråle, *Defenders of the Truth*, 299ff.

6 Richard Dawkins, *The Selfish Gene* (Oxford University Press, 1976).

7 For such a misreading see Rod Preece, 'Selfish Genes, Sociobiology, and Animal Respect', in Jodey Castricano (ed.), *Animal Subjects: An Ethical Reader in a Posthuman World* (Waterloo, Ontario: Wilfrid Laurier University Press, 2008), 39–62.

8 For some examples of this see Lucy G. Sullivan, 'Myth, Metaphor and Hypothesis: How Anthropomorphism Defeats Science', *Philosophical Transactions of the Royal Society of London* 349 (1995): 215–18. See also N. Katherine Hayles, 'Desiring Agency: Limiting Metaphors and Enabling Constraints in Dawkins and Deleuze/Guattari', *Substance* 94/95 (2001): 144–59.

9 Donna Haraway, *Primate Visions: Gender, Race, and Nature in the World of Modern Science* (London: Routledge, 1989).

10 Quoted ibid., 309.

11 Haraway, 'Morphing in the Order', 217.

12 Haraway, *Primate Visions*, 215–16.

13 Ibid., 213.

14 Haraway, 'Morphing in the Order', 207.

15 Ibid., 217.

16 Dawkins, *Selfish Gene*, 196.

17 Christa Grewe-Volpp, 'Nature "out there" and as "a social player": Some Basic Consequences for Literary Ecocritical Analysis', in Gersdorf and Mayer (eds.), *Nature in Literary and Cultural Studies*, 71–86, 78–9.

18 *Donna Haraway: Live Theory*, 26.

19 Haraway, *Primate Visions*, 377.

20 Latour, *Politics of Nature*, 4.

21 Peter Marren, 'Darwin's War-Horse: Beetle-Collecting in 19th-Century England', *British Wildlife* 19 (2008): 153–9, 157.

22 Eileen Crist, 'Against the Social Construction of Nature and Wilderness', *Environmental Ethics* 26 (spring 2004): 5–24, 7.

23 Hess, 'Three Natures', 7.

24 See Bruno Latour, 'The Promises of Constructivism', in D. Ihde and Evan Selinger (eds.), *Chasing Technoscience: Matrix for Materiality* (Bloomington: Indiana University Press, 2003); also at www.bruno-latour.fr/articles/article/087.html

16 Evolutionary theories of literature

1 See, for instance, Philip Pomper and David Gary Shaw (eds.), *The Return of Science: Evolution, History and Theory* (Lanham, MD: Rowman & Litttlefield, 2002); Joseph Carroll, *Literary Darwinism: Evolution, Human Nature and Literature* (New York: Routledge, 2004).

2 Glen A. Love, *Practical Ecocriticism: Literature, Biology, and the Environment* (Charlottesville: University of Virginia Press, 2003), 154.

3 Ibid., 50.

4 Dylan Evans, 'From Lacan to Darwin', in Jonathan Gottschall and David Sloan Wilson (eds.), *The Literary Animal: Evolution and the Nature of Narrative* (Evanston, IL: Northwestern University Press, 2005), 38–55, 50.

5 Jonathan Gottschall, 'Quantitative Literary Study: A Modest Manifesto and Testing the Hypotheses of Feminist Fairy Tale Studies', in Gottschall and Wilson (eds.), *Literary Animal*, 199–224, 220.

6 Evans, 'From Lacan to Darwin', 50.

7 Joseph Carroll, 'Human Nature and Literary Meaning: A Theoretical Model Illustrated with a Crtitique of *Pride and Prejudice*', in Gottschall and Wilson (eds.), *Literary Animal*, 76–106, 91.

8 Marcus Nordlund, 'The Problem of Romantic Love: Shakespeare and Evolutionary Psychology', in Gottschall and Wilson (eds.), *Literary Animal*, 107–25. 107.

9 Love, *Practical Ecocriticism*, 50.

10 Carroll, 'Human Nature and Literary Meaning', 81.

11 Quoted in Love, *Practical Ecocriticism*, 59.

12 Tony Jackson, 'Questioning Interdisciplinarity: Cognitive Science, Evolutionary Psychology, and Literary Criticism', *Poetics Today* 21 (2000): 319–47, 335.

13 Nordlund, 'Problem of Romantic Love', 119.

14 For a survey of evolutionary theories of art see Brain Boyd, 'Evolutionary Theories of Art', in Gottschall and Wilson (eds.), *Literary Animal*, 147–76.

15 Carroll, *Literary Darwinism*, 145. The use of scientific vocabulary may be skin-deep. For instance, David Sloan Wilson, speculating that literature is part of a hypothetical 'nongenetic evolutionary process', is arguably only rewording a familiar notion of 'culture'. Superficially Darwinian terms like 'adaptation' and 'evolution' are appropriated to a conservative and traditional defence of literature as a source of moral and cognitive stability ('Evolutionary Social Constructivism', *Literary Animal*, 20–37, 33).

16 Timothy Morton, 'Queer Ecology', *PMLA* 124 (2010), quotations taken from a pre-publication ms copy.

17 Interdisciplinarity and science: two essays

1 Marshall, *Story Line*, 6.
2 In Branch and Slovic (eds.), *ISLE Reader*, 188–202.
3 In S. J. Gould, *Ever Since Darwin: Reflections in Natural History* (Harmondsworth: Penguin, 1980), 207–13.
4 Julie Thompson Klein, *Crossing Boundaries: Knowledge, Disciplinarity and Interdisciplinarities* (Charlottesville: University Press of Virginia, 1996), 14.
5 For an overview of Gould's work and thought see Michael B. Shermer, 'This View of Science: Stephen Jay Gould as Historian of Science and Scientific Historian, Popular Scientist and Scientific Popularizer', *Social Studies of Science* 32.4 (August 2002): 489–524.
6 'Posture Maketh the Man', 208.
7 Ullica Segerstråle nevertheless offers a reading of Gould's scientific career as simultaneously a quest for social justice – '[Gould's] continuous search for theoretical alternatives to the adaptionist program [in theories of evolution], starting with punctuated equilibria and continuing with the idea of historical contingency (particularly in *Wonderful Life*) can be seen as one long argument for social reform and social justice. If everything is optimally adapted in the best of all possible worlds, there is no point in trying to effect social change. But if instead of adaptation you emphasize discontinuity, contingency, and chance, you indicate that in a radically new environment new types of individuals will flourish' (*Defenders of the Truth*, 378).
8 S. J. Gould, *An Urchin in the Storm: Essays about Books and Ideas* (New York: Norton, 1988), 154.
9 See Scott Slovic, 'Ecocriticism: Storytelling, Values, Communication, Contact', www.asle.org/site/resources/ecocritical-library/intro/defining/slovic/
10 J. Elder, *Reading the Mountains of Home* (Cambridge, MA: Harvard University Press, 1999); Terry Gifford, *Connecting with John Muir: Essays in Post-Pastoral Practice* (Athens: University of Georgia Press, 2006).
11 Slovic, 'Ecocriticism: Storytelling, Values, Communication, Contact'.
12 See Chris Stringer and Peter Andrews, *The Complete World of Human Evolution* (London: Thames & Hudson, 2005), 127.
13 See Jessica Mordsley, 'Tracing Origins in Paleoanthropology', in Neil Badmington (ed.), *Derridanimals, Oxford Literary Review* 29 (2007): 77–101.
14 Charles Bazerman, 'Intertextual Self-Fashioning: Gould and Lewontin's Representations of the Literature', in Jack Selzer (ed.), *Understanding Scientific Prose* (Madison: University of Wisconsin Press, 1993), 20–41, 38.
15 Gould, *The Hedgehog, the Fox*, 107.

The animal mirror

1 James Rachels, *Created from Animals* (Oxford University Press, 1991), 129.
2 Peter Singer, *Animal Liberation*, 2nd edn (London: Pimlico, 1995); Tom Regan, *The Case for Animal Rights* (Berkeley: University of California Press, 1983); Carol Adams, *The Sexual Politics of Meat* (New York: Continuum, 1990); Mary Midgley, *Animals and Why They Matter* (Harmondsworth: Penguin, 1984).
3 J. Baird Callicott, 'Animal Liberation: A Triangular Affair', *Environmental Ethics* 2 (1980): 311–38.
4 Regan, *Case for Animal Rights*, 362. For an overview of the conflicts see Mark Sagoff, 'Animal Liberation and Environmental Ethics: Bad Marriage, Quick Divorce', *Osgood Hall Law Journal* 22 (1984): 297–307.

18 Ethics and the non-human animal

1 David Garnett, *A Man in the Zoo* [and] *Lady into Fox* (London: Vintage, 2000), 23. See also Randy Malamud, *Reading Zoos: Representations of Animal and Captivity* (New York: New York University Press, 1998) and Diana Starr Cooper's account of the circus as an institution making an art form out of the human–animal distinction, *Night after Night* (Washington, DC: Shearwater Books, 1994).
2 Keith Thomas, *Man and the Natural World: Changing Attitudes in England 1500–1800* (Harmondsworth: Penguin, 1983), 36.
3 Soper, *What is Nature?*, 83.
4 C. Wolfe, *Animal Rites: American Culture, the Discourse of Species and Posthumanism* (University of Chicago Press, 2003), 43.
5 See Cynthia Chris, *Watching Wildlife* (Minneapolis: University of Minnesota Press, 2006).
6 See E. F. Bleiler (ed.), *Best Ghost Stories of Algernon Blackwood* (New York: Dover, 1973).
7 Thomas, *Man and the Natural World*, 16.
8 Editorial, *New Scientist*, 24 May 2008, 3.
9 See Matthew Calarco, *Zoographies: The Question of the Animal from Heidegger to Derrida* (New York: Columbia University Press, 2008), 3–13.
10 Editorial introduction to Wolfe (ed.), *Zoontologies*, xi.
11 Jacques Derrida, 'The Animal that Therefore I am (more to follow)', in Peter Atterton and Matthew Calarco (eds.), *Animal Philosophy: Ethics and Identity* (London: Continuum, 2004), 113–26, 125–6.
12 Anna Tsing, quoted in Donna Haraway, *When Species Meet* (Minneapolis: University of Minnesota Press, 2008), 218.
13 Rare examples would be the work of Cary Wolfe; Jean Hochman's chapter 'The Lambs in *The Silence of the Lambs*', in his *Green Cultural Studies: Nature in Film, Novel and Theory* (Moscow, ID: University of Idaho Press, 1998); Chen

Hong, 'To Set the Wild Free: Changing Images of Animals in English Poetry of the Pre-Romantic and Romantic Periods', *ISLE* 13.2 (summer 2006): 129–49. For more, see the Animal Studies Bibliography referred to in further reading for this chapter.

14 John Simons, *Animal Rights and the Politics of Literary Representation* (Basingstoke: Palgrave, 2002), 59.
15 For an overview of such arguments see ibid.
16 Wolfe, *Animal Rites*, 1.
17 Ibid., 124.
18 Ibid., 133–4.
19 Luc Ferry, *The New Ecological Order*, trans. Carol Volk (University of Chicago Press, 1995), 139.
20 Wolfe, *Animal Rites*, 38.
21 David Wood, '*Comment ne pas manger*: Deconstruction and Humanism', in H. Peter Steeves (ed.), *Animal Others: On Ethics, Ontology, and Animal Life* (Albany: SUNY Press, 1999), 15–35, 32.
22 A similar argument leads Rebecca Raglon and Marian Scholtmeijer, in another essay on animals in Armbruster and Wallace (eds.), *Beyond Nature Writing* ('Heading off the Trail: Language, Literature, and Nature's Resistance', 248–62), to write that, 'while each story can work on a symbolic, metaphoric, or psychological level . . . in each story's deepest level all such meanings fall away, and we are left to contemplate the unknowable, mysterious aspect of termite, turtle, or chimpanzee' (261). These are valuable points, but they may reduce interpretation to an entirely negative gesture – to take us to the edge of anthropocentric instrumentalism in language and leave whatever is outside (e.g., all living things) 'mysterious', 'unknown', 'other', 'challengingly unhuman', etc. This might soon become a rather repetitive mode of attention, affirming a merely negative irony, again and again.
23 See Akira Mizuta Lippit, *Electric Animal: Toward a Rhetoric of Wildlife* (Minneapolis: University of Minnesota Press, 2000), 71.

19 Anthropomorphism

1 Jack London, *The Call of the Wild, White Fang and Other Stories*, ed. Earle Labor and Robert C. Leitz III (Oxford University Press, 1998), 19.
2 See Crist, *Images of Animals*, 11–50.
3 Stephen Mithen, 'Anthropomorphism and the Evolution of Cognition', *Journal of the Royal Anthropological Institute* 2 (1996): 717–21.
4 Heidegger, *Gesammtausgabe* 66 (Frankfurt-on-Main: Klostermann, 1997), 161.
5 J. A. Baker and Robert MacFarlane, *The Peregrine* (Harmondsworth: Penguin, 1967); Richard Mabey, *The Book of Nightingales* (1993; London: Sinclair-Stevenson, 1997); Diane Ackerman, *The Moon by Whale Light: And Other Adventures Among Bats, Penguins, Crocodilians, and Whales* (1991; London, Random House, 1993).

6 Thomas Nagel, 'What Is It Like To Be A Bat?', *Philosophical Review* 83.4 (October 1974): 435–50.

7 Quoted in Karl Kroeber, 'Ecology and American Literature: Thoreau and Un-Thoreau', *American Literary History* 9.2 (1997): 309–28, 320.

8 Kalevi Kull and Peeter Torop, 'Biotranslation: Translation Between *Umwelten*', in Susan Petrilli (ed.), *Translation Translation* (Amsterdam: Rodopi, 2003), 313–28. See also Tino Maran's article on the promise of biosemiotics, 'Where Do Your Borders Lie? Reflections on the Semiotic Ethics of Nature', in Gersdorf and Mayer (eds.), *Nature in Literary and Cultural Studies*, 455–76.

9 In *Animal Others*, 271–84.

10 Richard Jefferies, *Field and Hedgerow*, new edn (1889; London: Lutterworth, 1948), 116–24.

11 See Claire Colebrook, *Gilles Deleuze* (London: Routledge, 2002), 29–54.

12 Simons, *Animal Rights*, 171–2.

13 Ibid., 172.

14 See, for example, Alice Kuzniar, 'A Higher Langauge: Novalis on Communion with Animals', *German Quarterly* 76 (2003): 426–42; Jacqui Griffith, 'Almost Human: Indeterminate Children and Dogs in "Flush" and "The Sound and the Fury"', *Yearbook of English Studies* 32 (2002): 163–76. For another reading of Virginia Woolf's *Flush* that takes its attempt to represent animal subjectivity more at face value, see Craig Smith, 'Across the Widest Gulf: Nonhuman Subjectivity in Virginia Woolf's "Flush"', *Twentieth-Century Literature* 48 (2002): 348–61.

15 Gilles Deleuze and Felix Guattari, *A Thousand Plateaus: Capitalism and Schizophrenia*, trans. Brian Massumi (Minneapolis: University of Minnesota Press, 1987), 233–309.

16 Phillips, *Truth of Ecology*, 205–10.

17 See Donna Haraway, *When Species Meet* (Minneapolis: University of Minnesota Press, 2008), 27–30.

18 Gareth Lovett Jones, *The Wind in the Pylons*, vol. I (Aylesbury: Hilltop Publishing, 2003), 233.

19 Contrast Tonia L. Payne's reading of two short stories by Ursula K. Le Guin on long-term interstellar travel and the breakdowns that ensue from human beings living as sole species in an environment, '"We are dirt: we are earth": Ursula Le Guin and the Problem of Extraterrestrials', in Gersdorf and Mayer (eds.), *Nature in Literary and Cultural Studies*, 229–48.

20 See also Val Plumwood's powerful reading of the film *Babe* (1995, dir. Chris Noonan) in *Ecological Culture*, 160–6.

20 The future of ecocriticism

1 Orr, *Earth in Mind*, 12.

Further reading

Introduction

General sources

Association for the Study of Literature and the Environment, www.asle.org/
ASLE's Resources site offers an online bibliography and also lists online
material introducing ecocriticism, www.asle.org/site/resources/
ecocritical-library/intro/

Journals

Green Letters: Studies in Ecocriticism (journal of the UK branch of ASLE),
www.green-letters.org.uk/
Indian Journal of Ecocriticism, http://osle-india.org/journal.html
ISLE (*Interdisciplinary Studies in Literature and the Environment*), founded in
1993, the official journal of ASLE, http://isle.oxfordjournals.org/
Journal of Ecocriticism, http://ojs.unbc.ca/index.php/joe

Useful non-literary journals: *Environmental Ethics*; *Environmental Politics*;
Environmental Values.

General critical anthologies

Armbruster, Karla, and Kathleen R. Wallace (eds.), *Beyond Nature Writing:
Expanding the Boundaries of Ecocriticism* (Charlottesville: University
Press of Virginia, 2001).
Branch, Michael P., and Scott Slovic (eds.), *The ISLE Reader: Ecocriticism,
1993–2003* (Athens: University of Georgia Press, 2003).
Bryson, J. Scott (ed.), *Ecopoetry: A Critical Introduction* (Salt Lake City: University
of Utah Press, 2002).
Coupe, Lawrence (ed.), *The Green Studies Reader: From Romanticism to
Ecocriticism* (London: Routledge, 2000).
Gersdorf, Catrin, and Sylvia Mayer (eds.), *Nature in Literary and Cultural Studies:
Transatlantic Conversations on Ecocriticism* (Amsterdam: Rodopi, 2006).

Glotfelty, Cheryll, and Harold Fromm (eds.), *The Ecocriticism Reader: Landmarks in Literary Ecology* (Athens: University of Georgia Press, 1996).

Ingram, Annie Merril, et al. (eds.), *Coming into Contact: Explorations in Ecocritical Theory and Practice* (Athens: University of Georgia Press, 2007).

Kerridge, Richard, and Neil Sammells (eds.), *Writing the Environment: Ecocriticism and Literature* (London: Zed Books, 1998).

Murphy, Patrick D. (ed.), *Literature of Nature: An International Sourcebook* (Chicago: Fitzroy Dearborn, 1998). Especially useful for its international range.

Tallmadge, John, and Henry Harrington (eds.), *Reading Under the Sign of Nature: New Essays in Ecocriticism* (Salt Lake City: University of Utah Press, 2000).

Other useful overviews

Buell, Lawrence, *The Future of Environmental Criticism: Environmental Crisis and Literary Imagination* (Oxford: WileyBlackwell, 2005).

Garrard, Greg, *Ecocriticism* (New York: Routledge, 2004).

Heise, Ursula K., 'Greening English: Recent Introductions to Ecocriticism', *Contemporary Literature* 47.2 (2006): 289–98.

Definitions of 'nature'

Soper, Kate, *What is Nature?* (Oxford: Blackwell, 1995).

Williams, Raymond, *Keywords* (London: Flamingo, 1993).

   'Ideas of Nature', in *Problems in Materialism and Culture: Selected Essays* (London: Verso, 1996), 67–85.

Worster, Donald, *Nature's Economy: A History of Ecological Ideas*, 2nd edn (Cambridge University Press, 1994).

Climate change

Australian National University, Climate Change Institute, www.anu.edu.au/ climatechange/

Behringer, Wolfgang, *A Cultural History of Climate*, trans. Patrick Camiller (Cambridge, MA: Polity, 2010). A suggestive if necessarily rather speculative account of effects of changes in climate upon mainly European cultural history over the millennia.

Bhaskar, Roy, et al. (eds.), *Interdisciplinarity and Climate Change* (London: Routledge, 2010).

Chakrabarty, Dipesh, 'The Climate of History: Four Theses', *Critical Inquiry* 35 (winter 2009): 197–222.

Cohen, Tom, and Claire Colebrook (eds.), 'Critical Climate Change', a
        forthcoming open access book series on climate change in the
        humanities with Open Humanities Press. See openhumanities.org
'Institute on Critical Climate Change in the Humanities,' www.
        criticalclimatechange.com/
King's College Cambridge, 'Global Warming Resources', www.kings.cam.ac.
        uk/global-warming/
Shearman, David, and Joseph Wayne Smith, *The Climate Change Challenge and
        the Failure of Democracy* (Westport, CT: Praeger, 2007). On how climate
        change forms a crisis as to the legitimacy of dominant forms of
        government and economics, especially liberal democracy.

Romantic and anti-romantic

The two most sustained critiques of modern ecocriticism to date both focus on its
romanticism:

Morton, Timothy, *Ecology without Nature: Rethinking Environmental Aesthetics*
        (Cambridge, MA: Harvard University Press, 2008).
Phillips, Dana, *The Truth of Ecology: Nature, Culture, and Literature in America*
        (Oxford University Press, 2003).

1   Old world romanticism

Bate, Jonathan (ed.), *Green Romanticism*, special issue of *Studies in Romanticism*
        35.3 (1996).
Harrison, Gary (ed.), 'Romanticism, Nature, Ecology', in *Romantic Circles*,
        Commons section, www.rc.umd.edu/pedagogies/commons/ecology/
        harrison/harrison.html. A useful collection of recent essays.
Hutchings, Kevin, 'Ecocriticism in British Romantic Studies', *Literature Compass*
        4.1 (2007): 172–202. A detailed and comprehensive survey, especially
        strong on the issues of animal rights in the romantic period and new
        developments such as attention to 'urban ecology' in the London of
        Leigh Hunt and Thomas de Quincey.
McKusick, James C., *Green Writing: Romanticism and Ecology* (New York: St
        Martin's, 2000).
Morton, Timothy, 'Environmentalism', in Nicholas Roe (ed.), *Romanticism: An
        Oxford Guide* (Oxford University Press, 2004), 696–707.

'Deep ecology'

Drengson, Alan, and Yuichi Inoue (eds.), *The Deep Ecology Movement: An
        Introductory Anthology* (Berkeley, CA: North Atlantic Books, 1995).

Luke, Timothy W., 'Deep Ecology as Political Philosophy', Chapter 1 of his *Ecocritique: Contesting the Politics of Nature, Economy, and Culture* (Minneapolis: University of Minnesota Press, 1997). Very critical.

Salleh, Ariel, 'Class, Race, and Gender Discourse in the Ecofeminism/Deep Ecology Debate', in Max Oelschalager (ed.), *Postmodern Environmental Ethics* (Albany: SUNY Press, 1995).

Zimmerman, Michael, *Contesting Earth's Future: Radical Ecology and Postmodernity* (Berkeley: University of California Press, 1994). Assesses debates between 'deep ecology', 'social ecology' and ecofeminism.

2 New world romanticism

Abrams, Robert E., 'Image, Object, and Perception in Thoreau's Landscapes: The Development of Anti-Geography', *Nineteenth-Century Literature* 46 (1991): 245–62.

Cranston, C. A., and Robert Zeller (eds.), *The Littoral Zone: Australian Contexts and their Writers* (Amsterdam: Rodopi, 2007). As Libby Robbin observes in a review, 'Neither the transcendental romantic wilderness view (the American canon) nor the pastoral romantic (the classic British genre) work for the Australian landscape and its peoples': *Australian Humanities Review* 42 (August 2007), www.australianhumanitiesreview.org/archive/Issue-August-2007/EcoHumanities/Robin.html#book

Cronon, William, 'The Trouble with Wilderness; or, Getting Back to the Wrong Nature', in William Cronon (ed.), *Uncommon Ground: Rethinking the Human Place in Nature* (New York: Norton, 1995). A seminal and in its time very controversial attack on romantic and evasive conceptions of 'wilderness' in US culture.

Mazel, Don, *American Literary Environmentalism* (Athens: University of Georgia Press, 2000). On the wilderness 'mystique' and how conceptions of the environment in the US reflect an often nationalist cultural politics.

Petrulionis, Sandra Harbert, and Laura Dassow Walls (eds.), *More Day to Dawn: Thoreau's Walden for the Twenty-First Century* (Amherst: University of Massachusetts Press, 2007).

Scheese, Don, *Nature Writing: The Pastoral Impulse in America* (New York: Twayne, 1996).

Wilson, Eric, *Romantic Turbulence: Chaos, Ecology and American Space* (New York: St Martin's, 2000). Locates American Romantic writers (mainly Emerson, Fuller, Melville, Thoreau, Whitman) in the historical development of ecological consciousness, with consideration of the literary forms read as enacting such understanding.

3   Genre and the question of non-fiction

Farber, Paul Lawrence, *Finding Order in Nature: The Naturalist Tradition from Linnaeus to E. O. Wilson* (Baltimore, MD: Johns Hopkins University Press, 2000).

Gifford, Terry, *Pastoral* (London: Routledge, 1999). A study of the various senses and histories of the genre.

Morris, David Copland, 'Inhumanism, Environmental Crisis, and the Canon of American Literature', *ISLE* 4.2 (autumn 1997): 1–16. 'Inhumanism' names the stance or discipline, mainly associated with the poet Robinson Jeffers (1887–1962), of affirming views of life that resist a human-centred perspective.

Selzer, Jack (ed.), *Understanding Scientific Prose* (Madison: University of Wisconsin Press, 1993). Innovative essays analyse the discourse of a famous essay on the nature of evolution ('Spandrels of San Marco and the Panglossian Paradigm' by Stephen Jay Gould and Richard C. Lewontin), attentive to the intellectual and conceptual effects of kinds of rhetoric in the writing of science.

Sweeting, Adam, and Thomas C. Crochunis, 'Performing the Wild: Rethinking Wilderness and Theater Space', in *Beyond Nature Writing: Expanding the Boundaries of Ecocriticism* (Charlottesville: University Press of Virginia, 2001), 325–40. On some surprising connections between the conventions of theatrical realism (e.g. the pretence that spectators are absent) and space-based notion of wilderness.

4   Language beyond the human?

Berghaller, Hannes, '"Trees are what everyone needs": The Lorax, Anthropocentrism, and the Problem of Mimesis', in Catrin Gersdorf and Sylvia Mayer (eds.), *Nature in Literary and Cultural Studies: Transatlantic Conversations on Ecocriticism* (Amsterdam: Rodopi, 2006), 155–75. Another critique of Buell's 'realism'.

Berry, Wendell, *Standing by Words: Essays* (Washington, DC: Shoemaker & Hoard, 1983). Relates the disastrous environmental illiteracy of modern societies to a 'disintegration of language'.

Kenneally, Christine, *The First Word: The Search for the Origin of Language* (London: Viking, 2007).

Morton, Timothy, chapter on 'ecomimesis' in *Ecology without Nature: Rethinking Environmental Aesthetics* (Cambridge, MA: Harvard University Press, 2008), 29–79. Attacks some ecocriticism for merely indulging rather than critically examining the produced effect of some nature writing that language may convey the natural world directly, without mediation.

Nielsen, Dorothy M., 'Prosopopoeia and the Ethics of Ecological Advocacy in the Poetry of Denise Levertov and Gary Snyder', *Contemporary Literature* 34

(1993): 691–713. On poetic techniques that aim to transgress given
distinctions between human and non-human (for instance, is Levertov's
calling trees 'awake' a literal or figurative expression?).

5   The inherent violence of western thought?

Clark, Timothy, *Martin Heidegger* (London: Routledge, 2001). An introduction
focussed on Heidegger and the literary.
De Bruyn, Ben, 'The Gathering of Form: Forests, Gardens and Legacies in Robert
Pogue Harrison', in Timothy Clark (ed.), *Deconstruction,
Environmentalism and Climate Change*, special issue of *Oxford Literary
Review* 32.1 (2010), 19–36. An introductory overview of Harrison's
work.
Foltz, Bruce V., *Inhabiting the Earth: Heidegger, Environmental Ethics, and the
Metaphysics of Nature* (Atlantic Highlands, NJ: Humanities Press, 1995).
Harrison, Robert Pogue, *The Dominion of the Dead* (University of Chicago Press,
2003). On the place and power of the dead in human cultures.
   Gardens: An Essay on the Human Condition (University of Chicago Press,
2008).
Zimmerman, Michael, *Heidegger's Confrontation with Modernity: Technology,
Politics, Art* (Bloomington: Indiana University Press, 1990).
   'Rethinking the Heidegger – Deep Ecology Relationship', *Environmental
Ethics* 15.3 (autumn 1993): 195–224.

6   Post-humanism and the 'end of nature'?

Badmington, Neil (ed.), *Posthhumanism* (Basingstoke: Palgrave, 2000).
Bartlett, Laura, and Thomas B. Byers, 'Back to the Future: The Humanist
   "Matrix"', *Cultural Critique* 53 (winter 2003): 28–46. A reading from a
post-humanist stance of the film *The Matrix* (dirs. Andy and Larry
Wachowski).
Dougherty, Stephen, 'Culture in the Disk Drive: Computation, Mimetics, and the
Rise of Posthumanism', *Diacritics* 31.4 (winter 2001): 85–102.
Palmer, Louis H., III, 'Articulating the Cyborg: An Impure Model of
Environmental Revolution', in Steven Rosendale (ed.), *The Greening of
Literary Scholarship* (University of Iowa Press, 2002), 165–77.
Strickler, Breyan, 'The Pathologization of Environmental Discourse: Melding
Disability Studies and Ecocriticism in Urban Grunge Novels', *ISLE* 15.1
(winter 2008): 111–34.
Westling, Louise, 'Literature, the Environment, and the Question of the
Posthuman', in Catrin Gersdorf and Sylvia Mayer (eds.), *Nature in
Literary and Cultural Studies: Transatlantic Conversations on Ecocriticism*
(Amsterdam: Rodopi, 2006), 25–48.

The boundaries of the political

The political and ethical remain the dominant categories in which the environmental crisis is debated, so books, articles and websites are numerous. Particularly useful may be the following.

Dobson, Andrew, *Green Political Thought*, 4th edn (London: Routledge, 2007).
Dryzek, John S., and David Schlosberg (eds.), *Debating the Earth: The Environmental Politics Reader*, 2nd edn (Oxford University Press, 2005).
Elliott, Lorraine, *Global Politics of the Environment*, 2nd edn (New York: Palgrave Macmillan, 2004).
Linkola, Pentti, *Can Life Prevail?: A Radical Approach to the Environmental Crisis*, trans. Eeuto Rautio (London: Integral Tradition Publishing, 2009). The work of this 'deepest' of deep ecologists is not exactly 'recommended' but highlighted for a provocative extremism useful for forcing readers to clarify their own position: 'Never before in history have the distinguishing values of a culture been things as concretely destructive for life and the quality of life as democracy, individual freedom and human rights – not to mention money' (154).

See also the entries for Ulrich Beck as further reading for Chapter 8 below.

7   Thinking like a mountain?

Fromm, Harold, 'Aldo Leopold: Aesthetic "Anthropocentrist"', in Michael P. Branch and Scott Slovic (eds.), *The ISLE Reader: Ecocriticism 1993–2003* (Athens: University of Georgia Press, 2003), 3–9. An attack on Leopold's arguably dated notions of the ecological as still inherently aesthetic and anthropocentric.
Moore, Kathleen Dean, and Lisa H. Sideris (eds.), *Rachel Carson: Legacy and Challenge* (Albany: SUNY Press, 2008).
Ryden, Kent C., '"How could a weed be a book?": Books, Ethics, Power, and a Sand County Almanac', *ISLE* 15.1 (winter 2008): 1–10. On the trope of 'reading' nature in Leopold and the development of a non-human-centred ecological literacy.

8   Environmental justice and the move 'beyond nature writing'

Beck, Ulrich, *Risk Society: Towards a New Modernity* (London: Sage, 1992). *World Risk Society* (Cambridge, MA: Polity, 1998).

These books outline Beck's theses on 'risk society': that modern societies are characterised by manufactured risks – pollution, climate change, new illnesses – that undermine their own proclaimed bases in reason and equity. See Ursula K.

Heise's chapter, 'Narrative in the World Risk Society', in her *Sense of Place and Sense of Planet* (Oxford University Press, 2008), 119–59.

Bennett, Michael, and David W. Teague (eds.), *The Nature of Cities: Ecocriticism and Urban Environments* (Tucson: University of Arizona Press, 1999).

Dwyer, June, 'Ethnic Home Improvement: Gentrifying the Ghetto, Spicing up the Suburbs', *ISLE* 14.2 (summer 2007): 165–82.

Grewe-Volpp, Christa, 'Nature "out there" and as "a social player": Some Basic Consequences for a Literary Critical Analysis', in Catrin Gersdorf and Sylvia Mayer (eds.), *Nature in Literary and Cultural Studies: Transatlantic Conversations on Ecocriticism* (Amsterdam: Rodopi, 2006), 71–86. Relates to the tension between objectivist/realist and constructivist approaches to the natural world. Argues for ways of conceptualising it both as an material entity and as an agent in human culture in its own right. See 'The antinomy of environmental criticism' at the end of Chapter 8.

Harvey, David, *Justice, Nature and the Geography of Difference* (Oxford and New York: Blackwell, 1996). On social and environmental justice.

Outka, Paul, *Race and Nature from Transcendentalism to the Harlem Renaissance* (New York: Palgrave, 2008).

Yamashiro, Shin, 'An Introduction to "Environmental Justice" in North American Ecocriticism: Its Origin and Practice', in Nirmal Selvamony et al. (eds.), *Essays in Ecocriticism* (New Delhi: Sarup & Sons, 2007), 40–56.

'Social ecology'

Foster, John Bellamy, *Ecology Against Capitalism* (New York: Monthly Review Press, 2002).

   Marx's Ecology: Materialism and Nature (New York: Monthly Review Press, 2000). Refutes the common view that Marx ignored ecological issues.

Institute for Social Ecology, www.social-ecology.org/

Light, A. (ed.), *Social Ecology after Bookchin* (New York: Guildford Press, 1998).

Zimmerman, Michael, *Contesting Earth's Future: Radical Ecology and Postmodernity* (Berkeley: University of California Press, 1994). Assesses debates between 'deep ecology', 'social ecology' and ecofeminism.

9 Two readings: European ecojustice

Goodbody, Axel (ed.), *The Culture of German Environmentalism: Anxieties, Visions, Realities* (New York and Oxford: Berghahn, 2002).

Williams, Raymond, *The Country and the City* (1973; London: Hogarth, 1993).

Collections of ecocritical essays with a particularly European focus are:

Catrin Gersdorf and Sylvia Mayer (eds.), *Nature in Literary and Cultural Studies: Transatlantic Conversations on Ecocriticism* (Amsterdam: Rodopi, 2006). *Natur-Kultur-Text: Beiträge zu Ökologie und Literaturwissenschaft* (Heidelberg: Universitätsverlag, 2005).

See also Richard Kerridge (ed.), *Crowded Space*, forthcoming from the University of Virginia Press, on ecocriticism in the UK.

10   Liberalism and green moralism

Hinchman, Lewis P., and Sandra K. Hinchman, 'Should Environmentalists Reject the Enlightenment?', *Review of Politics* 63 (2001): 663–92.

Roszak, Theodore, Mary E. Gomes and Allen D. Kanner (eds.), *Ecopsychology: Restoring the Earth, Healing the Mind* (San Francisco, CA: Sierra Club Books, 1995). Essays on the controversial relation of individual psychic health to the health of the planet (listed here because this issue involves notions of selfhood at odds with the individualistic norms of autonomy/independence central to the dominant liberal tradition in politics).

Thiele, Leslie Paul, 'Nature and Freedom: A Heideggerian Critique of Biocentric and Sociocentric Environmentalism', *Environmental Ethics* 17 (1995): 171–90.

Wissenburg, Marcel, *Green Liberalism: The Free and the Green Society* (University College London Press, 1998). An attempt to reconcile liberalism and environmental politics. For a critique, see Robyn Eckersley, *The Green State: Rethinking Democracy and Sovereignty* (Cambridge, MA: MIT Press, 2004), Chapter 4.

11   Ecofeminism

Alaimo, Stacy, 'Cyborg and Ecofeminist Interventions: Challenges for an Environmental Feminism', *Feminist Studies* 20 (1994): 133–54. On the debate between Donna Haraway's post-humanist 'cyborg' manifesto and some ecofeminist arguments.

Mortimer-Sandilands, Catriona, 'Queering Ecocultural Studies', *Cultural Studies* 22 (2008): 455–76.

Sandilands, Catriona, 'Desiring Nature: Queering Ethics: Adventures in Erotogenic Environments', *Environmental Ethics* 23 (2001): 169–88.

Warren, Karren J. (ed.), *Ecofeminism: Women, Culture, Nature* (Bloomington: Indiana University Press, 1997). A useful critical anthology.

12   'Post-colonial' ecojustice

Chavkin, Allan, *Leslie Marmon Silko's Ceremony: A Casebook* (Oxford University Press, 2002).
'Green Postcolonialism', special issue of *Interventions* 9.1 (2007), ed. Graham Huggan and Helen Tiffin.
Guha, Ramachandra, 'Radical American Environmentalism and Wilderness Protection: A Third World Critique', *Environmental Ethics* 11 (1989): 71–83.
Kamada, Roy Osamu, 'Postcolonial Romanticisms: Derek Walcott and the Melancholic Narrative of Landscape', in J. Scott Bryson (ed.), *Ecopoetry: A Critical Introduction* (Salt Lake City: University of Utah Press, 2002), 207–20.
Nixon, Rob, 'Environmentalism and Postcolonialism', in Ania Loomba, Suvir Kaul, Matti Bunzl, Antoinette Burton and Jed Esty (eds.), *Postcolonial Studies and Beyond* (Durham, NC: Duke University Press, 2005), 233–51.
Ombaka, Christine, 'War and Environment in African Literature', in Patrick Murphy (ed.), *Literature of Nature: An International Sourcebook* (Chicago: Fitzroy Dearborn, 1998), 327–36.

Overpopulation

Bandarage, Asoka, *Women, Population, and Global Crisis: A Political–Economic Analysis* (London: Zed Books, 1997). A synthesis of Third World, feminist, socialist and ecological thinking and solutions, criticising the assumption that overpopulation is one of the root causes of global crisis.
Meadows, D., J. Randers and W. Behrens III, *The Limits to Growth: The 30-Year Update* (London: Earthscan, 2005).

For changing literary representations of overpopulation, see Ursula K. Heise, *Sense of Place and Sense of Planet* (Oxford University Press, 2008); also Frederick Buell, *From Apocalypse to Way of Life: Environmental Crisis in the American Century* (New York: Routledge, 2004), 143–50.

13   Questions of scale: the local, the national and the global

Ball, Eric L., 'The Place Within: Scott Russell Sanders on Literature and Art of Place', *ISLE* 15.2 (summer 2008): 137–55.
Murphy, Patrick D., 'Grounding Anotherness and Answerability through Allonational Ecoliterature Formations', in Catrin Gersdorf and Sylvia Mayer (eds.), *Nature in Literary and Cultural Studies: Transatlantic Conversations on Ecocriticism* (Amsterdam: Rodopi, 2006), 417–34. An application of thinking of Mikhail Bakhtin to environmental politics, the state and the ethical claims of non-human others.

Smith, Mick, 'Against the Enclosure of the Ethical Commons: Radical
  Environmentalism as an "Ethics of Place"', *Environmental Ethics* 18
  (1997): 339–53.
Talent, David, 'The Nation and Beyond: Transnational Perspectives on United
  States History', *Journal of American History* 86 (1999): 965–75.

Science and the struggle for intellectual authority

14   Science and the crisis of authority

Demeritt, David, 'The Construction of Global Warming and the Politics of
  Science', *Annals of the Association of American Geographers* 91 (2001):
  307–37.
Oates, Matthew, 'The Dying of the Light: Values in Nature and the Environment',
  British Wildlife 18.2 (December 2006): 88–95. Argues how the would-be
  scientific terminology of nature conservation obscures what are actually
  decisions about ethical and political values.
Walls, Laura Dassow, 'Seeking Common Ground: Integrating the Sciences and
  the Humanities', in Annie Merril Ingram et al. (eds.), *Coming into
  Contact: Explorations in Ecocritical Theory and Practice* (Athens:
  University of Georgia Press, 2007), 199–208.
Woods, Gioia, 'Sci-Animism: American Poetry and Science', *ISLE* 15.2 (summer
  2008): 199–210.

15   Science studies

Asdal, Kristin, 'The Problematic Nature of Nature: The Post-Constructivist
  Challenge to Environmental History', *History and Theory* 42.4
  (December 2003): 60–74. Good critical introduction to Haraway and
  Latour in relation to ecological thinking (focussed on issues of gender in
  particular).
Gifford, Terry, 'The Social Construction of Nature', *ISLE* 13.2 (1996): 27–35.
Grafen, Alan, and Mark Ridley (eds.), *Richard Dawkins: How a Scientist Changed
  the Way We Think* (Oxford University Press, 2007).
Guillory, John, 'The Sokal Affair and the History of Criticism', *Critical Inquiry* 28
  (2002): 470–508. Overview of a notorious controversy in the mid 1990s
  about the nature and status of 'science studies'.
Latour, Bruno,*Remodelling the Social: An Introduction to Actor-Network-Theory*
  (Oxford University Press, 2007). Perhaps Latour's most accessible book.
  'The Impact of Science Studies on Political Philosophy', *Science, Technology,
  and Human Values* 16.1 (winter 1991): 3–19.
Rose, Dan, 'The Repatriation of Anthropology' [on Latour's *We Have Never Been
  Modern*, 1993], *American Literary History* 8.1 (spring 1996): 170–83.

16   Evolutionary theories of literature

Cohen, Michael P., 'Reading after Darwin: A Prospectus', in Annie Merril Ingram
et al. (eds.), *Coming into Contact: Explorations in Ecocritical Theory and
Practice* (Athens: University of Georgia Press, 2007), 221–33.
Seamon, Roger, review of Joseph Carroll, *Literary Darwinism*, *Journal of
Aesthetics and Art Criticism* 63 (2005): 298–300.

17   Interdisciplinarity and science: two essays on human evolution

Moeran, Joe, *Interdisciplinarity* (New Critical Idiom), 2nd edn (London:
Routledge, 2010).

Further material on/in 'narrative scholarship':

Adelson, Glenn, and John Elder, 'Robert Frost's Ecosystem of Meanings in
"Spring Pools"', *ISLE* 13.2 (2006): 1–17.
Roorda, Randall, 'Antinomies of Participation in Literacy and Wilderness', *ISLE*
14.2 (summer 2007): 71–87.

The animal mirror

Animal Studies Bibliography (online), Michigan State University,
http://ecoculturalgroup.msu.edu/bibliography.htm
Institute for Critical Animal Studies, www.criticalanimalstudies.org/
'The aim of the Institute for Critical Animal Studies (ICAS) is to provide
a space for the development of a "critical" approach to animal studies,
one which perceives that relations between human and nonhuman
animals are now at a point of crisis which implicates the planet as a
whole.'

18   Ethics and the non-human animal

Danta, Chris, and Dimitris Vardoulakis (eds.), 'The Political Animal', special issue
of *SubStance* 37.3 (2008).
Derrida, Jacques, *The Animal That Therefore I Am*, trans. David Wills (New York:
Fordham, 2008). A sustained deconstruction of the intellectual
underpinnings of speciesism.
Haraway, Donna, *The Companion Species Manifesto: Dogs, People and Significant
Otherness*, 2nd edn (Chicago University Press, 2003). Focussed on the
human–dog relationship, Haraway studies how the two species
co-evolved with each other as workers/helpers, companions/friends or
threats and enemies. See also her *When Species Meet (Posthumanities)*
(Minneapolis: University of Minnesota Press, 2008).

Raglon, Rebecca, and Marian Scholtmeijer, '"Animals are not believers in ecology": Mapping Critical Differences between Environmental and Animal Advocacy Literatures', *ISLE* 14.2 (summer 2007): 121–40.

Ryder, Richard D., *Animal Revolution: Changing Attitudes Towards Speciesism*, 2nd edn (London: Berg, 2000).

The Animal Series (general editor Jonathan Burt) of Reaktion Books offers numerous short monographs, often written by literary critics, on groups of animals that have been prominent in human culture (e.g. *Crow*, *Eel*, *Cockroach*, *Bee*, *Hare*, etc.). These are more texts of cultural history than of natural history.

19 'Anthropomorphism'

Crist, Eileen, *Images of Animals: Anthropomorphism and Animal Mind* (Philadelphia: Temple University Press, 1999).

Haraway, Donna, 'Otherworldly Conversations: Terran Topics, Local Terms', in *The Haraway Reader* (New York: Routledge, 2004), 125–50. On the 'animal–industrial' complex, modes of discourse about animals and animal subjectivity ('What is inter-subjectivity between radically different kinds of subjects?' [143]).

McMurry, Andrew, '"In their own language": Sarah Orne Jewett and the Question of Nonhuman Speaking Subjects', *ISLE* 6.1 (1999): 51–63.

Rees, Amanda, 'Anthropomorphism, Anthropocentrism, and Anecdote: Primatologists on Primatologists', *Science, Technology, and Human Values* 26 (2001): 227–47. On the peculiar difficulties posed in the study of creatures similar to ourselves.

Index

Abbey, Edward, 25, 27, 28, 29–30, 33, 69, 94
Abbot, Philip, 31
Aboriginal Australia, 155, 220
Abram, David, 48–54, 66, 210
Ackerman, Diane, 195
Adams, Carol, 180
Adorno, Theodor W., 36, 208
aesthetic, the aesthetic, 33, 41, 79, 80–2, 108, 217 (*see also* consumerism)
Africa, 120
African-American writing, 90
agency, question of non-human, 43–4, 117, 161–2, 164, 188, 191, 192, 194, 195, 198
Albanese, Catherine L., 104
Alderman, Harold, 207
Altmann, Jeanne, 159–60
Amazon region, 121
America, *see* United States. American studies, 132
animals, non-human, 42–4, 49, 50, 51, 53, 61, 66, 70, 79, 83, 103, 139, 166, 179, 206 (*see also* personhood: non-human animals as persons). Animal as uncanny, 185; 'animal hermeneutics', 195–8 (*see also* language: representing non-human animals); animal holocaust (in US), 26; animal names as insults, 184–5; animal rights, 8, 180, 186–7, 188, 203, 233; animal suffering, 179; in

children's books, 186; 'mecanomorphic' understanding of, 44; television documentaries on, 185
animism, 49, 50–1, 52
Ankersen, Thomas T., 219
Annan, Kofi, 10
anthropocentrism, 2, 3, 21, 28, 32, 34, 42, 46, 50, 54, 56, 57, 58, 80, 94, 105, 116, 122, 153, 164, 190, 191, 192, 195, 197, 229
anthropomorphism, 21, 51, 54, 79, 158, 162, 179, 192–201 (*see also* personhood: non-human animals as persons)
Argentina, 130
Aristotle, 56
Armbruster, Karla, 88, 215
Arndt, Ernst Moritz, 26
artificial intelligence, 63
artificial life, 63
Association for the Study of Literature and the Environment (ASLE), 4, 35, 38
Austin, Mary, 25, 27
Australia, Australian sense of environments, 26, 28, 71, 91, 92, 107, 130, 131, 154–5, 220, 234 (*see also* Bush, the)
Australopithecus africanus, 173, 174, 175
Australopithecus robustus, 174

Babe, 230
baboons, 159–60

244

Ruhl, Lealle, 118
Ruskin, John, 16, 17, 18, 26

Sagan, Carl, 144
Sagoff, Mark, 228
Sale, Kirkpatrick, 131, 132
Salleh, Ariel, 218
Sandilands, Catriona, 117, 118
Sartre, Jean Paul, 62
Sattelmeyer, Robert, 31
scenery, 79–80
scale, 136–9
Schiller, Friedrich, 22
Schneider, Joseph, 162, 221
Scholtmeijer, Marian, 48, 229
science, scientists, 8, 36, 38, 52, 64, 71,
    104, 107, 113, 125, 128,
    141–55, 165, 168, 203 (*see also*
    popular science). Green
    caricatures of science, 141; and
    interdisciplinarity, 171, 227;
    science as an ideology, 141,
    149–51, 176; scientific facts,
    establishment of, 159–61;
    scientific illiteracy, 176–7;
    scientific stance of neutral
    spectatorship, 100 (*see also*
    objectivity)
science fiction, 39, 52
science studies, 156–63, 226;
    caricatures of, 159
scientific revolutions, 57
scientism, 148
Scigaj, Leonard, M., 53, 209
Scott, Ridley, 70
Scottish, Scottishness, 91–2, 93
Segerstråle, Ullica, 156, 157, 227
Self, Will, 205
selfish gene, 157–8, 161, 193
'sentimental', 22
Serventy, Vincent, 28
Sessions, George, 24
sex/gender, 111
Shakespeare, William, 168
Shaw, David Gary, 226
Shearman, David, 222

Shelley, Mary (*Frankenstein*), 66–9
Shelley, P. B., 24
Sherman, Rachel A., 149
Shires, Linda, 100
Sierra Club, 25, 27, 136
Silko, Leslie Marmon, 48, 125, 220
Simons, John, 187, 197, 200, 201
Singer, Peter, 180, 185
situated science, situatedness
    (Haraway), 158, 160
Slaymaker, William, 120
Slovic, Scott, 174
Smith, A. D., 131
Smith, Craig, 230
Smith, Joseph Wayne, 222
Snyder, Gary, 18, 33, 47, 52–4, 107,
    138–9, 140
social ecology, 2, 82, 89, 131, 152, 220,
    238
sociobiology, 151, 156, 158, 160, 163,
    172, 176
Soper, Kate, 184, 210
Sophocles,
speciesism, 185, 186, 187, 199, 201, 242
Stafford, Fiona J., 216
Standard Social Science Model
    (SSSM), 165–7, 170
state, the, 54, 59, 104, 106, 130, 143
Stegner, Wallace, 82, 84
Stein, Rachel, 112–13
Sterling, Bruce, 213
Stewart, Frank, 209
Stiegler, Bernard, 65
Sting, 121
Storey, Robert, 168
Sturgeon, Noël, 217
Sullivan, Lucy G., 225
Sze, Arthur, 139

Taiwan, 85
Taylor, Bob Pepperman, 73, 103
technology, 64–5, 66
Tester, Keith, 151
'thinking like a mountain', 77–8, 118
Thomas, Keith, 183
Thomas, Michael J., 204

Cambridge Introductions to ...

Printed in Great Britain
by Amazon.co.uk, Ltd.,
Marston Gate.